Allegories of Encounter

ALLEGORIES OF ENCOUNTER

Colonial Literacy and Indian Captivities

Andrew Newman

Published by the
OMOHUNDRO INSTITUTE OF
EARLY AMERICAN HISTORY AND CULTURE,
Williamsburg, Virginia,
and the
UNIVERSITY OF NORTH CAROLINA PRESS,
Chapel Hill

The Omohundro Institute of Early American History and Culture is
sponsored by the College of William and Mary. On November 15, 1996,
the Institute adopted the present name in honor of a bequest from
Malvern H. Omohundro, Jr.

Cover illustrations: New England primer [1727] courtesy, American
Antiquarian Society; "Captivity of Mrs. Rowlands[on]" [detail] from John S. C.
Abbott, *King Philip* (1900), from Wikimedia Commons; antique book
© shutterstock/Honigjp31

Library of Congress Cataloging-in-Publication Data to come
Names: Newman, Andrew, 1968– author.
Title: Allegories of encounter : colonial literacy and Indian captivities /
Andrew Newman.
Description: Chapel Hill : Published by the Omohundro Institute of Early
American History and Culture, Williamsburg, Virginia, and the University of
North Carolina Press, [2019] | Includes bibliographical references and index.
Identifiers: LCCN 2018031157| ISBN 9781469643458 (cloth : alk. paper) |
ISBN 9781469647647 (pbk : alk. paper) | ISBN 9781469643465 (ebook)
Subjects: LCSH: Captivity narratives—United States—History and criticism. |
Indian captivities—United States. | Literacy—United States—History. |
United States—History—Colonial period, ca. 1600–1775.
Classification: LCC PN56.C36 N49 2019 | DDC 809.933/53—dc23
LC record available at https://lccn.loc.gov/2018031157

The University of North Carolina Press has been a member of the Green
Press Initiative since 2003.

ACKNOWLEDGMENTS

Like my first book, *Allegories of Encounter* originates in my dissertation. In other words, it began long ago; it is gratifying and humbling to reflect on the people and institutions that helped me to bring it to fruition.

I'm grateful to my graduate advisors at the University of California, Irvine: Brook Thomas, Sharon Block, and especially Michael Clark. For early fellowship support, thanks to the Huntington Library and the Andrew W. Mellon Foundation.

Thanks to the colleagues at Stony Brook who have read for, written for, and shared with me, including Patty Dunn, Justin Johnston, Daniel Levy, Ned Landsman, Adrienne Munich, Douglas Pfeiffer, Michael Rubenstein, Susan Scheckel, Michael Tondre, and three successive English Department chairs: Peter Manning, Stephen Spector, and Celia Marshik. The Office of the President and the Faculty of Arts, Humanities and Lettered Social Sciences generously provided a fellowship at the Humanities Institute of Stony Brook; special thanks to Director Kathleen Wilson, Program Coordinator Adrienne Unger, and my research assistants Georgia Cartmill and Karlianne Seri. Thanks also to Jay Levenson and the interlibrary loan department.

Thanks to the Faculty of Arts, Humanities and Social Sciences for a generous publication subvention.

This book developed in dialog with colleagues around the country, including Katy Chiles, Matt Cohen, Theresa Strouth Gaul, Sandra Gustafson, Tamara Harvey, Karen Marrero, Michele Currie Navakas, Phillip Round, and Nicole Tonkovich. For help with my Mohawk-language questions, thanks to the late Roy Wright. For their support, I'm especially indebted to Carla Mulford, Gordon Sayre, Teresa Toulouse, and Hilary Wyss. I hope that anyone I didn't name—including those who have rendered my department and me the professional service of evaluating my scholarship—will feel included in my general thanks to the wonderful community of early Americanists.

It's a privilege to publish with the Omohundro Institute, whose editorial staff has shaped *Allegories of Encounter* into the best book it had potential to be. I've had the good fortune to work with not one but three Editors of Books: Fredrika Teute offered encouragement and guidance early on, and I'm glad I was able to submit the manuscript to her. I'm grateful to Paul Mapp and Catherine E. Kelly for their support and guidance through the evaluation and production phases. Throughout, Nadine Zimmerli has been my primary editor, and she has a large share in whatever success this book enjoys. Collaborating with her has been one of my most rewarding professional experiences. I'm grateful to the two anonymous readers for their generous, transformative feedback. Thanks to M. Kathyrn Burdette for making my writing more straightforward, to Virginia Chew and Kelly Crawford, and to the editorial apprentices who chased down my citations and references: Daniella Bassi, Alison Bazylinski, Douglas Breton, Joan Jockel, Ryan Langton, Anne Powell, and Christopher Slaby. At the University of North Carolina Press, thanks to Executive Editor Chuck Grench, to Dino A. Battista for the marketing, and Kim Bryant for the cover design.

Early versions of parts of Chapters 1, 4, and 6 appeared in *Early American Literature* and *Legacy: A Journal of American Women Writers.* Thanks to the University of North Carolina Press and the University of Nebraska Press for permission to republish.

Finally, this book is dedicated to Mira Gelley and our sons Levi and Reuben (*gratias tibi,* Reuben, for the help with the Latin). Love for and from my family sustains me in everything I do.

CONTENTS

ILLUSTRATIONS

Figures

Table

ABBREVIATIONS

ACN   Gordon M. Sayre, ed., *American Captivity Narratives* (Boston, 2000)

CH   Evan Haefeli and Kevin Sweeney, eds., *Captive Histories: English, French, and Native Narratives of the 1704 Deerfield Raid,* Native Americans of the Northeast (Amherst, Mass., 2006)

EAL   *Early American Literature*

JR   Reuben Gold Thwaites, ed., *The Jesuit Relations and Allied Documents: Travels and Explorations of the Jesuit Missionaries in New France, 1610–1791* (Cleveland, Oh., 1898), Early Canadiana Online, http://eco.canadiana.ca

SGG   Neal Salisbury, ed., *The Sovereignty and Goodness of God, by Mary Rowlandson, with Related Documents,* Bedford Series in History and Culture (Boston, 1997)

UV   Vincent Carretta, ed., *Unchained Voices: An Anthology of Black Authors in the English-Speaking World of the Eighteenth Century* (Lexington, Ky., 2004)

WMQ   *William and Mary Quarterly*

Allegories of Encounter

INTRODUCTION

Captivity as Literacy Event

One of the most "Remarkable Occurrences" recounted in James Smith's 1799 captivity narrative took place in the captive's imagination: he fantasized that his captors intended to put him to death for reading.

According to Smith (1737–1814), sometime in the fall of 1755, not long after he had been captured and adopted by Kahnawake Iroquois migrants in the Ohio Country, he returned to their hunting camp from a chestnut-gathering outing to discover that his pouch of books was missing. Smith "enquired after them, and asked the Indians if they knew where they were; they told me that they supposed the puppies had carried them off. I did not believe them; but thought they were displeased at my poring over my books, and concluded that they had destroyed them, or put them out of my way." Smith made a drastic inference from a misplaced object.[1]

Subsequently, the eighteen-year-old Smith went out to gather more nuts—a juvenile activity, in contrast to the hunting carried out by the men—and returned to find that the Kahnawakes had fashioned a wooden structure consisting of two forked poles planted perpendicularly, with "a strong pole across." Smith "could not conceive the use of this piece of work, and at length concluded it was a gallows, I thought that I had displeased them by reading my books, and that they were about puting [*sic*] me to death." The following morning, however, he "observed them bringing their skins all to this place and hanging them over this pole, so as to preserve them from being injured by the weather, this removed my fears." What otherwise might be characterized as an "ethnographic" or "proto-ethnographic" observation about the Kahnawakes' method of preserving skins instead is a radically subjective expression of the observer's feelings. It tells us much more about Smith than about the Indians. Specifically, it

---

1. James Smith, *An Account of the Remarkable Occurrences in the Life and Travels of Col. James Smith (Now a Citizen of Bourbon County, Kentucky): During His Captivity with the Indians, in the Years 1755, '56, '57, '58, and '59* (Lexington, Ky., 1799), 28–29.

attests to the value he placed on his books in the circumstances of his captivity and his forced integration into a native American society.[2]

This passage was the point of departure for the research that led to this book. It prompted the following questions: How is it that Smith was so disconsolate about the disappearance of his books that he fantasized that a drying rack was actually a gallows and that the people who had declared him to be their kin intended to put him to death for reading? To what degree is Smith's outlandishly alarmist response indicative of the significance of literacy to the protagonists and authors of captivity narratives? How did native Americans perceive the literacy practices of their captives? Finally, since we learn so much about captivity from the writings of the captives, what can captivity reveal about writing, reading, and books? How does this specific, extreme variety of experience illuminate the functions of literacy in the cultures the captives represent, and more generally?

The Captive's Literacy

The captivity narrative was an enormously popular genre in colonial and early Anglo-America. The Garland Library of Narratives of North American Indian Captivities (1976–1980) comprises 111 volumes and 311 titles; one scholar lists the total number of "captivity titles" published between the sixteenth and the early twentieth centuries at more than a thousand, an estimate that does not include the accounts of captivity embedded in colonial writings on other subjects, such as wars or Christian missions, in English and other colonial languages. One of the selling points of captivity, for contemporary audiences and for modern readers, is its inversion of the relations of power between colonists and native Americans. Whereas the European and Euro-American colonists ultimately prevailed in the wars in which captivity accounts are set, through captivity the Indians variously ransomed, abused, tortured, executed, enslaved, and acculturated colonists as individuals and in small groups. This turning of the tables was the basis of the genre's utility both in religious messaging and

2. On "Food Nuts of the Iroquois," see Arthur C. Parker, *Iroquois Uses of Maize and Other Food Plants* (Albany, N.Y., 1910), 99–102; Smith, *Account*, 29. On "ethnography" in early American writing, see Yael Ben-Zvi, "Ethnography and the Production of Foreignness in Indian Captivity Narratives," *American Indian Quarterly*, XXXII (2008), x–xv; Gordon M. Sayre, *Les Sauvages Américains: Representations of Native Americans in French and English Colonial Literature* (Chapel Hill, N.C., 1997), 27–31, 79–143.

in wartime propaganda. It also affords a unique vantage point—not only, as has often been observed, on native American peoples but also on colonial ones. That is, captivity accounts showcase the behaviors of colonists under conditions of isolation, powerlessness, and duress.[3]

A prominent category of such behaviors, particularly in the subset of nonfictional narratives that were authored by the captives themselves, is *literacy practices*, which is a term that I have adopted from sociolinguistics and academic literacy studies. Literacy practices are "the general cultural ways of using reading and writing which people draw upon" in *literacy events*, or "the particular activities where reading and writing have a role." Although such activities may seem incongruous with the conditions of captivity, it is not surprising that someone who demonstrated his or her affiliation with print culture by composing and publishing a narrative would depict literacy practices within that narrative. By reading and writing, captives performed their participation in *discourse communities;* in this way, the representations of literacy events anticipate the captive's eventual reintegration into his or her discourse community as an author, which is always part of the captive's story, in the same way that the first-person tale of adventure always implies the successful return of the hero.[4]

The captives studied below did not necessarily identify with purpose-oriented, functional, specialized discourse communities as conceptualized within academic literacy studies. Some identified with collectivities, such as the Society of Jesus, that were closer to this model than others, such as British men of letters. But these captives were all participants in "imagined communities," in the sense of Benedict Anderson's newspaper-reading public. Smith's notional discourse community, for example, included fellow readers that he presumably never met—the former owners of his copies of Robert Russell's popular *Seven Sermons* and his "English Bible," which Indians had taken as plunder from "the field of battle" at "Braddock's Defeat" and "the frontiers of Virginia," respectively.[5]

3. Annette Kolodny, "Review Essay," *EAL*, XIV (1979), 232; Roy Harvey Pearce, "The Significances of the Captivity Narrative," *American Literature*, XIX (1947), 1–20.

4. David Barton, "Preface: Literacy Events and Literacy Practices," in Mary Hamilton, David Barton, and Roz Ivanič, eds., *Worlds of Literacy* (Philadelphia, 1994), vii–x; see also Brian V. Street, *Literacy and Development: Ethnographic Perspectives* (New York, 2001), 10–11; Shirley Brice Heath, "Protean Shapes in Literacy Events: Ever-Shifting Oral and Literate Traditions," in Deborah Tannen, ed., *Spoken and Written Language: Exploring Orality and Literacy* (Norwood, N.J., 1982), 91–117.

5. Smith, *Account*, 13, 17, 24. John M. Swales lists six criteria for discourse communities:

The participants in these imagined discourse communities shared not only a canon of readings but also discursive practices, as well as *language ideologies,* or "representations, whether explicit or implicit, that construe the intersection of language and human beings in a social world." This term encompasses value judgments about media, such as the view that writing is a more reliable medium than speech. Smith's claim that the light of scripture outshines "the light of Nature" expresses a language ideology. So, too, does his somewhat contradictory statement that "nature always outshines art." Language ideologies play an important role in the exclusions that define communities. Smith's fear of execution for reading attributed a language ideology to the Indians and implied a corresponding, antithetical one of his own—a belief that "reading his books" was irreconcilable with his becoming an Indian. This ideology was shared among the captives studied below: the use of alphabetic script was a defining difference between their culture and that of their captors.[6]

In this regard, the captives' depictions of their own literacy practices reveal an overlooked aspect of the role of literacy in colonial contact situations. The scholarship on "the encounter between Europeans and Native Americans from the vantage of book history" has focused on two fronts. In diplomacy, including land transactions, colonists often used writing to authorize unfair agreements, even if the records contain traces of complex negotiations employing various media such as spoken languages, gifts, and wampum. In evangelism, missionaries, especially Protestant ones, used literacy as a "weapon of conquest" in the arsenal of cultural imperialism, even as native proselytes appropriated it to their own uses, including the formation of native Christian communities. But captives' primary uses of literacy were not instrumental in the sense of furthering the objectives of settler colonialism. They were more self-contained and reflexive. Cap-

---

(1) "a broadly agreed set of common public goals," (2) "mechanisms of intercommunication" to (3) "provide information and feedback," (4) proprietary "genres," (5) a specialized "lexis," and (6) "a threshold level of members with a suitable degree of relevant content and discoursal expertise" (Swales, *Genre Analysis: English in Academic and Research Settings* [New York, 1990], 24–27). Benedict Anderson suggests that "all communities larger than primordial villages of face-to-face contact (and perhaps not even these) are imagined." He sees the "daily" ritual of newspaper reading as a "vivid figure for the secular, historically clocked imagined community" of the modern nation (Anderson, *Imagined Communities: Reflections on the Origin and Spread of Nationalism* [London, 1991], 6, 35).

6. Kathryn A. Woolard, "Introduction: Language Ideology as a Field of Inquiry," in Bambi B. Schieffelin, Woolard, and Paul V. Kroskrity, eds., *Language Ideologies: Theory and Practice* (New York, 1998), 8; Smith, *Account*, 3, 94.

tives read books, especially but not exclusively religious ones, and sometimes they kept journals. The Indians themselves were generally involved in these practices, if at all, as observers and even enablers. The analysis of the representations of these literacy events therefore reveals the significance of alphabetic literacy to colonists, vis-à-vis native Americans, as part of the performance of cultural identity. Secondarily, it provides information about native American perceptions of European literacy practices that were not aimed at dispossessing them of their land or overwriting their beliefs.[7]

A prevalent image in early colonial relations is of Indians expressing awe and amazement at European literacy. Some well-known examples can be sorted into two different categories of literacy events: cross-cultural theological disquisitions, involving the presentation of holy books, and technological demonstrations of the communicative capacity of writing. In *The True Relation of the Conquest of Peru* (1534), Francisco Xeres reports that, following Friar Vicente Valverde's explanation (conveyed through an interpreter) of the theological basis for the Spaniards' conquest, the Incan emperor Atahualpa took his Bible, and, "without marveling at the letters and paper like other Indians, threw it five or six paces from himself." Xeres suggests that such disdain was exceptional; his generalization about Indians' "marveling" is perhaps corroborated by Thomas Hariot (1590), who reports that the Roanoke Indians, after he "made declaration of the contentes of the Bible," were "glad to touch it, to embrace it, to kisse it, to hold it to their brests and heades, and stroke over all their bodie with it; to shewe their hungrie desire of that knowledge which was spoken of." Similarly, John Smith's *Generall Historie of Virginia* (1624) and Gabriel Sagard's

7. David D. Hall, "Introduction," in Hugh Amory et al., eds., *A History of the Book in America*, I, *The Colonial Book in the Atlantic World* (Cambridge, 2000), 6 ("vantage"); Jill Lepore, *The Name of War: King Philip's War and the Origins of American Identity* (New York, 1998), 27 ("weapon"); Hilary E. Wyss, *Writing Indians: Literacy, Christianity, and Native Community in Early America*, Native Americans of the Northeast (Amherst, Mass., 2000); Wyss, *English Letters and Indian Literacies: Reading, Writing, and New England Missionary Schools, 1750–1830* (Philadelphia, 2012); Phillip H. Round, *Removable Type: Histories of the Book in Indian Country, 1663–1880* (Chapel Hill, N.C., 2010); Drew Lopenzina, *Red Ink: Native Americans Picking up the Pen in the Colonial Period* (Albany, N.Y., 2012). On the communicative dimensions of diplomacy, see James H. Merrell, *Into the American Woods: Negotiators on the American Frontier* (New York, 1999); Matt Cohen, *The Networked Wilderness: Communicating in Early New England* (Minneapolis, 2010); Birgit Brander Rasmussen, *Queequeg's Coffin: Indigenous Literacies and Early American Literature* (Durham, N.C., 2012), 49–78; Andrew Newman, *On Records: Delaware Indians, Colonists, and the Media of History and Memory* (Lincoln, Neb., 2012), 133–184; Jeffrey Glover, *Paper Sovereigns: Anglo-Native Treaties and the Law of Nations, 1604–1664* (Philadelphia, 2014).

History of Canada (1636) report the Powhatans' "wonder" and the Wendats' *"admiration"* at their successful use of written notes to transmit information; in Smith's phrase, they thought "the paper could speake," and this impression contributed greatly to their esteem for the Europeans.[8]

Captivity narratives show some continuity with these earlier accounts. Atahualpa's gesture is seemingly reprised by the Wampanoag squaw sachem Weetamoo, as depicted in Mary Rowlandson's *Soveraignty and Goodness of God* (1682), when she "snatched" Rowlandson's Bible "hastily out of my hand, and threw it out of doors." In *A Narrative of the Lord's Wonderful Dealings with John Marrant, a Black* (1785), the daughter of a Cherokee "king," like Hariot's Roanoke Indians, "kissed" Marrant's Bible "and seemed much delighted with it." Like Smith's Powhatans and Sagard's Hurons, the Shawnees in *A Narrative of the Incidents Attending the Capture, Detention, and Ransom of Charles Johnston* (1790) thought his writing indicated "something extraordinary about me, which, however, they could not comprehend."[9] To whatever extent these representations are reliable, however, what they depict is, not indigenous perceptions of alphabetic literacy, but responses of various native individuals to distinct literacy practices—solitary meditative reading, an enthusiastic recitation, and secular journal keeping—in contingent, specific situations.

Moreover, these captives' narratives and others illustrate the interpenetration between indigenous and colonial worlds and, accordingly, indicate the Indians' familiarity with colonial literacy practices. One of the striking manifestations of this familiarity is their repeatedly attested act of providing captives with books, from the Bible that "one of the *Indians* that came from *Medfield* fight" offered Rowlandson out of "his basket" to the copy of Fenelon's *Adventures of Telemachus* that Thomas Ridout's Shawnee "Indian

---

8. Francisco de Xerez, *Verdadera Relación de la conquista del Perú*, ed. Concepción Bravo, Crónicas de América, XIV (Madrid 1985), 111 ("No maravillándose de las letras ni del papel como otros indios, lo arrojó cinco o seis pasos de sí" [my translation]); Thomas Hariot, *A Briefe and True Report of the New Found Land of Virginia* . . . (Frankfurt, 1590), 27; Patricia Seed, "'Failing to Marvel': Atahualpa's Encounter with the Word," *Latin American Research Review*, XXVI, no. 1 (1991), 7–32; Karen Ordahl Kupperman, ed., *Captain John Smith: A Select Edition of His Writings* (Williamsburg, Va., and Chapel Hill, N.C., 1988), 62; Gabriel Sagard, *Histoire du Canada et voyages que les Frères Mineurs Récollects y ont faicts pour la conversion des Infidelles* (Paris, 1636), 794; James Axtell, "The Power of Print in the Eastern Woodlands," *William and Mary Quarterly*, XLIV (1987), 300–309; Peter Wogan, "Perceptions of European Literacy in Early Contact Situations," *Ethnohistory*, XLI (1994), 407–429.

9. *SGG*, 86; *UV*, 119; *A Narrative of the Incidents Attending the Capture, Detention, and Ransom of Charles Johnston.* . . . (New York, 1975), 32.

friend" lent him to "divert [his] solitary hours." In contrast to the early colonial accounts, then, captivity narratives represent the Indians' recognition of the importance of books, especially but not exclusively Bibles, to their captives.[10]

In light of recent discussions that, focusing on colonial encounters and "indigenous literacies," challenge the very premises of the field of book history, my usage of "book" is admittedly Eurocentric. Since this study is primarily concerned with the subjective experience of the colonists, it employs usages of the terms *literacy, writing,* and *book* that are appropriate to its methodology. My emphasis is not on the "inter-animation between European and indigenous American forms of literacy," and the literacy practices represented in captivity accounts were not typically part of multimedia "publication events" like the one Thomas Morton famously staged in 1627 at the Maypole in Merrymount, where colonial and "native audiences" converged. Even after the turn in early American studies to a more inclusive understanding of literacy or a broader category of "media," several studies have fruitfully explored the significance of alphabetic literacy and books, more narrowly conceived, to native American users. With titles such as *Removable Type, English Letters and Indian Literacies,* and *Red Ink,* they investigate the apparent tension between an exogenous medium and indigenous cultures, an opposition that has also largely shaped the study of native American literature. *Allegories of Encounter* argues that this supposed antithesis is a crucial subtext to the literacy practices of the Indians' colonial captives. The captives read and wrote with the presumption that their captors did not—or should not.[11]

---

10. *SGG,* 76; Thomas Ridout, *Ten Years of Upper Canada in Peace and War, 1805–1815: Being the Ridout Letters, with Annotations by Matilda Edgar. . . .* (Toronto, 1890), 356.

11. Hilary E. Wyss, "Indigenous Literacies: New England and New Spain," in Susan Castillo and Ivy Schweitzer, eds., *A Companion to the Literatures of Colonial America,* Blackwell Companions to Literature and Culture (Malden, Mass., 2005), 387; Rasmussen, *Queequeg's Coffin,* 11–12; Cohen, *Networked Wilderness,* 29–64 ("publication events"); Round, *Removable Type;* Wyss, *English Letters and Indian Literacies;* Lopenzina, *Red Ink.* On the issue of defining literacy within early American studies, see Andrew Newman, "Early Americanist Grammatology: Definitions of Writing and Literacy," in Matt Cohen and Jeffrey Glover, eds., *Colonial Mediascapes: Sensory Worlds of the Early Americas* (Lincoln, Neb., 2014), xiv, 76–98. As Lisa Brooks points out, criticism of native American literature has been informed by the language ideology according to which "literacy is a mark of coercive colonialism and modernity inherently antithetical to Indigenous traditions" (Brooks, "Writing and Lasting: Native Northeastern Literary History," in James H. Cox and Daniel Heath Justice, eds., *The Oxford Handbook of Indigenous American Literature* [New York, 2015], 536).

Staying in the Moment

For captive authors, captivity as a whole was a literacy event—"any action sequence, involving one or more persons, in which the production and / or comprehension of print plays a role"—culminating in the production of a narrative. Many narratives include representations of smaller literacy events. James Smith's *Account* describes his encounter with a fellow captive—"one Arthur Campbell"—whom he met at the Wyandot town of Sunyendeand, near Lake Erie. Campbell borrowed Smith's Bible "and made some pertinent remarks on what he had read. One passage was where it is said, 'It is good for a man that he bear the yoke in his youth.' He said we ought to be resigned to the will of Providence, as we were now bearing the yoke, in our youth. Mr. Campbell appeared to be then about sixteen or seventeen years of age." Here is an exemplary literacy event: participants, a specific text, a contingent, situated interpretation.[12]

Smith's narrative presents an explicit link to a book—not just "the Bible" as an abstract text that was materially embodied in millions of editions, or even the King James version, whose rendering of Lamentations 3:27 appears in the citation, but rather the specific "English Bible" that a member of an Indian war party had taken as plunder and handed "to a Dutch woman who was a prisoner." "As she could not read English," she passed it on as "a present" to Smith, who found it "very acceptable." Thus the episode is an example of intertextuality—"a relationship of copresence between two texts or among several texts." Yet this intertextuality does not conform to the conventional understanding; it does not arise from the influence of one author upon another, nor is it a simple quotation or allusion, "an economical means of calling upon the history or the literary tradition that author and reader are assumed to share." Instead, Lamentations 3:27 is an element in the narrated action of Smith's *Account*: he encountered it as a captive, not as an author.[13]

The sort of intertextuality exemplified by this intersection between Smith's captivity narrative and the Book of Lamentations may be specified

12. Heath, "Protean Shapes in Literacy Events," in Tannen, ed., *Spoken and Written Language*, 93; Smith, *Account*, 49. Campbell went on to become a Virginia militia colonel who led devastating raids against the Cherokees during the Revolutionary War. See Gary B. Nash, *The Unknown American Revolution: The Unruly Birth of Democracy and the Struggle to Create America* (New York, 2005), 354.

13. Smith, *Account*, 24; Gérard Genette, *Palimpsests: Literature in the Second Degree* (Lincoln, Neb., 1997), 1 ("copresence"); *Oxford Dictionary of Literary Terms*, 1st ed., s.v. "allusion."

with reference to some basic distinctions in narrative theory. One distinction is between *story*—"the content of the narrative expression"—and *discourse*—"the form of that expression." The Bible verse that Campbell read to Smith was part of the story of Smith's captivity rather than an allusion belonging to the narrator's discourse. A related concept is *diegesis,* a term Gérard Genette imported from film theory to refer to the course of events, or "storyworld," depicted by a narrative. In a film, a musical soundtrack is outside the diegesis, an added layer, whereas a song on a radio heard by one of the characters is within the diegesis. Smith's plundered copy of an "English Bible," as opposed to a Bible that might have sat on his bookshelf as he revised his captivity journal for publication, was part of his narrative's diegesis. It was an "existent," pertaining to the storyworld in which Smith was an adopted captive.[14]

This detour into narrative theory is intended as a simple heuristic for thinking about nonfictional narratives. Narratology has been principally preoccupied with fiction, but as numerous theorists have pointed out, nonfiction and fiction can be formally identical. There is no formal feature necessarily distinguishing a fictional autobiographical narrative, such as *The Life and Strange Surprizing Adventures of Robinson Crusoe . . .* (1719), "Written by Himself," from a nonfictional one. So nonfictional narratives may also be considered in terms of story (what is told) and discourse (how it is told), except there is also a third term—*actuality*. The story / discourse distinction largely corresponds to one that is more prominent in early American studies scholarship between history and literary historicism. Historians, including ethnohistorians, are largely concerned with the storyworld of captivity narratives as a representation of an actual time and place: the wars in which the narratives are set, the indigenous customs to which they attest. By contrast, whereas many literary scholars have analyzed the narratives' representations of colonial encounters, literary historicism, broadly, is concerned with discourse: situating narratives within the discursive or cultural contexts of their composition and publication, as well as within diachronic literary history, and interpreting them in terms of their "cultural work," their social and political significances.

14. Seymour Chatman, *Story and Discourse: Narrative Structure in Fiction and Film* (Ithaca, N.Y., 1980), 23, 34; Gérard Genette, *Narrative Discourse: An Essay in Method,* trans. Jane E. Lewin (Ithaca, N.Y., 1983), 27, 27n; Dan Shen, "Diegesis," in David Herman, Jahn Manfred, and Marie-Laure Ryan, eds., *Routledge Encyclopedia of Narrative Theory* (London, 2010); see also Shen, "Story-Discourse Distinction," ibid.

Put differently, historians and literary historicists tend to emphasize different "moments" in the life of these texts: the moments of representation and the moments of production and reception.[15]

Allegories of Encounter approaches accounts of captivity as primary sources in both the historian's and the literary scholar's senses of that term—as records of literacy practices and events and as the products of these events and practices, discursive objects of analysis in their own right. My focus on in situ literacy events means that I trace the "rhetorical paths of thought" between texts somewhat differently than in conventional literary historicism, including reception study. In addition to sociohistorical or cultural contexts, the captive practiced literacy under radically contingent historical circumstances, ones that were largely shaped by the native captors. Accordingly, I am interested in literacy events as part of a represented series of events unfolding within ethnohistorical contexts.[16]

15. Brook Thomas, *Civic Myths: A Law-and-Literature Approach to Citizenship* (Chapel Hill, N.C., 2007), 20 ("moments"); Tara Fitzpatrick, "The Figure of Captivity: The Cultural Work of the Puritan Captivity Narrative," *American Literary History*, III (1991), 1–26. Of course, it is also possible to discuss "actuality" with respect to fictional storyworlds—to speculate beyond the narrator's limitations or misrepresentations. Any attempt to distinguish between fiction and nonfiction runs into theoretical complications that are beyond the scope of this study. See Gérard Genette, "Fictional Narrative, Factual Narrative," trans. Nitsa Ben-Ari and Brian McHale, *Poetics Today*, XI (1990), 755–774; Henrik Skov Nielsen, James Phelan, and Richard Walsh, "Ten Theses about Fictionality," *Narrative*, XXIII (2015), 61–73. Some of the many historical studies that draw on captivity narratives are Brett Rushforth, *Bonds of Alliance: Indigenous and Atlantic Slaveries in New France* (Williamsburg, Va., and Chapel Hill, N.C., 2012); Christina Snyder, *Slavery in Indian Country: The Changing Face of Captivity in Early America* (Cambridge, Mass., 2012); William Henry Foster, *The Captor's Narrative: Catholic Women and Their Puritan Men on the Early American Frontier* (Ithaca, N.Y., 2003); Evan Haefeli and Kevin Sweeney, *Captors and Captives: The 1704 French and Indian Raid on Deerfield*, Native Americans of the Northeast (Amherst, Mass., 2003). An exception would be Haefeli and Sweeney's study of the publication and reception history of John Williams's *Redeemed Captive* (1707), which employs a methodology much more characteristic of literary scholarship. See Haefeli and Sweeney, "'The Redeemed Captive' as Recurrent Seller: Politics and Publication, 1707–1853," *New England Quarterly*, LXXVII (2004), 341–367. Two important books by literary scholars that take this historicist approach are Teresa A. Toulouse, *The Captive's Position: Female Narrative, Male Identity, and Royal Authority in Colonial New England* (Philadelphia, 2007); and Lisa Voigt, *Writing Captivity in the Early Modern Atlantic: Circulations of Knowledge and Authority in the Iberian and English Imperial Worlds* (Williamsburg, Va., and Chapel Hill, N.C., 2009).

16. Steven Mailloux, *Reception Histories: Rhetoric, Pragmatism, and American Cultural Politics* (Ithaca, N.Y., 1998), xiv. According to James L. Machor, "Reception study examines the sociohistorical contexts of interpretive practice" ("Introduction," in Machor and Philip Goldstein, eds., *Reception Study: From Literary Theory to Cultural Studies* [New York, 2001], xii). Historicism "stresses the importance of historical contexts to the understanding of any social or cultural phenomenon"; the so-called New Historicism, which had a formative influence on the contemporary field of early American literature, emphasizes the "'textual' nature of history," which in

For example, the literacy event involving Smith and Campbell takes on significance as part of a narrative episode set at Sunyendeand. Their Bible reading is startlingly juxtaposed with Smith's description of his participation in a "gauntlet" ritual with "the Indians," in which "one John Savage," a "middle-aged man," was compelled to run between two lines of Indians, getting beaten from both sides. According to Smith, he gave Savage his instructions and then "fell into one of the ranks with the Indians, shouting and yelling like them; and as they were not very severe on him, as he passed me, I hit him with a piece of pumpkin—which pleased the Indians much, but hurt my feelings." The pumpkin throwing appears in the paragraph immediately following the Bible reading, a juxtaposition that epitomizes Smith's poignant expression of cultural ambivalence. The harmless blow he inflicted upon a fellow colonist was painful to himself. The young adoptee had participated in a ritual that affirmed his attachment to his natal community, then turned about and joined "the ranks with the Indians." Of course, a narrative juxtaposition happens at the level of discourse; it is not necessarily indicative of an immediate temporal sequence. Rhetorically, the message about "bearing the yoke" in one's "youth" and the observation about Campbell's age resonate with Smith's description of John Savage as "a middle-aged man, or about forty years old." If Campbell's "pertinent remarks" on scripture carried into Smith's participation in the gauntlet, perhaps they helped him to rationalize his actions: by inflicting suffering on Savage, was he contributing to the edifying effects of Savage's experience? Or was he "bearing the yoke" himself by fulfilling a painful role as an adoptive Kahnawake?[17]

The successive paragraphs recounting the Bible reading and the gauntlet present an apparent negative comparison between colonial and Indian cultural practices, complicated by Smith's participation in both. This tension is torqued further by the next paragraph, which features another reference to scripture, this time not as a diegetic literacy event but rather as an extradiegetic narratorial commentary. Describing the "comparatively high living" they enjoyed at the time of the warriors' return, with a bountiful harvest and abundant game, Smith wrote that the Indians "appeared to be fulfilling the scriptures beyond those who profess to be-

---

practice often means reading literary texts in relation to supplemental, nonliterary ones. See *Oxford Dictionary of Literary Terms*, s.v. "historicism," "new historicism."

17. Smith, *Account*, 49–50.

lieve them, in that of taking no thought of to-morrow: and also in living in love, peace and friendship together, without disputes. In this respect they shame those who profess Christianity."[18] His reference is to Matthew 6:34 ("Take therefore no thought for the morrow") and more generally to Gospel sentiments. Its application to the peaceful feasting of a culturally heterogeneous assembly of native Americans in the Ohio Country, including Wyandots and Kahnawakes, the descendants of ancient enemies, is startlingly off-key with respect to the vilifying tendency of the captivity genre. Writing from Bourbon County, Kentucky, toward the end of the eighteenth century, Smith offered representations and commentary that were at odds with the political needs of an expansionist, Indian-hating readership.

In this way, one reference to scripture—an intradiegetic citation from the Book of Lamentations—connects to the story of Smith's captivity and pertains to the moment of representation, whereas a second, present-tense discursive allusion to Matthew 6 relates vaguely to the moment of production. Instructively, the first connection was made, not by the narrator, but by a person Smith (as protagonist of his narrative) encountered. This man took the book Smith handed to him, located a "passage," and applied it to his present experience, which Smith (as narrator) renders in the past tense: "He said we ought to be resigned to the will of Providence, as we were now bearing the yoke, in our youth." Smith's next Bible reference connects the past to the present moment of composition, shifting from the Indians to his readers and their contemporaries and accordingly shifting tenses within a sentence: "They appeared to be fulfilling the scriptures beyond those who profess to believe them." In this study, I similarly observe the distinction between story and discourse by shifting between the past tense of narrated events (Campbell *took* the book) and the present tense of narratorial commentary (Smith *renders*). This approach corresponds to the distinction between the past circumstances of the historical actors and the present context of the author.

Reception Allegories

These two Bible references, the diegetic one to the Old Testament and the extradiegetic one to the New, provide glimpses of allegoresis, or allegorical interpretation—the practice of attributing "another sense" to "any created entity," or "presuming the work or figure to be encoded with meaning intended by the author or a higher spiritual authority."[19] According to Smith, Arthur Campbell suggested that their captivity, authored by God ("the will of Providence"), might be understood in terms of one of the Lamentations, traditionally attributed to Jeremiah, following the Babylonians' destruction of Jerusalem. If Campbell understood his captivity more broadly as a parallel to the story of the Old Testament Jews, whose city was sacked and who were carried away captive, there was ample precedent for doing so. The Indians were unwittingly playing the part of the Babylonians, God's instrument for scourging the Jews. This role could scarcely be a greater contrast to the one Smith ascribed to them in his allegorical reading of the feast at Sunyendeand, which casts the Indians as exemplars of the Gospel. Smith offers this interpretation retroactively, though it is possible that it also occurred to him in the moment.

Literary allegory is notoriously difficult to define and characterize. *Allegories of Encounter* proposes a further complication by applying it to personal narratives and historical experience.[20] Allegory distinguishes between two levels of signification: the primary, literal (or surface) meaning and the secondary, figurative (or deeper) meaning. To take an example that would be familiar to eighteenth-century readers, John Bunyan's *Pilgrim's Progress from This World, to That Which Is to Come* (1678) is literally the narrative of a dream of Christian, a paradigmatic everyman character, and figuratively the story of any predestined soul. In its intended didactic, evangelical use, a reader might consider the deeper meaning of *The Pilgrim's Progress* in relation to his or her own life. I call this sort of perceived parallel between textual narratives and life experiences, actuated through the reception of a text, a *reception allegory*. The reception allegory can allow the protagonist of one's own life story to read ahead along a parallel track: to anticipate one's arrival in heaven so long as he or she keeps parallel to Christian's path to the Celestial City. Similarly, Christian captives, construing their story as a parallel to the captivity of Jews in Babylon, might anticipate their restoration to Zion. Reception allegories are

19. Rita Copeland and Peter T. Struck, "Introduction," in Copeland and Struck, eds., *The Cambridge Companion to Allegory* (Cambridge, 2010), 2.

20. "As every critic who has attempted a definition is forced to acknowledge," write Copeland and Struck, "the nature of allegorical writing is elusive, its surface by turns mimetic and antimimetic, its procedures intricate and at times seemingly inconsistent, and its meaning or 'other' sense—how it is encoded, or what it refers to extrinsically—often indeterminate" (ibid.).

not necessarily religious in content, nor do they necessarily involve texts, like *The Pilgrim's Progress* or the Old Testament, that are already seen as having allegorical structures of meaning.

One of the functions of such allegoresis, of construing a sequence of events as a parallel to a textual narrative, is to frame experience as a narrative: the story of oneself or themselves. A variant of this sort of reception allegory was practiced prominently by Puritan colonists in New England as an extension of the Christian tradition of typological interpretation. Typology warranted the inclusion of the Jewish Bible in the Christian canon by interpreting it as an allegory for the story of Christ, in its various historical and metaphysical dimensions: "In the Old Testament the New Testament is concealed; in the New Testament the Old Testament is revealed." That is, elements of the story of the Old Testament, or *types,* are fulfilled by elements of the New, or *antitypes.* Some Orthodox Puritans, especially in New England, understood the Old Testament to prefigure not only the story of Christ but also the story of themselves: "Many things that literally concerned the Jewes," wrote the first-generation ministers Richard Mather, Hugh Peters, and John Davenport, "were types and figures signifying the like things concerning the people of God in these latter dayes." Effectively, they inserted a tier within the symbolic structure, interpolating their lived history between parts one and two of the story of Christ, the First Coming, and end times.[21]

Understanding their own story as having eschatological significance meant, in part, that they were living an allegory: their literal story, taking place within temporal history, had another meaning. I call this perception

21. Northrop Frye, *The Great Code: The Bible and Literature* (New York, 1982), 79 ("revealed"). There is debate over the definitions of allegory and typology and over the relationship between the terms, often involving specialized uses in subfields that are outside the scope of this study. According to Frye, typology is distinct from allegory because it posits historical correspondences, insofar as "both testaments . . . deal with real people and real events" (85). However, Thomas P. Roche, Jr., insists, *"Typology is a function of allegory."* See Roche, "Typology, Allegory, and Protestant Poetics," *George Herbert Journal,* XIII (1990), 2; Frye, *Great Code,* 79; Jean Daniélou, "Qu'est-ce que la typologie?" in Paul Auvray, *L'Ancien Testament et les chrétiens* (Paris, 1951), 201; Richard Mather, Hugh Peters, and John Davenport, *An Apologie of the Churches in New-England for Church-Covenant; or, A Discourse Touching the Covenant between God and Men, and Especially concerning Church-Covenant* . . . (London, 1643), 2, cited in Karen E. Rowe, *Saint and Singer: Edward Taylor's Typology and the Poetics of Meditation* (New York, 1986), 13–14. See also Sacvan Bercovitch, *The Puritan Origins of the American Self* (New Haven, Conn., 1975), 35–36; Janice Knight, "The Word Made Flesh: Reading Women and the Bible," in Heidi Brayman Hackel and Catherine E. Kelly, eds., *Reading Women, Literacy, Authorship, and Culture in the Atlantic World, 1500–1800* (Philadelphia, 2008), 170–171.

experiential allegory. I employ these related, generalized terms—reception allegory and experiential allegory—instead of referring only to typology, because not all of the instances I analyze are typological in the narrow sense of invoking a Calvinist "theory of history" involving temporal fulfillments of Old Testament types. Indeed, *typology* may be an overly applied term in early American literary studies, especially scholarship on captivity narratives, where it sometimes seems simply to denote having reference to the Bible. Even in Puritan captivity narratives, not all such references, including parallels or identifications with biblical figures, are necessarily typological in the stricter sense. Moreover, although the Bible predominates, it is by no means the only allegorical correlate for the accounts discussed below.[22]

That said, for Christians of various denominations, captivity among Indians was an experience that was especially conducive to such allegoresis, partly because captivity was such a resonant biblical plot device. Titles like those of the famous narratives of Mary Rowlandson and John Williams (Figure 1) deploy key words—*Captivity, Restauration, Redeemed, Deliverance*—whose literal referents, both in the Old Testament and in colonial New England, are invested with their typological significances, as they pertain to Christ's redemption of the soul from its spiritual captivity to sin and to the progress of the people of God toward the millennium. *Allegories of Encounter* argues that such significances are part of the story of captivity as much as its discourse. Indeed, they contribute to shaping the course of events and not merely the narrative account. As the protagonists of experiential allegories, Rowlandson, Williams, and other captives were like lucid dreamers, aware and motivated by the significances of the stories they were in.

They maintained and developed this awareness, in part, through literacy practices: recollecting, referring to, reading, and composing texts. But a remarkable feature of colonial American captivity narratives is the extent to which the allegorical parallels were also colored by ethnohistory. Colonial narratives present representations of indigenous peoples that, beyond the basic feature of carrying away captives, recapitulate the details of representations from completely exogenous texts. Why does John Wil-

---

22. Frye, *Great Code*, 81; and see Teresa A. Toulouse's thoughtful distinctions between typology and other uses in Toulouse, "Mary Rowlandson and the 'Rhetoric of Ambiguity,'" in Michael Schuldiner, ed., *Sacvan Bercovitch and the Puritan Imagination*, Studies in Puritan American Spirituality, no. 3 (Lewiston, N.Y., 1992), 35–43.

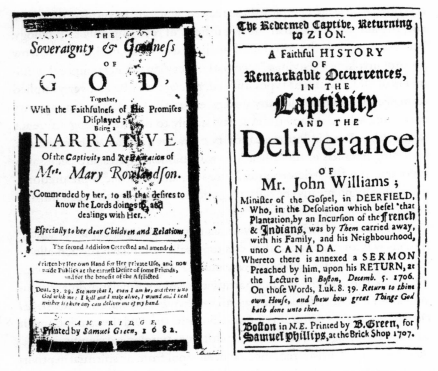

Figure 1 The title pages of Rowlandson's second New England edition (Cambridge, Mass., 1682) and Williams's first edition (Boston, 1707) identify their narratives as allegories. *Early American Imprints,* Ser. 1, nos. 332 and 1340. Reproduced with permission of Readex, a division of NewsBank, Inc.

liams represent his Mohawk and Abenaki abductors requesting his captive congregation sing a psalm, just like the Babylonians in the oft-cited 137th psalm? How does his young daughter, Eunice, come to seemingly switch tracks from one story line to another, from one that paralleled an Old Testament narrative to one that paralleled the *Life* of a medieval saint, Margaret of Antioch, and then perhaps one about a Mohawk woman, Kanenstenhawi? Why does John Marrant's 1785 narrative appear to borrow its depiction of his Cherokee captors' response to his Bible from an Anglo-African slave narrative? With the premise that stories occur and arise in the field as well as on the page, *Allegories of Encounter* investigates the ethnohistorical basis for representations of cultural contact.

This study is arranged in six paired chapters. In Part 1, Chapter 1 takes seriously Mary Rowlandson's characterization of her Bible as her *"Guid"* throughout her captivity, marking out the plotline she needed to follow toward "Restauration"; Chapter 2 demonstrates that captives of various Christian denominations did not need to have the familiar text of Psalm 137, "By the rivers of Babylon," before them to experience a radical actualization of its verses. Part 2 is a comparative diptych: Chapter 3 contrasts the literacy practices and competing story lines of the Jesuit Père Isaac Jogues and the Puritan minister John Williams, captured by Mohawks in 1642 and 1704, respectively; Chapter 4 argues that the lives of the "Mohawk Saint" Kateri Tekakwitha and the "unredeemed captive," Williams's daughter Eunice, intersected with the life stories of others through Catholic and Mohawk naming practices.[23] Part 3 focuses on representations of books in colonial encounters: Chapter 5 poses an "ethnohistoricist" intervention into the literary scholarship on Marrant's representation of the Cherokees' encounter with his Bible; Chapter 6 highlights the role of books — including secular works by Shakespeare and Fenelon and a transcript of debates on the Constitution — in captivities set in the eighteenth-century Ohio Country. Finally, the conclusion summarizes this book's arguments and methods with reference to the Civil War–era captivity narrative of Fanny Kelly.

Allegories of Encounter takes a dynamic approach to interpreting nonfictional narratives in which the relationship between literature and history is mediated by historical actors. The central figures in its case studies represent a number of distinct historical discourse communities across the seventeenth and eighteenth centuries, including New England Puritans, Jesuits, Iroquois Catholics, Protestant evangelicals, and devotees of literary culture. The specific practices and ideologies differ, but collectively, they illustrate the operation of media and stories in the retention, development, and performance of cultural identities in colonial contact situations. For European colonists, this function underscored the value of literacy — a value that the native American captors repeatedly recognized.

"I ran to see what was the matter," recounts James Smith, describing how a group called him over upon their return to the seasonal camp where his books had gone missing; "they shewed me my books, and said they were glad they had been found, for they knew I was grieved at the loss of them, and that they now rejoiced with me because they were found."

---

23. *SGG*, 90; Allan Greer, *Mohawk Saint: Catherine Tekakwitha and the Jesuits* (New York, 2005); John Demos, *The Unredeemed Captive: A Family Story from Early America* (New York, 1994).

More than intertexts, Russell's *Seven Sermons* and the Bible were elements that circulated through the storyworld of Smith's captivity: several times changing hands and, apparently, surviving for months when they had been abandoned in the woods. By restoring them to Smith, the Kahnawakes had paradoxically affirmed his inclusion by acknowledging and enabling his practice of cultural difference. This swing from an outsider's fear of execution to collective rejoicing exemplifies the dramatic significances of books in colonial captivities and in the narratives that recount them: as tokens of identity, cultural lifelines, and bases for dynamic symbolic interactions. In this way, the archive of captivity narratives furnishes an intriguing site to investigate the roles of texts in the encounters between people and the roles of people in the encounters between texts.[24]

24. Smith, *Account*, 39. "The first premise" of the sociological theory of symbolic interactionism "is that human beings act toward things on the basis of the meanings that the things have for them" (Herbert Blumer, *Symbolic Interactionism: Perspective and Method* [Berkeley, Calif., 1986], 2).

CHAPTER ONE

Rowlandson's Captivity, Interpreted by God

"Sending Me a Bible"

Mary Rowlandson's narrative of her captivity, *The Soveraignty and Goodness of God* (1682), is divided into twenty-one sections. The first presents her point-of-view account of a February 1676 raid by Narragansetts, Nipmucs, and Wampanoags on the Massachusetts frontier town of Lancaster. The next twenty are structured according to "the severall Removes we had up and down the Wilderness." For approximately twelve "removes," Rowlandson and her captors traveled "up," farther and farther from Lancaster. In the thirteenth remove, they traveled "down the [Connecticut] river"; in the fourteenth, they began "bending our course toward the Bay-towns," arriving in Boston in the twentieth.[1]

In the third remove, in the Nipmuc town of Memameset, "some Forces" that had carried away captives from Lancaster set off for a raid on the town of Medfield. Rowlandson recounts their return, the celebratory tally of English casualties, and "the hideous insulting and triumphing that there was over some *Englishmens* scalps that they had taken (as their manner) and brought with them." In the subsequent sentence, she declares that she "cannot but take notice of the wonderfull mercy of God to me in those afflictions, in sending me a Bible." She explains: "One of the *Indians* that came from *Medfield* fight, had brought some plunder, came to me, and asked me, if I wou'd have a Bible, he had got one in his basket." Rowlandson asked "whether he thought the *Indians* would let me read? He answered, yes." Presumably, the former owner of the Bible was dead; he was perhaps even betokened by one of the "*Englishmens* scalps," illustrating

---

1. *SGG*, 70, 87, 92. Unless otherwise indicated, all italics in quotations are in the original sources. See the map of "Mary Rowlandson's removes" in Lisa Brooks, *Our Beloved Kin: A New History of King Philip's War* (New Haven, Conn., 2018), 254, and especially on the companion site, http://ourbelovedkin.com. Along with Christine Delucia's *Memory Lands: King Philip's War and the Place of Violence in the Northeast*, Henry Roe Cloud Series on American Indians and Modernity (New Haven, Conn., 2018), *Our Beloved Kin* was published after my research for this chapter was completed.

that although the "afflictions" God visited upon New England were un-
sparing, his "mercy" was more selective. Rowlandson may refuse to recognize the provision of the Bible as an act of deliberate kindness on the
Indian's part, but it was the gesture of an intimate enemy, evincing a familiarity—most likely, an outcome of evangelization—with the nature of the
book in his basket and its significance to the captive Englishwoman.[2]

The Bible thus introduced into the narrative is the vehicle for an interpretation of Rowlandson's captivity that has precedence over all others,
because it was part of her story rather than part of the commentary upon
it and, in Rowlandson's view, because of its divine source. The narrator's
own exegesis is laced with quotations and references to scripture, as is the
"Preface to the Reader," authored by the pseudonymous "Per Amicam,"
and the sermon by Rowlandson's late husband Joseph that was appended
to early editions. However, the scriptures in the narrative that were drawn
from the very Bible she read during her captivity—the copy that was variously taken as plunder, tossed from a wigwam, and stored in Rowlandson's
"pocket" amid the remnants of corn cake and rotting bear meat—are different. The appearance of this Bible in a basket unsettles the premise of a
long-standing "critical debate" over *The Soveraignty and Goodness of God:*
the apparent dichotomy between "the dense web of biblical quotations
and allusions in the text" and Rowlandson's "direct experience."[3]

That is, one of the central conversations in the profuse body of scholarship devoted to Rowlandson's "hypercanonical" captivity narrative is
about the relationship between its biblical language and its depiction of
events. Some scholars have suggested that an orthodox minister, especially Increase Mather (widely identified as the author of the preface),
might have influenced the composition of the narrative or edited it directly, imbuing it with scriptures that brought it more in line with a con-

---

2. *SGG*, 76. On the participation of Christian Indians in King Philip's War, see Neal Salisbury, "Embracing Ambiguity: Native Peoples and Christianity in Seventeenth-Century North
America," *Ethnohistory*, L (2003), 248–251.

3. *SGG*, 83, 85, 86 ("pocket"); on the "critical debate," see *ACN*, 130. Bryce Traister argues
persuasively that the common rendering of the preface author's pseudonym as "Ter Amicam"
("Thrice a Friend") rather than "Per Amicam" ("By a Friend") derives from an error in reading
the type (Traister, "Mary Rowlandson and the Invention of the Secular," *EAL*, XLII [2007], 350).
The name "Per Amicam" is also consonant with the 1682 Cambridge title page, which informs
that the narrative was "made Publick at the earnest Desire of some Friends" (*SGG*, 62). On the
narrative's early publication history, see Kathryn Zabelle Derounian, "The Publication, Promo-
tion, and Distribution of Mary Rowlandson's Indian Captivity Narrative in the Seventeenth
Century," *EAL*, XXIII (1988), 239–261.

servative political interpretation of King Philip's War, an interpretation that was seconded by Joseph Rowlandson's jeremiad sermon. Others have countered that Rowlandson presents precisely the rhetoric one might expect from a minister's wife, and many have provided nuanced analyses of the literary manifestations of the collision between Mary Rowlandson's Puritan faith and her traumatic experiences as an Indian captive. But in Rowlandson's rendering, the provision of a Bible was an experience, a communication from God, as was the series of literacy events it enabled.[4]

Attention to Rowlandson's representation of literacy events adds to the understanding of the oft-noted polyphony of *The Sovereignty and Goodness of God*. Scholarship has observed three, overlapping categories of heteroglossia. First, there is the "linguistic and cultural dialogism" characterizing a colonial English woman's account of captivity among Algonquians: "This morning I asked my master whither he would sell me to my husband; he answered me *Nux*, which did much rejoyce my spirit." Second is the narrative's "peculiar double-voicedness," involving an "empirical" recounting of events and a "rhetorical" commentary suffused with borrowings from scripture, such as in this coupling of the destruction of Lancaster with a verse from Psalm 46: "Oh the dolefull sight that now was to

---

4. "Hypercanonization" is Jonathan Arac's term for the phenomenon wherein "a very few individual works monopolize curricular and critical attention" (Arac, *Huckleberry Finn as Idol and Target: The Functions of Criticism in Our Time* [Madison, Wis., 1997], 133). According to Teresa Toulouse, "No clear proof exists of Increase Mather's authorship of the anonymous preface to Mary Rowlandson's text." It is also possible that it was written by another conservative minister. See Toulouse, *The Captive's Position: Female Narrative, Male Identity, and Royal Authority in Colonial New England* (Philadelphia, 2007), 33. For suggestions of editorial interference, see Mitchell Robert Breitwieser, *American Puritanism and the Defense of Mourning: Religion, Grief, and Ethnology in Mary White Rowlandson's Captivity Narrative* (Madison, Wis., 1990), 8; Christopher Castiglia, *Bound and Determined: Captivity, Culture-Crossing, and White Womanhood from Mary Rowlandson to Patty Hearst* (Chicago, 1996), 50; Billy J. Stratton, *Buried in Shades of Night: Contested Voices, Indian Captivity, and the Legacy of King Philip's War* (Tucson, Ariz., 2013). Proponents of editorial integrity include Charles E. Hambrick-Stowe, *The Practice of Piety: Puritan Devotional Disciplines in Seventeenth-Century New England* (Williamsburg, Va., and Chapel Hill, N.C., 1982), 29; Kathryn Zabelle Derounian-Stodola and James Arthur Levernier, *The Indian Captivity Narrative, 1550–1900* (New York, 1993), 99; Gary L. Ebersole, *Captured by Texts: Puritan to Postmodern Images of Indian Captivity* (Charlottesville, Va., 1995), 259; Michelle Burnham, *Captivity and Sentiment: Cultural Exchange in American Literature, 1682–1861* (Hanover, N.H., 1997), 16–17. See also David Downing, "'Streams of Scripture Comfort': Mary Rowlandson's Typological Use of the Bible," *EAL*, XV (1980), 252–259; Kathryn Zabelle Derounian, "Puritan Orthodoxy and the 'Survivor Syndrome' in Mary Rowlandson's Indian Captivity Narrative," ibid., XXII (1987), 82–93; Dawn Henwood, "Mary Rowlandson and the Psalms: The Textuality of Survival," ibid., XXXII (1997), 169–186; Traister, "Mary Rowlandson and the Invention of the Secular," ibid., XLII (2007); Branka Arsić, "Mary Rowlandson and the Phenomenology of Patient Suffering," *Common Knowledge*, XVI (2010), 247–275.

behold at this House! *Come, behold the works of the Lord, what desolations he has made in the Earth.*" Third, the principal source for Rowlandson's rhetoric supplies "a variety of voices"; the Bible, especially the Book of Psalms, affords her public account an expansive, conflicted, expressive range that would be otherwise inappropriate for a Puritan woman. These three conceptualizations should entail a simultaneous recognition of the multiple voices of scripture and the multiple voices, in and through Rowlandson's narrative, employing scripture. The "double-voiced" narrator uses biblical rhetoric to depict and comment on a colonial, metaphysical heteroglossia featuring multilateral communicative events in which various participants—including Rowlandson, fellow captive readers, Christian Indians, and, above all, God—all employ the language of scripture.[5]

Although the several analyses of Rowlandson's biblical rhetoric or typology recognize that some of the "citations" appear in the context of her accounts of literacy events, they do not consistently distinguish these from the ones she employs in her narratorial commentary. In other words, these studies conflate her "use" of the Bible as an author with her experience of it as a captive reader; accordingly, they diminish her attempt to represent a voice other than her own. Yet God's message to the captive Rowlandson is a critical aspect, the upshot, of her narrative. "And here I may take occasion to mention one principall ground of my setting forth these Lines," Rowlandson declares after recounting one such literacy event, in the eighth remove: "even as the Psalmist sayes, *To declare the Works of the Lord, and his wonderfull Power* in carrying us along, preserving us in the *Wilderness,* while under the Enemies hand, and returning of us in safety again. And His goodness in bringing to my hand so many comfortable and suitable Scriptures in my distress." Rowlandson's "distress" was an experiential context for her reception of scriptures. Her uses of language from scripture challenge our critical vocabulary, because when verses appear as part of her narrated action, they are not quite "citations," "references," "quota-

5. The term "heteroglossia" was influentially introduced by the linguist and literary theorist Mikhail Bakhtin to refer to the "diversity of speech types"; for Bakhtin, a novel comprised "a social dialogue of 'languages'" (*The Dialogic Imagination: Four Essays* [Austin, Tex., 1981], 253, 364). On dialogism, see Burnham, *Captivity and Sentiment,* 35; *SGG,* 70, 86, 86n ("nux" means "yes"). On the dichotomy between orthodox and "empirical" rhetoric, see Henwood, "Mary Rowlandson and the Psalms," *EAL,* XXXII (1997), 170; Derounian, "Puritan Orthodoxy," ibid., XXII (1987), 82; and Downing, "'Streams of Scripture Comfort,'" ibid., XV (1980). On the ambiguity within the biblical rhetoric, see Teresa A. Toulouse, "Mary Rowlandson and the 'Rhetoric of Ambiguity,'" in Michael Schuldiner, ed., *Sacvan Bercovitch and the Puritan Imagination,* Studies in Puritan American Spirituality, no. 3 (Lewiston, N.Y., 1992), 37.

tions," or "allusions." Instead, in the language of narrative theory, they are "existents," elements in the story, part of the "substance of the content," whereas allusions and citations are part of the discourse, part of the "substance of expression."[6]

In some instances, it is difficult to tell which dimension, or narrative level, a particular reference to scripture belongs to—whether it is part of discourse or story. Rowlandson frequently introduces scriptures with variants of the phrase "now I may say," as when she recounts a meeting in captivity with her son Joseph: "We asked of each others welfare, bemoaning our dolefull condition, and the change that had come upon us. We had Husband and Father, and Children, and Sisters, and Friends, and Relations, and House, and Home, and many Comforts of this Life: but now we may say, as Job, *Naked came I out of my Mothers Womb, and naked shall I return: The Lord gave, and the Lord hath taken away, Blessed be the Name of the Lord.*" Rowlandson's use of the adverb *now* sticks a pin in her diegesis, marking a particular moment in the course of events, but it is unclear whether the reference to Job 1:21 was part of the conversation with her son that she represents through indirect discourse or whether it is part of a narratorial reflection on that moment.[7]

Rowlandson does recount eight distinct Bible-reading events, comprising nine specific "places" in the Old Testament that she visited during the time of her captivity (Table 1). Rowlandson exhibits a practice of "divinely-directed reading," in which she "opened my Bible to read, and the Lord brought" her particular scriptures. Some of the places in scripture she thus "lighted on" are so specifically "suitable" (in the now-obsolete sense of "accordant; corresponding; analogous") to her circumstances as to make it difficult for a modern reader to credit her disavowal of intention in selecting them. (In the case of the first reading, she im-

---

6. *SGG,* 46, 82; Sidonie Smith, "Reading the Posthuman Backward: Mary Rowlandson's Doubled Witnessing," *Biography,* XXXV (2012), 144 ("citations"); Downing, "'Streams of Scripture Comfort,'" *EAL,* XV (1980), 252 ("references," "quotations," "allusions"); *ACN,* 130 ("quotations and allusions"); Seymour Chatman, *Story and Discourse: Narrative Structure in Fiction and Film* (Ithaca, N.Y., 1980), 21, 23. Toulouse interprets "groups of texts" that include both diegetic and extradiegetic citations ("Mary Rowlandson and the 'Rhetoric of Ambiguity,'" in Schuldiner, ed., *Sacvan Bercovitch and the Puritan Imagination,* 37).

7. Didier Coste and John Pier, "Narrative Levels," in Peter Hühn et al., eds., *The Living Handbook of Narratology* (Hamburg, 2014), http://wikis.sub.uni-hamburg.de/lhn/index.php /Narrative_Levels; *SGG,* 81–82. See Janice Knight's discussion of this mode of Bible citation in Rowlandson: "The Word Made Flesh: Reading Women and the Bible," in Heidi Brayman Hackel and Catherine E. Kelly, eds., *Reading Women: Literacy, Authorship, and Culture in the Atlantic World, 1500–1800* (Philadelphia, 2008), 197n.

Table 1 Diegetic Scriptures in *The Sovereignty and Goodness of God*

Event	"Remove"	"Place"
1	3	1. Deuteronomy 28–30
2	3	2. Psalm 27
3	4	3. Jeremiah 31:16
4	8	4. Psalm 118:17–18
5	9	5. Psalm 55:22
6	12	6. Psalm 46:10
7	13	7. Isaiah 55:8
		8. Psalm 37:5
8	13	9. Isaiah 54:7

plicitly credits God for her thought to turn to Deuteronomy 28.) Nevertheless, she indicates that for scriptures to be "comfortable"—in the sense of "Strengthening or supporting (morally or spiritually); encouraging, inspiriting"—her reading of them needed to be joined by God. That is, the words of scripture comforted her, "quieted" her, and admonished her only through the affective agency of the Holy Spirit.[8]

The places in scripture that God selects for Rowlandson are consonant with the emphasis on the Old Testament by New England Puritan congregations. Cumulatively, these selections present an interpretation of Rowlandson's captivity in the form of a jeremiad—a "denunciation" of backsliding, an exhortation to reform, and a promise of redemption. They attribute her affliction and, by extension, the war that occasioned it, to God's righteous anger, construing "His vengeance [as] a sign of love, a father's rod used to improve the errant child." God's selections for Rowlandson are more consistently on-message than the anonymous preface that supposedly imposes its orthodoxy on the narrative. They pose a diegetic interpretation of her captivity, emerging from the inside out (or bottom up). For Rowlandson's readers, God's message, delivered to

8. *SGG*, 78, 112; Knight, "Word Made Flesh," in Hackel and Kelly, eds., *Reading Women*, 184 ("divinely-directed"). Rowlandson's practice does not quite amount to "'bibliomancy,' an act of divination in which a Bible verse is selected at random and then applied to the experience at hand," as Philip H. Round suggests. I agree, however, that in her "usage, the Bible becomes less a mundane object and more a talisman endued with great power" (Round, *Removable Type: Histories of the Book in Indian Country, 1663–1880* [Chapel Hill, N.C., 2010], 43).

Rowlandson in and through her captivity, should override all others. Accordingly, for her "dear Children and Relations" and for her own post-captivity self, she models the exemplary reading practices of an afflicted Puritan saint. Rowlandson also furnishes negative examples, in Ann Joslin, the desperate "Goodwife" who disregards a directive from scripture, and in the Christian, or "Praying," Indians, whose scriptural exegesis she represents as a horrifying travesty.[9]

"The Lord Helped Me Still to Go on Reading"
(Deuteronomy 28–30)

Reading the Bible in captivity would have facilitated Rowlandson's understanding of her situation as a narrative that she was living. Specifically, it identified her as the protagonist of a Puritan conversion narrative, which recapitulated the jeremiad plot sequence—backsliding, chastisement, renewal—on an individual level. Similarly, her Bible reading might have prompted her to construe her individual story as an epitome of her collectivity, her New England community. Her captivity was an experiential allegory: she was living out a story with multiple secondary and perhaps tertiary levels of signification.

These diegetic interpretations, her ongoing understanding of the significance of her captivity, are activated in the third remove, in her first literacy event as a captive reader, but Rowlandson presages the function of scripture within her story of captivity in a brief analepsis (or flashback) following the account of the death of her sister, Elizabeth Kerley, during the initial raid on Lancaster. "In her younger years," Rowlandson relates, "she lay under much trouble upon spiritual accounts, till it pleased God to make that precious scripture take hold of her heart, *2 Cor.* 12: 9. *And he*

9. Sacvan Bercovitch, *The American Jeremiad* (Madison, Wis., 1978), 6, 8 ("denunciation"); *SGG*, 62. According to Patricia Caldwell, "There is in fact more pain than triumph in New England's dependence on the Hebrew Scriptures, a stronger sense of identification with the Jews' suffering than with their having been chosen by God; more, in short, of Babylon than of Canaan" (Caldwell, *The Puritan Conversion Narrative: The Beginnings of American Expression* [New York, 1983], 172). In this regard, it is not "unusual," as Downing maintains, that Rowlandson exhibits a "heavy reliance on the Old Testament"; "fewer than one tenth" of her "Biblical references" are from the New Testament ("'Streams of Scripture Comfort,'" *EAL*, XV [1980], 254). In his vertical schema of narrative levels, Genette arranges them from the top down, with the extradiegetic level below the diegesis, but other theorists arrange them from the bottom up, an orientation that is more suggestive for my analysis (Coste and Pier, "Narrative Levels," in Hühn et al., eds., *Living Handbook of Narratology*, http://wikis.sub.uni-hamburg.de/lhn/index .php/Narrative_Levels).

said unto me, my grace is sufficient for thee. More than twenty years after I have heard her tell how sweet and comfortable that place was to her." This detail, which sounds as if it would once have been the climax of Kerley's conversion narrative, construes the reading of a Bible verse as the turning point in Kerley's life. Rowlandson's account of it is consistent with scholarly understandings of Puritan reading practices, in which the meeting of verse and reader is galvanized by the Holy Spirit, causing a scripture that she had presumably encountered many times suddenly to "take hold of her heart" and effect her conversion. Rowlandson's captivity parallels Kerley's spiritual "trouble"; it is a dramatic "objective correlative" for a crisis of faith and sets the stage for Rowlandson's re-encounter with scripture in the form of the Bible in the basket.[10]

Rowlandson accepted the Bible the Indian offered, "and in that melancholy time, it came into my mind to read first the 28. *Chap.* of *Deut.*" Her selection of a verse, prompted by God, already constitutes an interpretation of her experience, predicated on the ex post facto logic that, because she was suffering affliction, she must have been sinful: *"That there was no mercy for me, that the blessings were gone, and the curses come in their room, and that I had lost my opportunity."* The captive Rowlandson's starting point in scripture was a dire assessment of her situation.[11]

Deuteronomy 28 would have provided ample grist for her "dark heart" through its bearing on her immediate experiences. Some of the enumerated "curses" would have resonated with harrowing specificity. Verses 18 ("Cursed *shall* be the fruit of thy body"), 32 ("Thy sons and thy daughters *shall be* given unto another people"), and 41 ("Thou shalt beget sons and daughters, but thou shalt not enjoy them; for they shall go into captivity") would have hammered home the significance of her children's fate: "I had one Child dead, another in the Wilderness, I knew not where, the third they would not let me come near to." Verses 50–51, prophesying that a "nation of fierce countenance" would "eat the fruit of thy cattle" would have reminded her of the bacchanalistic consumption of the Lancaster livestock: "And as miserable was the waste that was there made, of Horses, Cattle, Sheep, Swine, Calves, Lambs, Roasting Pigs, and Fowls (which they had plundered in the Town) some roasting, some lying and burning,

10. *SGG*, 70. On the Holy Spirit in Puritan reading, see Matthew P. Brown, *The Pilgrim and the Bee: Reading Rituals and Book Culture in Early New England* (Philadelphia, 2007), 86; Caldwell, *Puritan Conversion Narrative*, 159 ("objective correlative").

11. *SGG*, 76–77.

and some boyling to feed our merciless Enemies; who were joyfull enough though we were disconsolate." In Rowlandson's circumstances, she would have understood the second-person "Thou" of scripture as referring to herself, not by analogy with the Old Testament Jews, but immediately.[12]

This reading cast Rowlandson's predicament as an antitypal fulfillment of Old Testament prophecy. Within the stricter definition of Christian typology, the destruction and captivation of the Israelites and their eventual redemption from captivity are historical events whose significance is revealed only through the New Testament; they can be understood to prefigure the plight of the sinner and his redemption through Christ. In the practice of Rowlandson's interpretive community, however, this system carried into "history after the Incarnation": the history that in 1675–1676 saw the temporal antitypes of the Old Testament Jews attacked by heathen enemies and carried in significant numbers into the antitypal "wilderness." Rowlandson was participating in a fulfillment that was itself a figural prophecy, "a harbinger of things to come," in the historical progress toward the Second Coming. Deuteronomy 28:45 marked her progress, at that instant, toward a temporal redemption: "All these curses shall come upon thee, and shall pursue thee, and overtake thee, till thou be destroyed: because thou hearkenedst not unto the voice of the LORD thy God, to keep his commandements, and his statutes which he commanded thee." If the afflictions visited upon Rowlandson, the devout minister's wife, seem incommensurate with her crimes, her self-reprobation was consonant with Deuteronomy 28:47: "Because thou servedst not the LORD thy God with joyfulness, and with gladness of heart, for the aboundance of all *things*." The lesson that she needed to learn was that "the comforts of the World" are God-given and can be withdrawn in an instant.[13]

Since her unfolding story was paralleled with an Old Testament narrative, she could "go on reading" to see how it would turn out. For this understanding of affliction to prompt reform, it had to be accompanied by an expectation of "mercy." Thus, "the Lord helped me still to go on reading till I came to *Chap.* 30 the first seven verses, where I found, *There was mercy promised again, if we would return to him by repentance; and though*

12. Ibid., 71, 77.

13. Bercovitch, *American Jeremiad*, 14 (see also 40–42); *SGG*, 112. According to Northrop Frye, "The general principle of interpretation is traditionally given as 'In the Old Testament the New Testament is concealed; in the New Testament the Old Testament is revealed'" (Frye, *The Great Code: The Bible and Literature* (New York, 1982), 79.

we were scattered from one end of the Earth to the other, yet the Lord would gather us together, and turn all those curses upon our Enemies." In guiding her through the chastening of Deuteronomy 28, the reminder of the covenant in 29, and the turning of the tables in 30:7, God provided her with a figural itinerary on which she might track her progress. "I do not desire to live to forget this Scripture," she wrote, "and what comfort it was to me." All the other scriptures that God communicated to her complemented and reinforced its message.[14]

This message definitively associated Rowlandson, and by extension her community, with the Jews of the Old Testament, who outraged their God by lapsing in their covenant but whose scourging brought them to reaffirm that covenant and was therefore a sign of divine favor. The rhetoric of Deuteronomy 28–30 suggests how Rowlandson might have understood her afflicted self to be representative of an afflicted community. The second-person singular "thou" spoke to Rowlandson, the reader, directly, but in its rhetorical context it composed a people as a singular subject— one person to be scourged and chastened. The verses also recognize the Jews' plurality. Rowlandson might have fearfully recognized herself in the "tender and delicate woman among you, which would not adventure to set the sole of her foot upon the ground for delicateness and tenderness" and would eat her own children "for want of all *things* secretly in the siege and straitness, wherewith thine enemy shall distress thee in thy gates" (Deut. 28:56–57). Here the second-person pronouns, *thou* and *you*, are simultaneously singular and plural. The nature of Rowlandson's affliction was such that she could only have understood it as part of a collective plight: the town sacked, along with other towns; many settlers killed or captured; a whole colony nearly overrun by the enemy. The message that God spelled out for her—that she should renew her covenant, obey God's statutes, and cast her entire dependence upon him—would naturally extend to her entire community of believers. Perhaps she left it to Increase Mather and her husband, in preface and sermon, to make that extension explicit. But why not consider that Rowlandson's narrative, with God speaking through its diegesis, drove the message of its frame instead of resisting it?[15]

14. *SGG*, 77. Caldwell observes that, in New England conversion narratives, "Scriptural passages become structural elements," and the convert moves "through the Bible, almost as through a physical space" (*Puritan Conversion Narrative*, 31).

15. As Knight observes, critics have debated whether Rowlandson "understood herself as a

Through her quietude, her ability to "still" her impatience, Rowland-son exhibited, in the terms of her husband's sermon, "the difference be-twixt a sinner forsaken and a Saint forsaken." If God forsakes the former utterly, for the latter, "he leaves some light, whereby they see which way he is gone; he leaves some glimmering light, by which they may follow after him, and find him." The story presented coherently by *The Soveraignty and Goodness of God* is that Mary Rowlandson was a forsaken saint who fol-lowed the light of scripture to her restoration and marked the trail for other saints to follow.[16]

"Did You Read This?" (Psalm 27, Jeremiah 31:16, Psalm 118:17–18)

Rowlandson's reading of Deuteronomy 28–30, from the prophesied de-struction through to the promised mercy upon the condition of repen-tance, running an affective course from severe self-reprobation through to "comfort" and hope, provided an exemplary model for her readers. As a minister's wife, she was also in a position to instruct the women and chil-dren among her fellow captives. The third and fourth removes present a "sad" case study: her neighbor Ann Joslin, who fails to heed God's message to "Wait on the LORD" (Psalm 27:14) and accordingly, unlike Rowland-son, fails the test of her captivity. In contrast, the eighth remove exhibits the devout literacy practices of Rowlandson's son Joseph, offering a model for the emotional disposition of the Puritan reader.

As narrator, Rowlandson primes her readers for their joint discovery of Psalm 27 with Ann Joslin by extradiegetically citing the penultimate verse of Psalm 27 near the beginning of the third remove: "Oh the num-ber of Pagans (now merciless enemies) that there came about me, that I may say as *David*, Psal 27. 13, *I had fainted, unless I had believed*, etc." Here the "et cetera" includes the continuation of verse 13—"to see the good-ness of the LORD in the land of the living"—as well as the final verse,

---

representative type of New England" or whether this "grand typological reading" was imposed from without, specifically by the ministerial preface and the jeremiad sermon that "contained — one might even say disciplined" her narrative. See "Word Made Flesh," in Hackel and Kelly, eds., *Reading Women*, 182–183. Readers have tended to look for signs of rhetorical and ideological struggle between Rowlandson and her orthodox editors or sponsors. According to Toulouse, "The tempting alternative of captive women's resistance rather than their orthodoxy has been variously considered in a range of studies" (*Captive's Position*, 10).

16. *SGG*, 160–161.

"Wait on the LORD: be of good courage, and he shall strengthen thine heart: wait, I say, on the LORD." She presented the events of the third remove, which included her self-recriminating acknowledgment of the Lord's righteousness and the death of her daughter Sarah, as a demonstration of this moral. For expressing her "earnest and unfeigned desire" for God's help through this "distressed time," he rewarded her with "a token for good," a reassuring encounter with her son Joseph, who was separately held captive. Next, God manifested "wonderfull mercy" in the midst of "afflictions" by providing the aforementioned Bible. This sets up her reading of Deuteronomy 28–30—a lesson in the importance of upholding faith in the midst of deserved judgment—which, in turn, sets up her interview with Joslin and their shared reading of Psalm 27.[17]

The faith itself, of course, was an index of God's favor, and for that reason, when Rowlandson encountered a group of eight captive children in the company of the "Goodwife *Joslin*," she was somewhat encouraged by the children's response to her query *"whether they were earnest with God for deliverance"*: they responded that "they did as they were able," which "was some comfort to me, that the Lord stirred up *Children to look to him*." The English captives were at the point of disbanding, as contingents of captors went their separate ways. Rowlandson's hope was that the English children would carry with them the root connection: God moving their hearts to depend upon Him for deliverance.[18]

Without this connection, one could not properly read the Bible. When Rowlandson invited Joslin to join her in a reading, Joslin was in a state of despair. She told Rowlandson "she should never see me again" and that she was contemplating an attempt "to run away"; Rowlandson tried to persuade her not to, pointing out that she was a week away from childbirth, with "another Child in her Arms," that they were separated from the nearest *"English Town"* by "near *thirty miles"* and "bad Rivers," and that they were "feeble" from their "poor and coarse entertainment." According to Rowlandson, "I had my Bible with me, I pulled it out, and asked her whether she would read; we opened the Bible, and lighted on *Psal. 27.* in which Psalm we especially took notice of that, *ver. ult., Wait on the Lord, Be of good courage, and he shall strengthen thine heart, wait I say on the Lord.*" Rowlandson does not record Joslin's response to her invitation to

---

17. Ibid., 74.
18. Ibid., 77.

read, and we may infer that Rowlandson took the more active part in the literacy event. Implicitly, the problem for Joslin was that she did not fully appreciate the significance of her situation as a metaphor for the helplessness and hopelessness of the justly damned soul, with no recourse but faith. She could not properly read because her soul was unprepared. For Rowlandson, the like circumstances were spiritually advantageous because they awakened her to the "state of holy desperation"—her utter dependency on God's saving grace.[19]

Unlike Rowlandson, therefore, Joslin did not "wait." Her actions show that the message of Psalm 27:14 did not get through to her. In the fourth remove, in a brief prolepsis (or flash-forward), Rowlandson recounts that she later heard that Joslin kept importuning her captors "to let her go home," and they then "gathered a great company together about her, and stript her naked, and set her in the midst of them." Eventually, "they knockt her on head, and the child in her arms with her." They torched both, warning the other captive children "that if they attempted to go home, they would serve them in like manner." According to Rowlandson, "the Children said, she did not shed one tear, but prayed all the while." Rowlandson suggests that Joslin died because she did not heed the scripture they had shared, but furnishes the reader with the heartening secondhand information that finally, in her dying moment, God enabled Joslin to communicate with him.[20]

Rowlandson never found herself in quite such an extremity—her child in her arms, the flames leaping around them, no recourse at her disposal but prayer. However, Joslin's end typified the peril of every unregenerate sinner, with the lesson that they must not wait until they feel the "flames of *Burning Fire*" (in Michael Wigglesworth's phrase) before they reconcile themselves to their absolute dependency upon God. Rowlandson's situation typified the desolation and precariousness of the readers' spiritual state and indicated the remedy. Her readers were actually in a more hazardous place than she, because they experienced the allegory at a reader's remove. Rowlandson had come to "a desolate place in the Wilderness,

19. Ibid. According to Charles Lloyd Cohen, "Holy desperation unleavened by hope metamorphoses into consternation that inhibits rather than furthers the goals of preparation. Sinners properly readied for faith respond to fears of damnation and cognition of weakness by hungering for Christ and resolving to spare no effort or means to reach him. The despondant [sic] misconstrue their situation and choose an unproductive course" (Cohen, *God's Caress: The Psychology of Puritan Religious Experience* [New York, 1986], 88; see also 80).
20. *SGG*, 77–78.

where there were no *Wigwams* or *Inhabitants* before; we came about the middle of the afternoon to this place; cold and wet, and snowy, and hungry, and weary, and no refreshing, for man, but the cold ground to sit on, and our poor *Indian cheer.*" This stage is a literal embodiment of an allegorical "wilderness" and therefore the ideal setting for a demonstration of exclusive dependence upon God.[21]

The spiritual understanding of that dependence required God to work at both ends of the communication. Fatigued, famished, and acutely worried about her surviving children, Rowlandson declares that in her present narration, "I cannot express to man the affliction that lay upon my Spirit, but the Lord helped me at that time to express it to himself." What she describes is a two-way channel of communication, with prayer calling and scripture responding. "I opened my Bible to read, and the Lord brought that precious scripture to me, *Jer.* 31.16. *Thus saith the Lord, refrain thy voice from weeping, and thine eyes from tears, for thy work shall be rewarded, and they shall come again from the land of the Enemy.*" This verse echoed Deuteronomy 30—the hopeful note in the jeremiad sequence of affliction, reform and redemption.[22]

Although Rowlandson's rhetoric acknowledges no intention, a captive woman separated from her captive children could hardly have found a more "suitable" verse: in Jeremiah 31, amid promises to "gather" and restore the "remnant of Israel" (7–8) from captivity in Babylon, God reassures a mother "weeping for her children" who "refused to be comforted for her children, because they *were* not" (31:15). In Rowlandson's representation, although the verse prohibited tears of anxiety, it became an occasion for tears of another sort. "This was a sweet Cordial to me, when I was ready to faint, many and many a time have I sat down, and wept sweetly over this Scripture." Shifting within this sentence from the simple past tense to the present perfect, she attests to the continued significance the verse has held for her in her postcaptivity life. It was one of several places of scripture that became actualized for her, invested with specificity, during her captivity; and her narrative might, in some measure, have activated these places for her readers, or demonstrated the process whereby verses of scripture might "take hold" in their lives.[23]

21. [Michael Wigglesworth], *Day of Doom; or, A Description of the Great and Last Judgment: With a Short Discourse about Eternity* ([Cambridge, Mass., 1666]), 68; *SGG*, 78.
22. *SGG*, 78.
23. Ibid., 146.

A further demonstration of successful communication, spirit to God, through the medium of scripture, occurs in the eighth remove, in another shared reading during a brief reunion with her son Joseph. "I asked him whither he would read; he told me, he earnestly desired it." Whereas in the third remove she had omitted mention of Joslin's response to the same question, here the adverb echoes her query to the captive children: being *"earnest with God"* was the prescribed emotional state, the necessary condition for effective prayer and heartfelt experience of scripture. As Increase Mather wrote in the preface to a tract printed during the year of Rowlandson's captivity, *An Earnest Exhortation to the Inhabitants of New-England* (1676), the people of New England *"had need then to pray earnestly, that past and present dispensations may be sanctified to us."* Rowlandson's captivity narrative became an exhibit in the argument for such sanctification, for an understanding of King Philip's War that would prompt spiritual reform, by first demonstrating the Christians' dependency: "Now the Heathen begins to think all is their own," wrote Rowlandson in the twentieth remove, recalling the point in the war when the Indians had the upper hand, "and the poor Christians hopes to fail (as to man) and now their eyes are more to God, and their hearts sigh heaven-ward; and to say in good earnest, *Help Lord, or we perish."* The failure of the "Christians' hopes" in "man" was a necessary step toward resting their hopes totally and "in good earnest" on God, as Rowlandson's scriptures repeatedly insisted.[24]

Being "earnest," Joseph was prepared, unlike Joslin, to be properly receptive to the verse God pointed out to him. "I gave him my Bible," wrote Rowlandson, "and he lighted upon that comfortable scripture, Psal. 118. 17, 18. *I shall not dy but live, and declare the works of the Lord: the Lord hath chastened me sore, yet he hath not given me over to death.* Look here, *Mother* (sayes he), did you read this?" Joseph and Mary Rowlandson's shared understanding of these lines, at that contingent moment, would have been different from that of churchgoers back home. The structure of the application was different. At home, the reader might understand the literal reference to David's temporal survival—"I shall not dy"—as a type for the promise of eternal life through Christ: "We, whose life is hid with Christ in

---

24. Ibid., 82, 106; Increase Mather, *An Earnest Exhortation to the Inhabitants of New-England* (Boston, 1676), 3; and see Abram Van Engen's related discussion of the use of the adverb "pathetically" in the printer Samuel Green's advertisement for Rowlandson's narrative on the back page of a 1681 edition of *Pilgrim's Progress* (Abram C. Van Engen, *Sympathetic Puritans: Calvinist Fellow Feeling in Early New England* [New York, 2015], 177–178).

God," wrote John Calvin in his commentary on Psalm 118, "ought to meditate upon this song all our days." But the captive Rowlandsons, like David,
felt they were "in imminent danger, exposed every moment to a thousand
deaths." Their empirical situation was comparable to the literal meaning
of the psalm; they were living the allegory. Calvin's further explication of
Psalm 118:18 characterizes the difference between the Rowlandsons and
Joslin, who did not recognize the meaning of her affliction: "Our champ-
ing the bit, and rushing forward impatiently, certainly proceeds from the
majority of men not looking upon their afflictions as God's rods, and from
others not participating in his paternal care." Rowlandson's readers were
not joining her, like Joslin and Joseph, in reading the Bible under the rod;
but in representing the literacy events through narrative, she invited her
readers, as well, to re-experience scriptures such as Psalms 27:14 and 118:
17–18 in light of the historical recapitulations of the afflictions visited
upon God's chosen people in New England.[25]

"I Repaired under These Thoughts to My Bible" (Psalm 55:2)

But scripture was only one kind of remedy, specific to "affliction that lay
upon" the "spirit" rather than the body. In the catalog of physical and
emotional ailments that Rowlandson experienced during her captivity,
scripture was effective in addressing the latter: her doubts and disappoint-
ments, her grief for her dead child and worry for her two surviving ones.
For bodily concerns, she had to look elsewhere: to the Indians. The succor
she received "while under the Enemies hand" was a point of divergence
between the Old Testament type and its temporal fulfillment in her experience.

On the one hand, if the Indian antagonists signify God's righteous judgment, then Indian "friends" symbolize mercy in the midst of judgment;
particularly in the absence of fellow Christians to do kind offices, they
indicate the Christian's dependence on God alone. In the ninth remove,
Rowlandson was camped *"about a mile"* from Joseph, and she went to visit
him, becoming lost along the way. She remarks that she "cannot but ad-
mire at the wonderfull power and goodness of God to me, in that, though
I was gone from home, and met with all sorts of *Indians,* and those I had

25. *SGG,* 82; John Calvin, *Commentary on the Book of Psalms,* trans. James Anderson, V (Edinburgh, 1849), 385–386.

no knowledge of, and there being no Christian soul near me; yet not one of them offered the least imaginable miscarriage to me." However, the actions of her "master," the Narragansett sachem Quinnapin, exceed this passive benignity; when she "turned homeward again," having failed to find her way, he escorted her to her son himself. She found Joseph sick, and while they "bemoaned one another a while," apparently they did not share a reading. Rowlandson returned to camp "as unsatisfied as I was before. I went up and down mourning and lamenting: and my spirit was ready to sink, with the thoughts of my poor children: my son was ill, and I could not but think of his mournfull looks, and no Christian Friend was near him, to do any office of love for him, either for Soul or Body." No "Christian Friend" was near Mary Rowlandson either—emphatically, she did not consider the Praying Indians to be such—but she "repaired under these thoughts to my Bible (my great comfort in that time) and that Scripture came to my hand, *Cast thy burden upon the Lord, and He shall sustain thee.* (Psal. 55. 22)." The psalm told her to give over her concerns to God.[26]

On the other hand, the kind actions of individual Indians seem to disrupt the correspondence between Rowlandson's narrative and scripture. "But," she begins the very next paragraph, "I was fain to go and look after something to satisfie my hunger." In other words, although she could look to the Bible to satisfy her soul, she must look elsewhere to sustain her body. What follows is the narrative's most favorable depiction of the Indians, in which they fill the office of Christian friends. One *"Squaw""shewed herself very kind"* to Rowlandson, giving her bear meat, and then, the next day, helping her to cook it, "and gave me some Ground-nuts to eat with it: and I cannot but think how pleasant it was to me." Another squaw, on *"One bitter cold day,"* *"laid a skin"* for Rowlandson by the fire, gave her more ground nuts, *"and bade me come again: and told me they would buy me, if they were able, and yet these were strangers to me that I never saw before."* Because of the contradicting conjunction that introduces this passage, it is not subordinated rhetorically to Psalm 55:22; that is, casting her "burden upon the LORD" does not entail going out and scrounging for food and shelter among the Indians. She is not directly crediting their benevolence to God, although such credit is everywhere implicit in the context of the narrative. Her representation of their actions exceeds the scope of her earlier statement about their restraint from "miscarriage" toward her.

26. *SGG,* 84.

There was no Old Testament type that the Indians who provided sustenance for Rowlandson were fulfilling. There is no mention of kindness on
the part of the Babylonians toward the captive Jews.[27]

Rowlandson found a more prototypical antagonist in her "mistriss,"
Weetamoo, the "squaw-sachem" of the Pocasset Wampanoags. Apparently, the Indian who bestowed upon Rowlandson a Bible and assured her
that "the *Indians* would let" her read was not speaking for Weetamoo. As
a "traditional sachem," she represented a class of persons, along with the
shamans, or powwows, with the most to lose to the spread of Christianity.
"The *Sachems* of the Country are generally set against us," wrote the missionary John Eliot in 1651. Possibly, Weetamoo saw the present war in the
context of a broader spiritual contest, which apparently the Algonquians
in New England were losing. Accordingly, when she returned from "the
burial of a *Papoos*" and found Rowlandson "sitting and reading in [her]
Bible," "she snatched it hastily out of my hand, and threw it out of doors;
I ran out and catch it up, and put it into my pocket, and never let her see
it afterward." From that point, the captive Rowlandson becomes a furtive reader. Her narrative represents a diversity of indigenous responses to
her devotional literacy practices: one Indian enabled them, another pro-
scribed them, others quietly tolerated them, and still others, as discussed
below, read scripture themselves.[28]

I Took My Bible to Read, but I Found No Comfort Here Neither (Psalm 46:10; Isaiah 55:8; Psalm 37:5; Isaiah 54:7)

The sequence of literacy events composes a narrative within Rowlandson's
narrative. Having explained the meaning of her afflictions and reassured
her that "There was mercy promised again," having urged her to "wait"
and demonstrated the consequences of failing to do so, and having provided her with spiritual sustenance and (perhaps) seen to her physical

27. As Burnham observes, "The representation of the Algonquians in Rowlandson's liminal
discourse exceeds and escapes their representation in her orthodox Puritan discourse" (*Captivity and Sentiment*, 37).

28. James Axtell, *The Invasion Within: The Contest of Cultures in Colonial North America* (New
York, 1985), 144 ("traditional"); Michael P. Clark, ed., *The Eliot Tracts: With Letters from John
Eliot to Thomas Thorowgood and Richard Baxter* (Westport, Conn., 2003), 202; *SGG*, 86. Accord-
ing to Tiffany Potter, "Even as she acknowledges the slave status of other white female captives,
Rowlandson will not see it in herself" (Potter, "Writing Indigenous Femininity: Mary Rowland-
son's Narrative of Captivity," *Eighteenth-Century Studies*, XXXVI [2003], 154, 159).

sustenance, God readied Rowlandson for a final test of faith—his apparent withdrawal.

The twelfth and thirteenth removes were particularly trying, and although Rowlandson stood in much need of *"Scripture-comfort,"* she initially found the Bible to be reticent. In the twelfth remove, Rowlandson became bitterly disappointed by what turned out to be a false start toward home, only to be forced to return to camp with Weetamoo while her "master" Quinnapin went ahead without them. "My Spirit was upon this, I confess, very impatient, and almost outrageous." Rowlandson uses the rhetoric of confession because her affective state, as she describes it, was completely contrary to the one repeatedly prescribed by God, as communicated through scripture. Accordingly, once she "had an opportunity" to read her Bible—presumably out of Weetamoo's sight—instead of offering comfort, scripture sternly silenced her: "That quieting Scripture came to my hand, *Psal. 46. 10, Be still, and know that I am God.* Which stilled my spirit for the present: But a sore time of tryal, I concluded, I had to go through." Rowlandson also cites this psalm extradiegetically, in the first remove: *"Come, behold the works of the Lord, what desolations he has made in the Earth"* (46:8). Its message is that, as bad as things may be, one must continue to confide in the power of God.[29]

In the thirteenth remove, the "sore time" included a temporary blindness, after a *"Squaw"* "threw a handfull of ashes" in Rowlandson's eyes: "I thought I should have been quite blinded, and have never seen more: but lying down, the water run out of my eyes, and carried the dirt with it, that by the morning, I recovered my sight again." This incident is keyed to two verses, one that seemingly occurs to Rowlandson as narrator and another that came to Rowlandson's mind as the protagonist of her own narrative. In the discourse, Rowlandson compares herself to Job: "I hope it is not too much to say with Job, *Have pitty upon me, have pitty upon me, O ye friends, for the Hand of the Lord has touched me."* In the story, Rowlandson compared herself with Samson; sometimes, while "sitting in their Wigwams" musing about her former life, she became forgetful about "what my condition was," only to go out and see "nothing but Wilderness, and Woods, and a company of barbarous heathens." This experience prompted consideration "of that, spoken concerning Sampson, who said, *I will go out and shake myself as at other times, but he wist not that the Lord was de-*

---

29. SGG, 70, 86.

parted from him." In Judges 16:20, Samson wakes up and steps out from the tent, not realizing that Delilah has had his hair cut off while he slept with his head in her lap; his strength sapped, he then falls into the power of the Philistines, who "put out his eyes" (Judges 16:21). Rowlandson's fault, seemingly, was in "forgetting where I was," lapsing into a sort of complacency, like Samson falling asleep in Delilah's lap, by imagining herself at home in an Algonquian wigwam instead of meditating on the lessons of her captivity. She therefore deserved to be blinded.[30]

This lapse sets up Rowlandson's experience of being unable to find solace even in her Bible—suddenly, her reading was no longer joined by the Holy Spirit, and the scriptures were reduced to mere words, perhaps, as she had implied, like Joslin's experience of Psalm 27. She felt discouraged about her prospects of being redeemed from captivity—"I began to think that all my hopes of Restoration would come to nothing"—and her "Spirit was now quite ready to sink." She asked her captors "to let me go out and pick up some sticks, that I might get alone, *And Poure out my heart unto the Lord.* Then also I took my Bible to read, but I found no comfort here neither, which many times I was wont to find: *So easie a thing it is with God to dry up the Streames of Scripture-comfort from us.*" God's absence, in Rowlandson's evolving story of herself, was a final test: first he afflicted her and gave her the strength to bear up under affliction; then he seemed— perhaps because she had lost patience and then focus—to abandon her.[31]

Paradoxically, however, God did not leave Rowlandson to suffer her abandonment alone. "Yet I can say," she wrote, in finding herself without "Scripture-comfort," "that in all my sorrows and afflictions, God did not leave me to have my impatience work towards himself, as if his wayes were unrighteous. *But I knew that he laid upon me less than I deserved.*" This divinely supported reaffirmation that she deserved nothing less than to be forsaken is the preliminary to Rowlandson's spiritual redemption, which is the preliminary to her physical one. The radio silence from Rowlandson's Bible is thus a dramatic precedent to the resumption of communication. To expand upon this doubly anachronistic metaphor, it is as if Rowlandson were a character in a film, perhaps a story of shipwreck, searching

30. Ibid., 86–88. I understand the significance of this verse to Rowlandson differently than Toulouse: "Curiously, the narrator represents her desire for an idealized home as analogous to Samson's desire for the foreign Dalilah" (*Captive's Position*, 59).
31. *SGG*, 88.

among the bands on her shortwave radio, hoping again to find a signal:
"Before this dolefull time ended with me, I was turning the leaves of my
Bible, and the Lord brought to me some Scriptures, which did a little re-
vive me, as that Isai. 55. 8. *For my thoughts are not your thoughts, neither are
your wayes my ways, saith the Lord.* And also that, *Psal.* 37. 5. *Commit thy
way unto the Lord, trust also in him, and he shall bring it to pass."* The verse
from Isaiah, which anticipated God's voice from the whirlwind in the
Book of Job, informed Rowlandson that even her attempt to make sense
of her captivity, to correlate afflictions with sinfulness, was a presumption
against God's prerogative; Psalm 37:5 affirmed, once again, that she should
just leave things to him.[32]

These lessons set up a culminating verse in Isaiah 54:7. Rowlandson's
"dolefull time" concluded once Weetamoo released her from a confinement "to the *Wigwam"* that she had imposed after hearing allegations that
Rowlandson intended to run away. She allowed Rowlandson to leave in
the company of an Indian who wished her to re-knit his stockings, and
she "was not a little refresht with that news, that I had my liberty again."
Now Rowlandson could take her Bible out of the "pocket" where she had
hidden it. "Being got out of her sight, I had time and liberty again to look
into my Bible: *Which was my Guid by day, and my Pillow by night."* It is on this
occasion that "that comfortable Scripture presented itself to me, *Isa.* 54. 7.
*For a small moment have I forsaken thee, but with great mercies will I gather
thee."* Rowlandson comments that God "made good to me this precious
promise, and many others." The divine instruction had concluded, and
with the fourteenth remove, she turns "toward the Bay-towns."[33]

No longer, by the close of the thirteenth remove, was she liable to forget where she was, and where she was not. Her thoughts of home were
now framed by her contrasting circumstances. She recalled being among
"Family" and "Neighbors," eating "the good creatures of God," and sleeping on "a comfortable Bed," but now "in stead of all this, I had only a little
Swill for the body, and then like a Swine, must ly down on the ground.
I cannot express to man the sorrow that lay upon my Spirit, the Lord

32. Ibid., 88. "Theologically speaking," Toulouse points out, "one might argue that at this
point the captive Rowlandson is appropriately represented as reaching the point of despair in
her own abilities, one of the necessary steps in the orthodox morphology of conversion" (*Captive's Position*, 57).
33. *SGG*, 90–91.

knows it." This sorrow, correcting her earlier impatience and forgetfulness, was appropriate to her condition. "Yet," she remarks of Isaiah 54:8, "that comfortable Scripture would often come to my mind"; her verb tense indicates that once God brought Isaiah 54:8 to her attention, she referred to it repeatedly during her captivity for reassurance. It is a culminating verse, concluding her course of directed readings on an appropriately hopeful note and presaging the turn homeward in the fourteenth remove.[34]

"A Right Improvement of His Word" (Micah 6:14, Amos 3:6)

The account of eight serial literacy events, comprising nine places of scripture, concludes in the thirteenth remove, but in the fifteenth, Rowlandson identifies two additional scriptures that God presented to her during her captivity. The circumstances of their occurrence are unclear, whether they came up in her reading or whether they simply came to mind, but they reassert the jeremiad message of her scriptural confirmation, enforcing the idea that Rowlandson has been in the hands of an angry God. In this regard, they exemplify the contrast between scriptural referents of Rowlandson's narrative and those of the anonymous "Preface to the Reader."

Rowlandson's narrative indicates the captive's spiritual progress by having her finally turn homeward and cross a boundary in her diegesis. Micah 6:14 and Amos 3:6 appear in the context of the narrator's reflection on the occasion of "cheerfully" revisiting the Baquaug River, which in the fifth remove had "put a stop" to the pursuing English army in a failed rescue that Rowlandson construes as a sign that "we were not ready for so great a mercy as victory and deliverance." In the brief fifteenth remove, Rowlandson was ready to cross the Baquaug in the other direction. With an apparent lull in the action, the narrator enters into some musings on hunger, which she turns into meditations on scripture. She remarks, "After I was thoroughly hungry, I was never again satisfied," and even when she had the opportunity to binge until "I could eat no more, yet I was as unsatisfied I was as when I began. And now could I see that Scripture verified (there being many Scriptures which we do not take notice of, or understand till we are afflicted) *Mic. 6.14. Thou shalt eat and not be satisfied.*" The

34. Ibid., 90.

"now" does seem to make the scripture part of her story; she underscores how her captivity afforded her a stringently privileged vantage point as a reader of scripture.[35]

Her new understanding of Micah 6:14 picked up on the metaphysics of satisfaction broached by the ninth remove when, in her "unsatisfied" condition, she first turned to scripture and then scrounged for food. The relationship between her spiritual and physical hunger is figurative, meaning that her literal hunger was a representation of her spiritual hunger. This logic informs the Puritan practice of ritual fasting, "whereby the body is denied and emptied in order then to be infused by a mediated likeness of the spirit through the sensory qualities of the preached and read Word." Ultimately, the only true satisfaction can be achieved through Christ, whose lack is symbolized by spiritual hunger and, further, for Rowlandson, by the inability to achieve physical satiety, as in Micah 6:14. In the words of John Downame's *Guide to Godlynesse* (1622), "Our bodily hunger . . . may make us more sensibly conceive our soules emptinesse of saving graces, that we may hunger and thirst after them, and use all good meanes whereby we may be filled and satisfied." But in comparison to Rowlandson's captivity, a ritual fast day was like an in vitro simulation of in vivo affliction. She understood, as never before, the meaning of hunger and, therefore, the meanings of scripture.[36]

Micah 6:14 is part of a prophetic denunciation, much like Deuteronomy 28, which explains the sentences following her citation: "Now I might see more than ever before, the miseries that sin hath brought upon us: Many times I should be ready to run out against the Heathen, but the Scripture would quiet me again, *Amos, 3.6. Shal there be evil in the City, and the Lord hath not done it?*" She refers to both original and occasional sin, the backsliding that provoked God's judgment. She indicates that, as with Isaiah 54:7, she referred to Amos 3:6 repeatedly as a captive: it reminded her that hating "the enemy" was beside the point, when spiritual reform was a necessary condition for victory. "The Lord help me to make a right improvement of His Word," she continues, "and that I might learn that

---

35. Ibid., 80, 93. On the "special significance" of Rowlandson's river crossings, see Ralph Bauer, *The Cultural Geography of Colonial American Literatures: Empire, Travel, Modernity*, Cambridge Studies in American Literature and Culture (Cambridge, 2003), 151.

36. Brown, *Pilgrim and the Bee*, 122–123 ("sensory qualities"). See the theological uses of "satisfy" in the *Oxford English Dictionary* online. As Arsić remarks, "There is virtually no Remove in *The Sovereignty and Goodness of God* that is not marked by reference to food" ("Phenomenology," *Common Knowledge*, XVI [2010], 249).

great lesson, *Mic. 6.8, 9. He hath showed thee (Oh Man) what is good, and what doth the Lord require of thee, but to do justly, and love mercy, and walk humbly with thy God? Hear ye the rod, and who hath appointed it."* Shifting again to the present tense, she uses Micah 6:8–9 to sum up the jeremiad message of the scriptures God communicated to her in her captivity: God was punishing her iniquity that she might return to "what is good."[37]

All of the places of scripture, from Deuteronomy in the third remove to Micah and Amos in the fifteenth, are consistent with this message. The narrative deviates from the supposedly more orthodox preface, which is more inclined to highlight Rowlandson's saintliness than her sinfulness and, accordingly, to compare her to righteous figures rather than to backsliding Jews in need of correction. The preface compares her to "just Lot," to *"Joseph, David* and *Daniel,"* and to "the three Children"—Shadrach, Meshach, and Abednego, the devout Jews who emerged unscathed from Nebuchadnezzar's fiery furnace in Daniel 3:20–28. Rowlandson also refers to the stories of Daniel and the three children, but only toward the close of her narrative, extradiegetically, as a way of crediting God for the Indians' restraint in not killing her and the lawyer John Hoar, who arrived with her ransom and other goods, and for their apparent disinterest in violating her chastity. The three children emerged from the furnace with nary "an hair of their head singed, neither were their coats changed, nor the smell of fire had passed on them," and Rowlandson would have readers understand that her chastity was similarly unscathed (Daniel 3:27).[38]

Overall, though, Rowlandson would scarcely have been so presumptuous as to make a categorical comparison between herself and the righteous types invoked by the preface. The difference in types creates a difference in message. Rowlandson emphasizes awful judgment: "But now I see the Lord had his time to scourge and chasten me," she remarks, looking back on her captivity. "The portion of some is to have their afflictions by drops, now one drop and then another; but the dregs of the Cup, the Wine of astonishment: like a sweeping rain that leaveth no food, did the Lord prepare to be my portion." By contrast, Per Amicam expects her story to inspire hope: *"Reader,* if thou gettest no good by such a Declaration as this," he proclaims, "the fault must needs be thine own." He directs the reader's attention to Rowlandson's Bible reading, albeit with a

37. *SGG*, 93–94.
38. Ibid., 64–65.

somewhat different takeaway: "Read, therefore, Peruse, Ponder, and from hence lay up something from the experience of another, against thine own turn comes, that so thou also through patience and consolation of the Scripture mayest have hope." Not merely offering an interpretation, the preface prescribed an approach to reading, presenting Rowlandson's narrative as a text to pore over and meditate upon. Per Amicam added an external layer of extradiegetic commentary, but he also insisted on the diegesis, on having the pious reader learn to emulate Rowlandson's devotional reading practices by sharing in her experience.[39]

"He Expounded This Place to His Brother" (2 Kings 6)

The representations of literacy events within *The Sovereignty and Goodness of God* implied that Rowlandson belonged to a discourse community within a discourse community. The community as a whole was centered around a single book and oriented toward its divine author; it shared literacy practices, rhetoric, and content. As evidence of her election to the inner circle, Rowlandson's narrative showcased a metaphysical intercommunication in which God selected scriptures for her reception and spiritually actuated her understanding. Conversely, as evidence of the Praying Indians' essential exclusion from her community, she represented their blasphemous selection of a scripture as a warrant for hypocrisy.[40]

Rowlandson presents her would-be exposé of the offensive discoursal pretensions of the Praying Indians in the nineteenth remove, which, in recounting a literacy event where Rowlandson herself was a marginal participant—the composition of a ransom note—introduces an unwanted, profane dimension to the narrative's intertextuality. In Rowlandson's representation, by producing a letter to Governor John Leverett and asking her to name the price of her own ransom, her captors parodied English practices: "They bade me stand up, and said, *they were the General Court.*

---

39. Ibid., 67–68, 112. Stratton has presented what he describes as "compelling circumstantial evidence," as well as textual evidence, that Increase Mather was "the primary author of the narrative itself." I don't find his evidence or his analysis persuasive, and I disagree with his contention that scholars who investigate Rowlandson's narrative as her personal expression are somehow complicit with "the colonial male subjectivity" and with the historical silencing of native peoples (*Buried in Shades of Night*, 112, 119, 121).

40. According to John M. Swales, "A discourse community has a threshold level of members with a suitable degree of relevant content and discoursal expertise" (Swales, *Genre Analysis: English in Academic and Research Settings* [New York, 1990], 27).

They bid me speak what I thought he would give." After hesitating, she "said *Twenty pounds,* yet desired them to take less; but they would not hear of that, but sent that message to *Boston,* that for *Twenty pounds* I should be redeemed." The extant letter, indeed, recorded this exchange: "We ask Mrs. Rolanson, how much your husband willing to give for you she gave an answer 20 pounds in goodes." The event was a remarkable inversion of the colonial chain of mediation. Much more typically, the Indians' spoken utterances are represented by European scribes, and Indians are the objects of representations by colonial writers.[41]

Rowlandson does not identify the "Praying-*Indian* that wrote their Letter for them," but the scolding response from the governor, complaining about its flouting of convention, does. "We received your letter by Tom and Peter, which doth not answer ours to you: neither is subscribed by the sachems nor hath it any date, which we know your scribe James Printer doth well understand should be." The Nipmuc James Printer (Wowaus) has emerged as one of the most fascinating persons associated with Rowlandson's captivity and her narrative. He was also the attributed writer—if not necessarily the author—of a much-studied note the English army found stuck to a bridge post outside the devastated town of Medfield. The message tauntingly repurposed the English Christians' jeremiad rhetoric: "Thou English man hath provoked us to anger and wrath," the note declared, according to a contemporary transcription, "and we care not though we have war with you this 21 years for there are many of us 300 of which hath fought with you at this town[.] we hauve nothing but our lives to loose but thou hast many fair houses cattell and much good things." After the war, "in one of the most sublime ironies" of the conflict, Printer resumed the profession from which he derived his English surname and ended up setting the type for the Cambridge publication of Rowlandson's narrative.[42]

41. *SGG,* 98, 136. On such chains of communication, see James H. Merrell, "'I Desire All That I Have Said . . . May Be Taken down Aright': Revisiting Teedyuscung's 1756 Treaty Council Speeches," *WMQ,* 3d Ser., LXIII (2006), 777–826; Andrew Newman, *On Records: Delaware Indians, Colonists, and the Media of History and Memory* (Lincoln, Neb., 2012), 133–183.

42. *SGG,* 98, 136. The Medfield note is cited in Jill Lepore, *The Name of War: King Philip's War and the Origins of American Identity* (New York, 1998), 94. According to Lepore, Noah Newman copied the note out in a 1676 letter to John Cotton (52n). An alternate transcription appears in Daniel Gookin, "History of the Christian Indians: A True and Impartial Narrative of the Doings and Sufferings of the Christian or Praying Indians, in New England, in the Time of the War between the English and Barbarous Heathen, Which Began the 20th of June, 1675," *Archaeologia Americana: Transactions and Collections of the American Antiquarian Society,* II (Cam-

Appearing before the Indian *"General Court"* and being compelled to name her own price might have been one of the culminating humiliations of her captivity, and in retrospect Rowlandson seemed especially resentful of the role of a supposed Christian. Following her reference to Printer, Rowlandson launches a digression that is unlike any other in the narrative; it is the most significant departure from the narrator's close attention to the events immediately concerning herself until the concluding statements. It is a catalog of the iniquities of the Praying Indians, with each item introduced by some variant of the phrase "There was another Praying-*Indian.*" Rowlandson's conspicuous hatred of the Christian Indians is consistent with the wartime "animosity and rage of the common people" that prompted some English, according to Daniel Gookin, to advise the "neighbour Indians" to "forbear giving that epithet of praying." The difference is that Rowlandson was behind enemy lines, and it is notable that, even as she seemingly represents her attitude's softening toward some of the "heathen"—especially Philip, her "master" Quinnapin, and the several hosts who supplied her with food—she conspicuously represents the Christian Indians as more malign.[43]

The first *"Praying-Indian"* in her list practices scriptural hermeneutics, a representation that vividly, for her readers, demarcates the bound-

---

bridge, Mass., 1836), 494–495. According to the nineteenth-century New England antiquarian Samuel Gardner Drake, this "insulting proclamation" was written by the "notorious" "James the Printer," "chief scribe to the hostile Indians" (Drake, *The History and Antiquities of Boston* [Boston, 1856], 421). Despite the invective, the attribution seems likely, although identifying Printer as the writer would not necessarily mean that he was the author, in the sense that the note expressed his personal views. The note has received a lot of attention from literary scholars. See Hilary E. Wyss, *Writing Indians: Literacy, Christianity, and Native Community in Early America*, Native Americans of the Northeast (Amherst, Mass., 2000), 43–44; E. Jennifer Monaghan, *Learning to Read and Write in Colonial America*, Studies in Print Culture and the History of the Book (Amherst, Mass., 2005), 63–64; Round, *Removable Type*, 41; Drew Lopenzina, *Red Ink: Native Americans Picking up the Pen in the Colonial Period* (Albany, N.Y., 2012), 178–179; Lisa Brooks, "Turning the Looking Glass on King Philip's War: Locating American Literature in Native Space," *American Literary History*, XXV (2013), 737–738; Cathy Rex, *Anglo-American Women Writers and Representations of Indianness, 1629–1824* (Surrey, U.K., 2015), 45–47. On Printer, see Lepore, *Name of War*, 126; see also *SGG*, 34, 49; Wyss, *Writing Indians*, 41–49; Lopenzina, *Red Ink*, 106–114; Brooks, "Turning the Looking Glass on King Philip's War," 718; Rex, *Anglo-American Women Writers*, 40–50.

43. *SGG*, 98; Gookin, "History of the Christian Indians," *Archaeologia Americana*, II, 449. In one respect, the ascription of a monetary value—neither "a little" nor "a great sum"—demeaned and interfered with the symbolic economy of the captivity, according to which her worthless life was only valuable insofar as it betokened the inestimable value of a soul captivated by sin. Breitwieser remarks on Rowlandson's mention of a distant event: "Such connections between personal and group experience, even at the sparse level of 'at the same time as,' are almost entirely absent from the narrative" (*American Puritanism and the Defense of Mourning*, 5).

aries of their discourse community. He told her, she claims, "that he had a brother, that would not eat Horse; his conscience was so tender and scrupulous (though as large as hell, for the destruction of poor *Christians*). Then he said, he read that Scripture to him, 2 Kings, 6.25. *There was a famine in* Samaria, *and behold they besieged it, until an Asses head was sold for fourscore pieces of silver, and the fourth part of a Kab of Doves dung, for five pieces of silver.* He expounded this place to his brother, and shewed him that it was lawfull to eat that in a Famine which is not at another time. And now, says he, he will eat horse with any *Indian* of them all." Rowlandson's views of this Indian are made clear by the items that follow it in her catalog: the "Praying-*Indian*" who "betrayed his own Father"; the one who was "hanged" for his participation in the battle of Sudbury; the one who wore "a string about his neck, strung with *Christians* fingers."[44] A person in such a series could not make a properly devout application of scripture. Rowlandson lets the absolute perversity, the blasphemy, of his scriptural warrant speak for itself, assuming that her Christian readers need no explanation.

For these conversations—between Rowlandson and the Indian, between the Indian and his brother—to take place, Rowlandson's interlocutor would need familiarity with the English Bible. But this diegetic reference to 2 Kings contrasts with all of the aforementioned uses of scripture within her captivity. Merely invoking scripture, Rowlandson suggests, is hardly evidence of conversion. Her principle is the same one voiced by Roger Harlakenden at the trial of Anne Hutchinson, as the judges were repeatedly baffled by Hutchinson's facility in citing scripture: "I may read scripture," declared Harlakenden, "and the most glorious hypocrite may read them and yet go down to hell." For Rowlandson's readers, whom she would have presumed to have a high degree of Bible literacy, the blasphemy of citing 2 Kings 6:25 as a warrant for violating dietary taboos would have been self-evident. Not only do the starving Samarians, besieged by the Syrian army, eat asses' heads and doves' dung, but they also practice infanticidal cannibalism. In the succeeding verses (26–29), a woman sitting on the city wall calls out to the king of Israel, explaining that she made a pact with another woman and gave up her own son to be boiled and eaten, but the other woman was now reneging on reciprocating. "And it came to pass, when the king heard the words of the woman, that he rent his

44. *SGG*, 98.

clothes; and he passed by upon the wall, and the people looked, and, behold, *he had* sackcloth within upon his flesh" (2 Kings 6:30). The diegetic reference to 2 Kings is one of several points where Rowlandson's narrative verges on the topic of cannibalism.[45]

Moreover, 2 Kings 6:25 is a drastic instance of the sort of faithless desperation, the unwillingness to "wait," manifested by Ann Joslin. In 2 Kings 7:1–2, the prophet Elisha relays God's word that "To morrow about this time *shall* a measure of fine flour *be sold* for a shekel, and two measures of barley for a shekel, in the gate of Samaria"—in other words, the siege would be miraculously lifted, and, as one seventeenth-century commentator glossed, "the next morrow there should be plenty of victuals and good cheap." Thus 2 Kings 6 hardly offers proof "that it was lawfull to eat that in a Famine which is not at another time"; quite the opposite. It is, indeed, difficult to believe that any professor of Christianity would cite 2 Kings 6 as a justification, and it seems likely that Rowlandson's representation was simply theological libel. But to her readers, it would have depicted a presumptuous aspirant to a discourse community, committing a revealing faux pas.[46]

Yet that ill-chosen, certainly not divinely directed, passage has unmistakable bearing on Rowlandson's own situation, insofar as she participated in famine with her captors and indeed depended on their willingness to share the scarce sustenance. (Notably, the cited passage, whether it was actually selected by a Christian Indian or apocryphally attributed to one by Rowlandson, casts the English army as the Syrians.) If Rowlandson's cultural dichotomies were challenged by the Indians' adaptation of English cultural accoutrements, including clothing and especially literacy, they were also degraded, as many commentators have pointed out,

45. David D. Hall, *The Antinomian Controversy, 1636–1638: A Documentary History* (Durham, N.C., 1990), 338.
46. Thomas Beard and Tho[mas] Taylor, *The Theatre of Gods Judgements: Wherein Is Represented the Admirable Justice of God against All Notorious Sinners* . . . (London, 1648), 131. Kristina Bross observes that the depicted exchange between the "Praying *Indian*" and his brother follows the same conventions as the interlocutions in John Eliot's *Indian Dialogues:* "One Indian raises an objection to a desired belief or behavior, and another convinces him of the 'right' path by citing and expounding scripture" (Bross, *Dry Bones and Indian Sermons: Praying Indians in Colonial America* [Ithaca, N.Y., 2004], 182). For other readings of this passage, see David R. Sewell, "'So Unstable and Like Mad Men They Were': Language and Interpretation in Early American Captivity Narratives," in Frank Shuffelton, ed., *A Mixed Race: Ethnicity in Early America* (New York, 1993), 48; Toulouse, *Captive's Position*, 68–69; Nan Goodman, "'Money Answers All Things': Rethinking Economic and Cultural Exchange in the Captivity Narrative of Mary Rowlandson," *American Literary History*, XXII (2010), 13.

by her hunger. If the scriptural basis didn't make it so inappropriate, the conclusion that "it is lawful to eat in a famine which is not at another time" might have been an apt rationalization for Rowlandson when she snatched a horse hoof from a captive child to gnaw on herself.

Ironically, it was plausibly easier for Rowlandson to reconcile herself to eating such foods as deer innards than to receiving the comfort foods of home, for such treats as pork or salt (like Rowlandson's Bible) arrived only as the result of the devastation of another frontier settlement. The nineteenth remove concludes with Rowlandson's account of two meals Indians invited her to. First, she partook in a feast of "Pork and Ground-nuts" in an Indian man's wigwam; while she ate, "another *Indian* said to me, he seems to be your good Friend, but he killed two *Englishmen* at *Sudbury*, and there lie their Cloaths behind you." Rowlandson "looked behind me, and there I saw bloody Cloaths, with Bullet holes in them; yet the Lord suffered not this wretch to do me any hurt; Yea, instead of that, he many times refresht me: five or six times did he and his Squaw refresh my feeble carcass." The second Indian's point would seem to be a trenchant one: How could Rowlandson enjoy such hospitality? Her use of the word "carcass" both reminds us of her necessity and associatively fills out the bloody clothes of her compatriots. Here again, cannibalism, particularly Christian flesh, is metonymically proximate to the scene of the feast. But Rowlandson leaves the ethical problem unaddressed, except to inform her readers that captivity really did, indeed, increase her appreciation for food: "Another *Squaw* gave me a piece of fresh Pork, and a little Salt with it, and lent me a Pan to Fry it in; and I cannot but remember what a sweet, pleasant and delightfull relish that bit had to me, to this day. So little do we prize common mercies when we have them to the full." The passage is at once consonant with the scripturally derived lesson about not taking God's favors for granted and also strangely dissonant, in that she seems to enjoy the favors of enemy Indians a little too much. Morsels of pork, like verses of scripture, derive their significance from the context of their consumption.[47]

47. *SGG*, 101. As Virginia DeJohn Anderson demonstrates, the Algonquians in New England, and Metacom in particular, had actually begun to raise their own livestock, especially hogs. During the privations of King Philip's War, however, the Indians raided English livestock for food. Livestock was a significant source of conflict between the Algonquians and frontier settlements like Rowlandson's Lancaster (Anderson, *Creatures of Empire: How Domestic Animals Transformed Early America* [New York, 2006], 231–240).

Conclusion

This chapter has read Mary Rowlandson's captivity narrative as a record of an extended literacy event. Its participants included fellow captives, various "heathens," and (to Rowlandson's consternation) "Praying" Indians. In Rowlandson's representation, though, the major players were herself and her God, who placed her in analogous circumstances and then redirected the prophetic denunciations and promises from the backsliding Jews of the Old Testament to her. Separating out the diegetic "places" of scripture elevates one voice from among the many that compose Rowlandson's narrative, furnishing a coherent, overarching interpretation of her captivity. Rowlandson might have been acting out an allegory, but her act of allegoresis became more muddled in her engagement with individual Indians—it was disrupted, in part, by acts of kindness.

Together with the preface by "Per Amicam," *The Soveraignty and Goodness of God* furnishes intertextual connections to numerous biblical types for Indian captivity, including the stories of Lot, Joseph, David, and Job. But the archetype, as it were, is furnished by the Babylonian captivity: the fulfillment of Jeremiah's prophecies and the context for the stories of Daniel and the three children. The most celebrated scriptural evocation of the situation of the Jews in Babylon was the 137th psalm. Accordingly, it was a "place" that was common to many captives and, as the next chapter demonstrates, the site of a remarkable interface between the colonial experience of captivity and its scriptural analogs.

CHAPTER TWO

Psalm 137 as a Site of Encounter

1 By the rivers of Babylon, there we sat down, yea, we wept, when we remembered Zion.

2 We hanged our harps upon the willows in the midst thereof.

3 For there they that carried us away captive required of us a song; and they that wasted us *required of us* mirth, *saying,* Sing us *one* of the songs of Zion.

4 How shall we sing the LORD'S song in a strange land?

5 If I forget thee, O Jerusalem, let my right hand forget *her cunning.*

6 If I do not remember thee, let my tongue cleave to the roof of my mouth; if I prefer not Jerusalem above my chief joy.

7 Remember, O LORD, the children of Edom in the day of Jerusalem; who said, Rase *it,* rase *it, even* to the foundation thereof.

8 O daughter of Babylon, who art to be destroyed; happy *shall he be,* that rewardeth thee as thou hast served us.

9 Happy *shall he be,* that taketh and dasheth thy little ones against the stones.

—Psalm 137, King James Bible

"Now I May Say As" (Psalm 137:1)

In a much-analyzed passage in the eighth remove of *The Soveraignty and Goodness of God* (1682), Mary Rowlandson recounts that her captors brought her in a canoe across the Connecticut River. On the opposite bank, the victorious war party was received by "a numerous crew of Pagans." There, "sitting alone in the midst" of her captors, as "they . . . rejoyced over their Gains and Victories," her "heart began to fail: and I fell a weeping, which was the first time to my remembrance, that I wept before them." Whereas previously she had exhibited a reticence that sounds to modern ears like symptoms of shock—"could I not shed one tear in their sight: but rather had been all this while in a maze, and like one astonished"—"now" she was able to fulfill the words of the psalmist: "but now I may say as, Psal. 137.1. *By the rivers of* Babylon, *there we sat down: yea, we wept when we remembered Zion.*"[1]

By referring to the 137th psalm, Rowlandson made a rhetorical gesture that was common during the early modern period and during the centuries that followed. From the Reformation and Counter-Reformation through twentieth-century protest movements, the 137th has been one of the most frequented points of reference in the Book of Psalms. The argument of this chapter, though, is that the references to Psalm 137 in Rowlandson and several other American captivity narratives are different from those in virtually any other context. Historically, culturally, geographically, the circumstances of Christian captives in the Eastern Woodlands corresponded to the language of the psalm so closely as to entail a partial collapse in the structure of the allegory between the biblical narratives and their own experience.[2]

That is, in the basic structure of allegory, the primary and secondary levels of signification are discrete; allegorical writing or reading entails a distinction between "what appears on the surface and another meaning to which the apparent sense points." Christian typology, as a "theory of history," thus discerns "another meaning" in the superficial narrative of the Old Testament, which prefigures the persons and events of the New. The New England Puritans' extension of this system into their own history is similarly premised on a figural "accord or similarity" between multiple series of events. Hence, in his *Magnalia Christi Americana; or, The Ecclesiastical History of New-England* (1702), Cotton Mather designated John Winthrop "Nehemias Americanus": the redemption of the Jews from captivity in Babylon and their resettlement in the Holy Land under Nehemiah was a type for the escape of the Puritans from despotism in England

1. *SGG*, 82.

2. Hannibal Hamlin refers to 137 as "perhaps the quintessential psalm of the Renaissance and the Reformation," observing that "over the centuries" it has been "one of the most translated, paraphrased, and adapted of all the Psalms" (*Psalm Culture and Early Modern English Literature* [New York, 2004], 219); see also Linda Phyllis Austern, Kari Boyd McBride, and David L. Orvis, "Introduction," in Austern, McBride, and Orvis, eds., *Psalms in the Early Modern World* (Surrey, U.K., 2011), 11–12; David W. Stowe, "Babylon Revisited: Psalm 137 as American Protest Song," *Black Music Research Journal*, XXXII (2012), 95–112.

and the founding of New England. Commenting on Winthrop's character as a magistrate, Mather wrote that "he made himself still an exacter *parallel* unto that governor of *Israel,* by doing the part of a *neighbour* among the distressed people of the *new plantation*." Mather's rhetoric recognizes the duality of levels of signification, the "parallel" courses of the Old Testament and providential history.[3]

The Puritans in England were not the only Christians to compare their persecutions or sufferings to the Babylonian captivity. These comparisons by the others were allegorical without necessarily being typological in the sense of positing that personal experiences were foretold by the Old Testament. For example, the Portuguese poet Luis de Camões, the English poet Robert Herrick, and the eponymous heroine of Samuel Richardson's 1740 novel *Pamela; or, Virtue Rewarded* all adapt Psalm 137 to express their respective plights, but their adaptations implicitly acknowledge the imprecision of the parallels between their situations and that of the Jews in Babylon. Camões, experiencing "Exile" in Goa in the mid-sixteenth century, borrows from the psalm to figure his longing for Lisbon: "Here in this murky chaos and delirium, / I carry out my tragic destiny, / but never will I forget you, Jerusalem!" Herrick, as an Anglican during the English Civil War, uses the psalm to represent the impossibility of making poetry during times of trouble: "Play I co'd once; but (gentle friend) you see / My Harp hung up, here on the Willow tree." Pamela, held captive by her would-be seducer, creates a Lincolnshire version of the psalm: *"WHEN sad I sat in B—n ball, / All watched round about; / And thought of every absent Friend, / The Tears for Grief burst out."* In each of these allegorical uses of the psalm, the distinction between levels of signification is clear: that is, the storylines of the poems and the psalm are distinct, and even divergent.[4]

---

3. Rita Copeland and Peter T. Struck, "Introduction," in Copeland and Struck, eds., *The Cambridge Companion to Allegory* (Cambridge, 2010), 2; Northrop Frye, *The Great Code: The Bible and Literature* (New York, 1982), 81; Erich Auerbach, *Scenes from the Drama of European Literature: Six Essays* (Minneapolis, 1984), 27; Cotton Mather, *Magnalia Christi Americana; or, The Ecclesiastical History of New-England, from Its First Planting in the Year 1620, unto the Year of Our Lord, 1698,* I, book 2 (Hartford, Conn., 1820), 109, 111.

4. Luís de Camões, *Selected Sonnets: A Bilingual Edition,* ed. and trans. William Baer (Chicago, 2008), 73, 181 ("Cá neste escuro caos de confusão, / cumprindo o curso estou da natureza. / Vê se me esqueceri de ti, Sião!"); John Masefield, ed., *The Poems of Robert Herrick* (London, 1906), 73, and see Achsah Guibbory, "Afterword: Herrick's Community, the Babylonian Captivity, and the Uses of Historicism," in Ruth Connolly and Tom Cain, eds., *"Lords of Wine and Oile": Community and Conviviality in the Poetry of Robert Herrick* (New York, 2011), 300–316; Samuel Richardson, *Pamela; or, Virtue Rewarded,* ed. Thomas Keymer and Alice Wakely (New York, 2001), 317,

Compared to these situations, the Christians' captivities among Algonquian and Iroquoian peoples furnished, in Mather's phrase, an "exacter *parallel*" to the Babylonian captivity as recounted in the psalm. For instance, John Underhill's 1638 relation of the Pequot War alludes to the psalm in recounting the experience of "two *English* Maides" the Pequots captured in a raid on Wethersfield, Connecticut. According to Underhill, "The *Indians* carried them from place to place, and shewed them their Forts, and curious Wigwams, and houses, and incouraged them to be merry, but the poore soules, as Israel, could not frame themselves to any delight or mirth under so strange a King, they hanging their Harpes upon the Willow trees, gave their mindes to sorrow, hope was their chiefest food, and teares their constant drinke." Here he alludes to the second and fourth verses of Psalm 137, drawing on the language of the Sternhold and Hopkins psalter (1562): "We ha[n]ged out harps and instruments, the willow trees upon" and "Alas (sayd we) who can once frame, his sorowful hart to syng: / The prayses of our loving God, / thus under a straunge kyng?" Although it may seem that Underhill's allusion transposes figurative language from one rhetorical context to another—surely the Jews did not actually hang harps upon willow trees?—Puritans probably understood Psalm 137:2 not as a metaphor but as a literal depiction of a symbolic act. Of the "harps," Calvin writes in his commentary, "We have in this another proof mentioned by the Psalmist of their faith and fervent piety, for the Levites when stripped of all their fortunes had preserved their harps at least as a piece of precious furniture, to be devoted to a former use when opportunity presented itself." Of the willows, he writes: "This denotes the pleasantness of the banks, which were planted with willows for coolness." In the context of Underhill's extradiegetic allusion, the literal harps and willows become figurative, just as in Herrick's poem, but the girls' situation, captured by pagans and carried along the rivers of New England, might have tracked more closely with scripture.[5]

319; and see Michael Austin, "Lincolnshire Babylon: Competing Typologies in Pamela's 137th Psalm," *Eighteenth-Century Fiction*, XII (2000), 501–514.

5. John Underhill, *Newes from America; or, A New and Experimentall Discoverie of New England; Containing, a True Relation of Their War-Like Proceedings These Two Yeares Last Past, with a Figure of the Indian Fort, or Palizado* (London, 1638), 24–26; Thomas Sternhold, *The Whole Booke of Psalmes Collected into Englysh Metre by T. Starnhold, I. Hopkins, and Others . . .* (London, 1562), 350–351; John Calvin, *Commentary on the Book of Psalms*, trans. James Anderson, V (Edinburgh, 1849), 191. Cotton Mather's commentary does not address 137:2 but displays a similar literalness in reading 137:1: "When they were transported into *Babylon*, they had the Sides of *Euphrates*,

In Rowlandson's narrative, the levels of signification verge even more closely, such that a literal description might leap from one to the other—and remain literal. The locution "now I may say as" indicates this occurrence. Rowlandson literally sat down among rejoicing "Pagans" at a riverside and "wept." There remains a slight rhetorical incompatibility in the graft between her first-person narrative and the plural "we" of the psalm, but the association of New England with "Zion," and therefore the application of "Babylon" to the so-called "wilderness" of her captivity, was for Rowlandson's community conventional. Carried away from a community that identified with the ancient Israelites newly resettled in their promised land, Rowlandson, according to her narrative, was already in the midst of divinely directed readings in the Bible that God had sent her in the third remove, as discussed in the previous chapter; arriving on the far side of the Connecticut River and sitting among her captors, she would have recognized her place in her story. Although to that point she had been dry-eyed, "now" she could hardly have refrained from weeping. Otherwise, she would not have been able to "say as, Psal. 137. 1, *By the rivers of* Babylon, *there we sat down: yea, we wept when we remembered Zion.*" That is, the typology might have triggered her emotional breakthrough.[6]

But the concurrence between Rowlandson's narrative and Psalm 137, however compelling, is brief. The Indian who inquired about her tears and reassured her "none will hurt you" deviates from the typological script; another, who gave her "two spoon-fulls of Meal to comfort me," and a third, who gave her "half a pint of Pease," depart still further. Rowlandson knew her cues, but the Indians did not. So Rowlandson must end her citation of Psalm 137 with the first verse.[7]

Other captives traveled further into the psalm throughout the European colonization of the Americas. Even apart from a Calvinist jeremiad framework, the psalm's opposition between a detested "Babylon" and a longed-for "Zion" was generally "suitable" to the plight of Christian captives of any denomination. Moreover, verses 3–4, representing the request

---

and several of its Rivers assigned for their Habitation" (Mather, *Biblia Americana*, ed. Henry Clark Maddux, IV [Tübingen, 2013], 754).

6. *SGG*, 82. "When Rowlandson finally finds release from psychological numbness," writes Dawn Henwood, "she captures the pathos of that moment and its conflicting emotions in the language of the Psalms" ("Mary Rowlandson and the Psalms: The Textuality of Survival," *EAL*, XXXII [1997], 172).

7. *SGG*, 82.

for songs, and 8–9, expressing a wished-for infanticidal vengeance, had specific correlations with colonial conflicts.

"'Sing Us One of Zion's Songs'" (Psalm 137:3)

In contrast to Rowlandson's narrative, the Puritan minister John Williams's famous *Redeemed Captive, Returning to Zion* (1707) cites the third verse. Williams was captured, along with a large number of his congregants, in a February 1704 raid on the frontier town of Deerfield, Massachusetts, during the War of Spanish Succession, which, in its North American theater (known as Queen Anne's War), pitted New England against New France and its native American allies. Eventually, Mohawks of Kahnawake delivered him to New France, but en route, as he declares, pointing to the contrast with his treatment by Jesuits in the French colony, his Haudenosaunee and Algonquian abductors permitted the English captives to assemble and pray, and even put "Bibles, psalm books, catechisms, and good books ... into their hands with liberty to use them." Williams identifies the scripture "spoken from" at one such Sabbath-day meeting as *Lamentations* 1:18: "'The LORD is righteous; for I have rebelled against his commandment: Hear, I pray you, all people, and behold my sorrow: My virgins and young men are gone into captivity.'" Williams's choice of scripture unambiguously ascribes the plight he shared with his congregation to the just wrath of God, correlating the destruction of Deerfield and the captivity of its community with the destruction of Jerusalem and the Babylonian captivity. It serves as a fitting segue to Psalm 137.[8]

"The enemy," Williams writes, "who said to us, 'Sing us one of Zion's songs,' were ready some of them to upbraid us because our singing was not so loud as theirs." Here the interior quotation marks signal not so much a verbatim representation of the captors' speech as a form of indirect discourse, a paraphrase of an utterance, substituting whatever the Indians did say for lines attributed, in the psalm, to the Babylonians. The quotation is from the third verse of the version of Psalm 137 as it appeared in a recently published and widely adopted metrical psalter, Nahum Tate and Nicholas Brady's *New Version of the Psalms of David* (1696):

---

8. According to Evan Haefeli and Kevin Sweeney, the raid was carried out by a force of "250 to 300 Hurons, Mohawks, Abenakis, Frenchmen, Pennacooks, and Iroquois of the Mountain" and resulted in 50 casualties and 112 captives (*CH*, 1, 105).

> Mean while our Foes, with Pride inspir'd
> The Authors of our slavish Wrongs,
> Musick and Mirth of us requir'd;
> "Come, sing us one of *Sion's* Songs."

The Tate and Brady psalter might have been one of the "psalm books" that were "put into" the captives' hands, but Williams is not declaring that either captors or captives referred explicitly to the psalm during the captivity.[9]

Represented in this way, the captors' supposed request for a song may seem like a typological conceit. The situation and setting (by the Connecticut, the same river where Rowlandson sat down and wept) were strikingly evocative of Psalm 137, so Williams's diegetic citation may be a fitting allusion. However, "'sing us one of *Sion's* Songs'" is also a plausible representation of the captors' request, if not of their words. Williams's account is corroborated, albeit not quite independently, by the narrative of his son Stephen, who was ten at the time of their capture. "They gave my father liberty to preach. There we sang a psalm for they required of us a song." At a Puritan prayer meeting, a request for a song was necessarily a request for a psalm. Since sacred song was an important medium of evangelization for both Catholic and Protestant missionaries, the Catholic Mohawks and especially the Abenaki refugees from New England, who "knew the English, their religion, and their language and had reason to resent them," would have known that singing was one of the core elements of Christian devotional practice.[10]

Indeed, the Christian colonists shared with the Algonquian and Iroquoian peoples they encountered a belief in the spiritual power of song. This commonality underlies one of the remarkable points of convergence between Psalm 137 and American captivity narratives: the native American custom of requiring captives to sing. The captors' request in *The Redeemed Captive* is a credible ethnohistorical detail, as is their deprecation of the English singing, insofar as it is consistent with other colonial depictions of the role of song in war. A report in the *Jesuit Relations* of

9. Ibid., 102; N[ahum] Tate and N[icholas] Brady, *A New Version of the Psalms of David, Fitted to the Tunes Used in Churches* (London, 1696), 293–294; Hamlin, *Psalm Culture*, 83–84. On the Tate and Brady psalter, see John Julian, *A Dictionary of Hymnology*, II (New York, 1907), 919–920.

10. *CH*, 159, 162. Stephen Williams's account of the first phase of his captivity, before he separated from his father, might have been influenced by *The Redeemed Captive*. See Haefeli and Sweeney, *Captors and Captives*, 74.

1643–1644, composed by Barthélemy Vimont, the Jesuit superior at Quebec, recounts how, while Father Joseph-François Bressani was tortured by Mohawks, "they ordered him to sing." He might have been instructed to play his part in a ritual: if the torture was an attempt to reach through the captive's body to his *orenda*, or *manit*, the Iroquois and Algonquian terms for spiritual power, the singing was an expression of this power. The captive's song might have been a means for the captors to assert their spiritual ascendance—and an opportunity for the captive to bid defiance.[11]

The association of singing with orenda or manit is apparent later in the same report, in the account of three Iroquois prisoners captured by a party of Algonquin and Huron French allies. According to Vimont, a Huron who was injured by one of the captives ate a portion of his own damaged lung: "He swallowed it, singing: 'That is very strange medicine.'" Vimont then describes the arrival of the war party with their captives at Trois-Rivières. The triumphant warriors "sang all together,—making the prisoners dance in time to their voices, and to the noise that they made." Meanwhile, the captives "sang as boldly as the victors,—showing by the swaying of their bodies, and the look in their eyes, that the fire and death that they expected caused them no fear." The singing was the primary medium for a spirit contest.[12]

The Iroquois captives knew how to play their role, but European captives needed instruction. The New Englanders John Gyles, Nehemiah How, Susannah Willard Johnson, and Titus King—all taken captive by the

---

11. *JR*, XXVI, 43. On singing and colonial contact, see Glenda Goodman, "'But They Differ from Us in Sound': Indian Psalmody and the Soundscape of Colonialism, 1651–75," *WMQ*, 3d Ser., LXIX (2012), 793–822; Olivia Bloechl, "Wendat Song and Carnival Noise in the Jesuit *Relations*," in Joshua David Bellin and Laura L. Mielke, eds., *Native Acts: Indian Performance, 1603–1832* (Lincoln, 2011), 117–143; Christine DeLucia, "The Sound of Violence: Music of King Philip's War and Memories of Settler Colonialism in the American Northeast," *Common-Place*, XIII, no. 2 (Winter 2013). According to Joel W. Martin, "Torture and ritual cannibalism allowed grieving Iroquois to vent their rage against enemies and assimilate the *orenda*, or spiritual power, of captives" (*The Land Looks after Us: A History of Native American Religion* [Oxford, 2001], 45). According to José António Brandão, "Even if it is not clear that torture served a religious purpose, it seems evident that aspects of the torture process reflected Iroquois spiritual beliefs" (Brandão, *Your Fyre Shall Burn No More: Iroquois Policy towards New France and Its Native Allies to 1701* [Lincoln, Neb., 1997], 40). As Goodman observes, using the Algonquian word equivalent to *orenda*, native peoples in eastern North America believed that "singing tapped into the spiritual power, or manit, that flowed through the world" ("'But They Differ from Us in Sound,'" 794).

12. "L'avalla en chantant voila une medecine bien extraordinaire"; "chantans tous ensemble, et faisans dancer les prisonniers à la cadece de leurs voix, et de leur bruit"; "chantoient aussi courageusement que les victorieux, faisans paroistre au bransle de leur corps et au regard de leurs yeux que le feu, et la mort qu'ils attendoient, ne leur faisoient point de peur": *JR*, XXVI, 56–59.

so-called "Eastern Indians" across more than a half century of French and Indian Wars—attest to what may be a variant of the captive song ritual, in which the captive is taught and "compelled" to "Sing an Indian Song." According to Gyles, "When any great number of Indians met, or when any captives had been lately taken, or when any captives desert and are re-taken, they have a dance, and torture the unhappy people who have fallen into their hands." It is on these occasions that the captive is forced to join the dance and to sing. How could not learn the Abenaki words and so was permitted to "sing it in English, which was, I don't know where I go; which I did, dancing round that Ring three Times." King's narrative presents both a transliteration ("Pumatuck a chesuk wigazeul a Dam bor") and translation ("Sorroy you are taken you wanter go hum to See the girles"). He concluded that "this was only to make a Lettel Sport for themsels." However, Johnson wondered "whether this task was imposed on us for their diversion, or a religious ceremonial." She found it "very painful and offensive." During the "war dance," Johnson and her fellow captives "were obliged to join, and sing our songs, while the Indians rent the air with infernal yelling." Cumulatively, these accounts suggest that the practice of making European captives sing might have been both for the captors' "diversion" and "a religious ceremonial"—having a laugh at their expense was a form of spiritual belittlement.[13]

Possibly—although the question lies beyond the scope of this chapter—Psalm 137 itself may be read as ethnohistorical evidence concerning the role of song in cultural conflict in the ancient Near East. Biblical scholars generally consider 137, the one psalm that is datable on the basis of

13. *CH*, 101n ("Eastern Indians"); James Hannay, ed., *Nine Years a Captive; or, John Gyles' Experience among the Malicite Indians, from 1689 to 1698* (Saint John, N.B., 1875), 14–15; *Narrative of Titus King*, Garland Library of Narratives of North American Indian Captivities, CIX (New York, 1977), 8–9; Victor Hugo Paltsits, ed., *A Narrative of the Captivity of Nehemiah How in 1745–1747*, Narratives of Captivities (1748; rpt. Cleveland, Oh., 1904), 33; [Susannah Willard] Johnson, *A Narrative of the Captivity of Mrs. Johnson . . .*, 3d ed. (Windsor, Vt., 1814), 50. As Yael Ben-Zvi argues, although such details have led scholars to construe Gyles, Johnson, and other captivity narratives as "ethnographic," their function is to establish cultural difference: "rather than reflecting essential foreignness, these texts produce it" ("Ethnography and the Production of Foreignness in Indian Captivity Narratives," *American Indian Quarterly*, XXXII [2008], ix). Johnson's first-person narrative voice of the narrative is an "artifice"; the narrative was authored by New Hampshire lawyer John G. Chamberlain; his "likely collaborators," according to Lorrayne Carroll, were "Joseph Dennie, Royall Tyler, and those members of the New Hampshire bar who frequented Craft's Tavern in Walpole" (Carroll, "'Affecting History': Impersonating Women in the Early Republic," *EAL*, XXXIX [2004], 521). On the Johnson narrative's description of the "war dance," see Yael Ben-Zvi, "Ethnography," xii.

textual evidence, to reflect the experience of Judean exiles in Babylon. As they labored on the irrigation canals, their captors might have requested a song, according to one biblical scholar, in order to "mortify the exiles with the impotence of their song, their God, and their identity." A perhaps less-informed but more historically germane (because it stems from colonial New England) interpretation is furnished by Cotton Mather's *Biblia Americana*. In his reading of Psalm 137:3, Mather also saw the request to sing as a form of humiliation. He reflected on a visit by some Palatine "Beggars": "Their Way of Begging was, to sing a *Psalm* in High-Dutch, which they did so melodiously, that at every Door in my Neighbourhood, the People would require a *Psalm* of them, e're they gave them any thing." He speculated: "Doubtless I now see, how it was with the poor Jews in *Babylon*. They were *Beggars* there. . . . the Gentry would not give them a Bitt of Bread, | until they had sung 'em a *Psalm* which these People were very ready at." Mather noted that the Hebrew translates, *"Sing us the Words of a Song."* He made a characteristic Puritan distinction between superficial forms and sincere belief: "A Mark of *Babylonians!* Among *Babylonians,* they regard nothing but *Words,* and *Forms.* All that they mind is a *Lip-labour;* an external Service in Religion." Thus he emphasized the belief that the spiritual efficacy of psalms derived only from inspired singing.[14]

In the case of Williams's captive congregation, their heartfelt emotion was, presumably, humility. Whether or not their captors requested them to do so, Williams's congregation did, according to his narrative, sing at least one psalm in captivity—not to defy their abductors, but to prostrate themselves before their God. Williams would have chosen a psalm in keeping with the theme of their prayer meetings, "a patient bearing the indignation of the Lord till He should plead our cause." The Mohawk and Abenaki captors of the Deerfield congregation would have witnessed an emotional outpouring, "an apotheosis of obedience and faith," and in addition to their exposure to Christian practices, they would have

---

14. John Ahn, "Psalm 137: Complex Communal Laments," *Journal of Biblical Literature,* CXXVII (2008), 281. According to Alexander Kirkpatrick, the phrase "By the rivers" denotes "Not only the Euphrates and its tributaries, such as the Chebar (Ezek. i. I; iii. 15), but the numerous canals with which the country was intersected. Babylonia was characteristically a land of streams, as Palestine was a land of hills; it was the feature of the country which would impress itself upon the mind of the exiles." See *The Book of Psalms, with Introduction and Notes by A. F. Kirkpatrick* (Cambridge, 1901), 780–781; Mather, *Biblia Americana,* IV, *Ezra–Psalms,* 755. On psalms and inspiration, see Glenda Goodman, "'The Tears I Shed at the Songs of Thy Church': Seventeenth-Century Musical Piety in the English Atlantic World," *Journal of the American Musicological Society,* LXV (2012), 702.

understood it through the schema of their own culture as spirit singing, although in a different key than their own. They would have heard "grave, and solemne, and plaine Tunes" such as John Cotton prescribed in *Singing of Psalmes a Gospel-Ordinance* (1647), "as doe fitly suite the gravitie of the matter, the solemnitie of Gods worship, and the capacitie of a plaine People." It is plausible that their native American captors chose to "upbraid" the English Christians for their apparent lack of spirit.[15]

The first three verses of Psalm 137 conformed so closely to the circumstances of American captivity narratives that, if a captor requested a Christian captive to sing a song by a river, an obvious one would come to mind. Cotton asserted that there was a psalm for every "estate and condition that ever befell the Church and people of God, or can befall them." In her 1728 narrative, the Quaker Elizabeth Hanson, who was captured in a raid on Dover Township, New Hampshire, during the continuing French and Indian wars, recounts that with her family she was brought across "some very great runs of water and brooks." "At the side of one of these runs or rivers the Indians would have my eldest daughter Sarah to sing them a song. Then was brought into her remembrance that passage in the 137th Psalm, 'By the rivers of Babylon there we sat down, yea we wept when we remembered Zion; we hanged our harps on the willows in the midst thereof, for there they that carried us away captives required of us a song, and they that watched us required of us mirth.'" The diction of the narrative seems to bend toward the King James version of the psalm, with the introduction of the word "rivers" into the phrase "runs or rivers." Hanson does not indicate whether Sarah complied with the request.[16]

In Hanson's representation, this interaction became a literacy event. Although Hanson, in hearing her daughter's story, was dismayed by her subjection to a reenactment of Psalm 137:1–3 ("my heart was very full

---

15. *CH*, 102; Goodman, "'The Tears I Shed,'" *Journal of the American Musicological Society*, LXV (2012), 692; John Cotton, *Singing of Psalmes, a Gospel-Ordinance; or, A Treatise, wherein Are Handled These Foure Particulars . . .* (London, 1647), 56.

16. Cotton, *Singing of Psalmes*, 25; [Cotton?], preface to *The Whole Booke of Psalmes . . .* (Cambridge, Mass., 1640), [ix], cited in Goodman, "'The Tears I Shed,'" *Journal of the American Musicological Society*, LXV (2012), 707. According to Alden Vaughan and Edward Clark, although Hanson, the wife of a reportedly "'stiff Quaker,'" was "not, strictly speaking, a Puritan," her narrative was "characteristically Puritan in its pietistic rhetoric and general theme." Vaughan and Clark base their edition on the first American edition, published in 1728. As they point out, the English editions were stylistically redacted. See Elizabeth Hanson, "God's Mercy Surmounting Man's Cruelty," in Alden T. Vaughan and Edward W. Clark, eds., *Puritans among the Indians: Accounts of Captivity and Redemption, 1676–1724* (Cambridge, Mass., 1981), 229, 233.

of trouble"), she was also pleased by the stimulus-response relationship between the circumstances and the recollection of a particular place of scripture. She "was glad" that Sarah "had so good an inclination," meaning that, when her captors by the river demanded a song, the words of Psalm 137:1–3 were "brought to her remembrance." In early modern usage, "remembrance" denoted a fallible faculty, a site where sometimes, with the right stimulus and perhaps some effort, a face, a name, or some errant principles might come back into view. When Rowlandson notes that the moment after crossing the Connecticut River was "the first time to my remembrance" she wept before her captors, she is expressing some doubt concerning her memory or offering a disclaimer. Hanson was pleased that the riverine location and the captors' demand elicited the retrieval of a verse from a place where it was stored, an estranged Bible. She commended her daughter's "further" inclination, "in longing for a Bible that we might have the comfort in reading the Holy Text at vacant times for our spiritual comfort under our present affliction." This desire for one was a propitious indication of her spiritual condition. Implicitly, Sarah's response to the Indians' request was confined to these mental processes—the "remembrance" of the scripture and the longing for a Bible; she didn't actually vocalize a song that was, in part, about the inhibition in vocalizing "songs of Zion" in captivity. Just as Rowlandson's intersection with the psalm is confined to verse 1 (sitting by the river and weeping), Hanson's concludes with verse 3: the request for a song.[17]

"We Sang the 'Canticles of the Lord in a Strange Land'" (Psalm 137:4)

One captive who reported consciously breeching the inhibition expressed in the fourth verse—"How shall we sing the LORD'S song in a strange land?"—was the Jesuit Isaac Jogues, who was captured by Mohawks in 1642 while returning from Montreal to his mission among the Hurons. In a 1643 letter to the father provincial of France, written in Latin from Dutch Rensselaer, he recounts: "They ordered us to sing as other captives are wont to do; we at last complied, for alas, what else could we do? but we sang the 'Canticles of the Lord in a strange land.'" His citation is from

---

17. Hanson, "God's Mercy Surmounting Man's Cruelty," in Vaughan and Clark, eds., *Puritans among the Indians*, 233.

the fourth verse of Psalm 136 *("Super flumina Babylonis")*, the counterpart to the Protestant Psalm 137 in the Latin Vulgate: "Quomodo cantabimus canticum Domini in terra aliena?" Here the citation functions as a sort of disclaimer, indicating that they sang sacred songs among the Mohawks, not with inappropriate joyfulness, but only because they had no choice.[18]

The psalm's dichotomy between Babylon and Zion was applicable to innumerable contrasting pairs—wilderness/settlement, exile/home, sin/virtue, earth/heaven. In a passage recounting a seasonal journey with the family that adopted him, Jogues cites the psalm at length to characterize the contrast between his subjection to sinfulness and confinement in the hunting camp and the religious freedom he experienced in the woods: "How often, in those journeys, and in that quiet wilderness, 'did we sit by the rivers of Babylon, and weep, while we remembered thee, Sion,' not only exulting in heaven, but even praising thy God on earth! 'How often, though in a strange land, did we sing the canticles of the Lord;' and mountain and wildwood resound with the praises of their Maker, which from their creation they had never heard!" In the woods, Jogues was in a "strange land" literally, but in Zion figuratively. While in the "prison" of the village or the "Babylon" of the hunting camp—"where constant worship was paid to the devil and to dreams"—he might sing the "Lord's song" *(Canticum domini)* only under compulsion; in the sylvan temple he had sanctified by carving crosses on trees, he could joyfully chant *Alleluia.*[19]

Two further references to captive settlers actually singing Psalm 137 appear in popular histories; these accounts suggest the epistemological difficulty presented by such diegetic allusions, because, although it is possible that the captives chose to sing the psalm, it's more likely that the psalm informed the representation of the event. Charles W. Baird's *History of the*

18. *ACN,* 104; "P. Isaacus Jogues," in Philippo Alegambe, ed., *Mortes illustres et gesta eorum de Societate Jesu* (Rome, 1657), 624 ("Haec ubi ut cantaremus, sicut solent caeteri captivi, imperavit, tandem [quid enim aliud faceres] cantamus, sed de Canticis Domini in terra aliena"). The Vulgate and Protestant Bibles used different numbering systems for the Book of Psalms, one following the Greek Septuagint and the other following the Hebrew Bible.

19. *ACN,* 111, 113, 117. "Quoties in illis itineribus et quieto secessu, super flumina Babylonis sedimus, et fleuimus dum recordaremur tui Sion, non solum in Coelo exultantis, sed etiam in terris laudantis Deum tuum? Quoties, licet in terra aliena, cantavimus canticum Domini; et sylvae et montes resonarunt laudibus sui creatoris, quas à constitutione sua non audiverant"; "tugurio nimirum ubi perpetuus ferè cultus Daemoni, et somniis exhibebatur": "P. Isaacus Jogues," in Alegambe, ed., *Mortes illustres,* 628, 630. In his commentary on the Mass, John England understands the "Canticles of the Lord" to refer to "The Alleluia, which signifies, 'Praise the Lord'" (England, *The Roman Missal: Translated into the English Language for the Use of the Laity . . .* [Philadelphia, 1843], 37).

Huguenot Emigration to America (1885) recounts the oral tradition that, during the Second Esopus War (1663), a group of captive Walloons staved off execution by "entertaining their captors, and obtaining a momentary reprieve, by singing the one hundred and thirty-seventh psalm." Similarly, Joseph Addison Waddell's *Annals of Augusta County* reports that in 1764 a Shawnee war party, "after crossing the Ohio" with captives from a raid on Kerrs Creek, Virginia, "elated with their success, demanded that the captives should sing for their entertainment, and it is said that Mrs. Gilmore struck up, with plaintive voice, the 137th Psalm of Rouse's version, then in use in all the churches." These instances of psalm singing are possibly embellishments on historical traditions—they are suspiciously evocative of David Gamut's psalm singing in James Fenimore Cooper's *Last of the Mobicans* (1826).[20]

Yet even Cooper's patently fictional representations had some basis in nonfictional sources. When Cooper had the Hurons and Iroquois mistake Gamut's psalmody for a "death song," he was probably drawing on John Heckewelder's *Account of the History, Manners, and Customs of the Indian Nations Who Formerly Inhabited Pennsylvania and the Neighboring States* (1819), according to which the Delawares' prisoners of war sang under torture. The idea of the captive Walloons and Mrs. Gilmore singing Psalm 137 may also seem far-fetched, but at least the occasions for them to do so—at a scene of intended "execution" (as in Baird) or upon the triumphant return of a war party having just crossed a river (as in Wadell)—have credible precedents in other sources.[21]

Such American references to Psalm 137 (or 136, for the Catholic Jogues) are more literal or radical than European ones, since, for Christian captives, Indian Country was a "strange land" indeed. But the abstract, rhetorical question, "How shall we sing the LORD'S song in a strange land?" could equally apply to various situations, and the hypothetical conse-

20. Charles W. Baird, *History of the Huguenot Emigration to America*, I (New York, 1885), 198; J. A. Waddell, *Annals of Augusta County, Virginia . . .* (Richmond, Va., 1886), 124. The use of the psalter by Francis Rous marks the community as Scots-Irish Presbyterian (Julian, *Dictionary of Hymnology*, II, 908).

21. James Fenimore Cooper, *The Last of the Mobicans: A Narrative of 1757* (Albany, N.Y., 1983), 175; John Heckewelder, *History, Manners, and Customs of the Indian Nations Who Once Inhabited Pennsylvania and the Neighboring States*, Historical Society of Pennsylvania, *Memoirs*, XII (Philadelphia, 1881), 217. Christina Snyder notes that "Creeks expected a captive to endure the torture stoically while singing his death song" (Snyder, "Conquered Enemies, Adopted Kin, and Owned People: The Creek Indians and Their Captives," *Journal of Southern History*, LXXIII (2007), 266.

quences of doing so, the disabled "right hand," the palsied "tongue," are compelling figures without direct literal referents in Indian captivity. In the aforementioned poem by Robert Herrick, the references to his "hand" and "tongue" are no more literal than the one to his "Harp": "Griefe, (my deare friend) has first my Harp unstrung; / Wither'd my hand, and palsie-struck my tongue." His allusion to Psalm 137, as an Anglican during the English Civil War, exemplifies John Calvin's reflection on the fourth verse in his *Commentary on the Book of Psalms*: "To those, whether Frenchmen, Englishmen, or Italians, who love and practise the true religion, even their native country is a foreign clime when they live under that tyranny." The sense of being in "a strange land" and the impropriety of joyful song (interpreted metaphorically or literally) could apply to any Christian in circumstances of exile or oppression.[22]

In this regard, perhaps no Christian communities had greater occasion to identify with the Jewish captives in Psalm 137 than did the Praying Indians of New England during King Philip's War, especially those who were "rounded up" and interned under deplorable conditions on Deer Island in Boston Harbor. There is, however, no extant record of these Christians singing or referring to Psalm 137 in their devotions. The only evidence of literacy events involving Christian Indians and this psalm from this period is in the translations of the Book of Psalms (published in 1658) and the entire Bible (1663). Likely, the person who set the type for Psalm 137 (Figure 2), as he would later for Rowlandson's *Soveraignty and Goodness of God*, was the Nipmuc James Printer, working in the shop of James Green. The phrase "in a strange land" might have held specific resonances for these translators and their readers. The Algonquian rendering, *penuwohkomuk*, is a compound composed of *peen8*, meaning "strange" or "foreign," and *akômuk*, meaning "on the other side of" or "beyond" the location of the speaker—a foreign elsewhere. Just as Christians across various denominations activated the allegory of the fourth verse during the sectarian conflicts in Europe, it might also have been significant to the dispossessed, displaced, estranged Christian Indians held in captivity by Christian colonists.[23]

22. Masefield, ed., *Poems of Robert Herrick*, 74; Calvin, *Commentary on the Book of Psalms*, trans. Anderson, V, 193. According to Hamlin, the verse could speak for virtually every Christian community, "depending on time and place" (*Psalm Culture*, 219).

23. *SGG*, 23 ("rounded up"); see also Nan Goodman, "The Deer Island Indians and Common Law Performance," in Joshua David Bellin and Laura L. Mielke, eds., *Native Acts: Indian Performance, 1603–1832* (Lincoln, Neb., 2011), 53–80. Daniel Gookin does recount that the native

PSAL. CXXXVII.

KIike ſepuwehtu ut Bábilon, na nuta-
pinnean, nux nammaumun, mehquon-
tamog Sion.

2 Nutakoochittomun   nut-harpſumun-
nonaſh anumuſſukuppehtu, ut noeu.

3 Newutche nag monchanukqueagig en
nummiſſinnanéanonut, na natootomungquño-
nog ketoohomaonk, kah nag paguánukqueág-
ig noowáóg, unnoobhomaiinnean paſuk Sio-
ne unnoohomaonk.

4 Toh woh kittinne ketoohhomauonan Jehovah ukketoohomooonk ut penuwóhkom-
uk.

5 Wananumunan, woi Jeruſalem, num-
munadcheu wannehhikqutch nuhtompuh-
pequaonk.

6 Matta waanumunnooon, neenan piſſogq-
ſhonſh woſkeche nuttoonit: mátta anuwon-
tammooon Jeruſalem negonohtag noowee-
koutamoonk.

7 Mehquanum, woi Jehovah wunneecha-
noh Edom, ut ukkeſukkodtumit Jeruſalem,
anoowahettit nookinnumook nookinnumook
anohteaſhik.

8 a Woi ken wuttaunoh Babilon mos ke-
nuſhit: wunnaiyeu noh onkquatunkquean,
ne anheog.

9 b Wunnaiyeu nnoh tohqunont kuppe-
iſſeſumoh, kah anóhkonont quſſukquánit.

Figure 2 The Massachuset-language version of Psalm 137 from *The Holy Bible Containing the Old Testament and the New: Translated into the Indian Language* . . . (Cambridge, Mass., 1663), produced by John Eliot and native translators. Courtesy of the Henry E. Huntington Library

"To Think of Bringing up Children to Be Dashed against the Stones by Our Barbarous Enemies"

Psalm 137:8–9, "one of the most difficult texts in the Hebrew Bible / Old Testament," expresses a curse "in the form of a beatitude." The verses thus combine history with prophecy, indicting the Babylonians for dashing Jewish "little ones against the stones" and conferring a prospective blessing on the champions who shall repay the Babylonians in kind. In this respect, they anticipate a foundational motif in American literature. Just as the scripture recorded the "barbarous customs of Oriental warfare," so did captivity narratives testify to the braining of English children. Rowlandson recounts that her captors "knockt" her young nephew William "on the head" and later threatened to do the same to her wounded daughter Sarah, who died in transit. Williams reports that the "enemies who entered the house" were "so cruel and barbarous as to take and carry to the door two of my children and murder them, and also a Negro woman." Hanson, surprisingly, attributes motives to the killers of "two of my children": They "killed one child immediately as soon as they entered the door, thinking thereby to strike in us the greater terror and to make us more fearful of them"; a second child could not be quieted, "and the Indians, to ease themselves of the noise and to prevent the danger of a discovery that might arise from it, immediately before my face knocked its brains out." Such braining of

---

preacher Symon Beckom "read and taught" the refugee congregation from the Praying Town of Wamesit "out of" Psalms 35, 46, and 118; "Scriptures, being considered, were very suitable to encourage and support them in their sad condition" (Gookin, *An Historical Account of the Doings and Sufferings of the Christian Indians in New England, in the Years 1675, 1676, 1677* [New York, 2003], 485). See Edward E. Andrews, *Native Apostles: Black and Indian Missionaries in the British Atlantic World* (Cambridge, Mass., 2013), 50–51; Kevin Robert Cattrell, "Colonial New England Psalmody and the Poetics of Discord in Translation" (Ph.D. diss., Rutgers University, 2011), 85–88. On Gookin's *Historical Account*, see J. Patrick Cesarini, "'What Has Become of Your Praying to God?' Daniel Gookin's Troubled History of King Philip's War," *EAL*, XLIV (2009), 489–515. On Printer as typesetter, see Drew Lopenzina, *Red Ink: Native Americans Picking up the Pen in the Colonial Period* (Albany, N.Y., 2012), 112–116; see also Kristina Bross, *Dry Bones and Indian Sermons: Praying Indians in Colonial America* (Ithaca, N.Y., 2004), 52–83. See also *The Holy Bible Containing the Old Testament and the New: Translated into the Indian Language and Ordered to Be Printed by the Commissioners of the United Colonies in New-England* . . . (Cambridge, Mass., 1663), Bbbb3r; Lopenzina, *Red Ink*, 114. The word *akômuk* was also used in the translation of the phrase "beyond Jordan" (Deuteronomy 3:20). My thanks to Jessie Little Doe Baird and the Wampanoag Language Recovery Project for the translation (Jessie Little Doe Baird to Andrew Newman, "Translation," May 16, 2017). The Massachuset translators included John Sassamon, whose murder triggered the war, and especially Job Nesuton, who died fighting for the colonists in 1675.

Christian babies is a prevalent feature of the captivity narrative genre, increasingly so over the course of its development and especially its expression in fiction.[24]

Representations of infanticide served to vilify Indians, especially, in early national historical romances, to highlight the contrast between good ones and bad ones. In Cooper's portrayal of the massacre of British soldiers and their families after the surrender of Fort William Henry, just before the Huron villain Magua carries Cora and Alice Munro away into captivity, one of his tribesmen "tore the screaming infant" from the arms of its mother and "dashed the head of the infant against a rock, and cast its quivering remains to her very feet." Similarly, Catharine Maria Sedgwick's novel *Hope Leslie; or, Early Times in Massachusetts* (1827) employs the motif to humanize the Pequot Mononotto and demonize his Mohawk allies: whereas Mononotto is deterred from his bloody purpose by a "piteous supplication" from the Fletcher infant, "one of the Mohawks fiercely seized him, tossed him wildly around his head, and dashed him on the door-stone." Here, inverting the sequence in the psalm, the attribution of atrocity to the Indians seemed to counterbalance and justify the commission of atrocities by the colonists: "'We have had blood enough,' cried Mononotto, 'you have well avenged me, brothers.'" The Pequot chief accepts the slaughter of a single English infant as compensation for the destruction of his people in the 1637 massacre at Mystic.[25]

As much as such fictional representations seem hyperbolic, they were clearly inspired by nonfictional accounts (Figure 3). In Cooper's case, he was merely borrowing from his historical sources: "Children they took from their Mothers and Dasht their Brains out against the Stons," wrote one soldier of the Fort William Henry massacre in his diary; another wrote a poem according to which children were "dash'd, impetuous, on the

---

24. Ahn, "Psalm 137," *Journal of Biblical Literature*, CXXVII (2008), 267 ("difficult"); John Barton and John Muddiman, eds., *The Oxford Bible Commentary* (New York, 2001), 402 ("curse"); Kirkpatrick, *Book of Psalms*, 783; *SGG*, 69, 74; *CH*, 96; Hanson, "God's Mercy Surmounting Man's Cruelty," in Vaughan and Clark, eds., *Puritans among the Indians*, 231–232. On the infanticide motif, see Anna Mae Duane, *Suffering Childhood in Early America: Violence, Race, and the Making of the Child Victim* (Athens, Ga., 2010), 59; Laurel Thatcher Ulrich, *Good Wives: Image and Reality in the Lives of Women in Northern New England, 1650–1750* (New York, 1991), 175; Kathryn Zabelle Derounian-Stodola and James Arthur Levernier, *The Indian Captivity Narrative, 1550–1900* (New York, 1993), 71–72; Colin Ramsey, "Cannibalism and Infant Killing: A System of 'Demonizing' Motifs in Indian Captivity Narratives," *Clio*, XXIV (1994), 55–68.

25. Cooper, *Last of the Mohicans*, 175; Catharine Maria Sedgwick, *Hope Leslie; or, Early Times in Massachusetts* (Mineola, N.Y., 2011), 67.

Figure 3 Lieutenant General Louis-Joseph de Montcalm trying to stop
the 1757 massacre after the siege of Fort William Henry. Ca. 1870.
Engraving by A. Bobbet, after a painting by F. O. C. Darley.
Library of Congress, Prints and Photographs Division

Wave-worn Cliff!" Newspaper accounts of the massacre emphasized such
details, ginning up anti-French and anti-Indian fervor.[26]

To whatever extent these nonfictional and, secondarily, literary representations were based upon historical events, they were also inflected by
Psalm 137. The philological evidence of this derivation is in the use of the
verb "dashed" and the insistence on "stone." The two successively mur-
dered infants in Ann Eliza Bleecker's 1779 epistolary novel *The History of
Maria Kittle* are "dashed" against a "stone wall" and "against the stones";
in Sedgwick, the infant is "dashed" against a "door-stone." It is as if the

26. Duane, *Suffering Childhood in Early America*, 59–60; David R. Starbuck, *Massacre at Fort
William Henry* (Hanover, N.H., 2002), 12, 13; Ian K. Steele, *Betrayals: Fort William Henry and
the "Massacre"* (New York, 1990), 117, 127. Mary Chapman's interpretation of the instance in
The Last of the Mohicans depends on the mistaken premise that Cooper was echoing scripture,
but not "historical evidence" (Chapman, "'Happy Shall He Be, That Taketh and Dasheth Thy
Little Ones against the Stones': Infanticide in Cooper's *The Last of the Mohicans*," in Susan C.
Greenfield and Carol Barash, eds., *Inventing Maternity: Politics, Science, and Literature, 1650–
1865* [Lexington, Ky., 1999], 240).

authors are searching about the woods for an appropriately biblical sub-strate for their violence. Cooper may be just echoing his sources on the Fort William Henry massacre, but with David Gamut about to take the stage, the psalms were part of the rhetorical ambient for his represen-tation, and the nonfictional accounts might themselves have been influ-enced by the Bible. When, in 1755, the New Jersey diarist Esther Edwards Burr wrote about the fears "a tender Mother undergoes for her children at such a day as this, to think of bring[ing] up Children to be dashed against the stones by our barbarous enemies," she was, perhaps not quite deliber-ately, paraphrasing scripture.[27]

Yet although the psalm was rhetorically proximate to the colonial and early national representations of Indian atrocities, the connection was better left implicit, because it allegorized not only the barbarity of the enemy but also the savagery of the colonists. More generally, despite the widespread popularity of Psalm 137, its virulently ambivalent concluding verses are not much cited, alluded to, or adapted, and in some modern versions they are even omitted. Whereas the "tender pathos of the open-ing verses enlists our sympathy," wrote the Cambridge theologian Alex-ander Kirkpatrick in 1901, "the crash of bitter denunciation in the closing stanza shocks and repels." Psalm 137:8–9 epitomizes the Old Testament at its most unchristian. Calvin addressed this problem by scouring the New Testament for some antitypal vindication for the verses, settling upon Matthew 7:2: "It may seem to savour of cruelty, that he [the psalmist] should wish the tender and innocent infants to be dashed and mangled upon the stones, but . . . this is but the declaration of a just judgment, as when our Lord says, 'With what measure yet mete, it shall be measured to you again.'" This expression of the Gospel offered a faint, abstract cor-roboration for the visceral concluding verses of Psalm 137.[28]

The difficulty posed by the concluding verses is illustrated by the

27. Ann Eliza Bleecker, *The History of Maria Kittle* (Hartford, Conn., 1797), 20, 21. According to Chapman, the "reiteration of the verb *dash,* like the recurrence of the trope of infanticide itself, in fictional and nonfictional accounts of colonial American history suggests discursive rather than strictly documentary significance" ("'Happy Shall He Be,'" in Greenfield and Ba-rash, eds., *Inventing Maternity,* 239). I believe this use of the term "trope" is an oversimplifica-tion. Burr cited in Michelle Burnham, *Captivity and Sentiment: Cultural Exchange in American Literature, 1682–1861* (Hanover, N.H., 1997), 61.

28. Cattrell, "Colonial New England Psalmody," 49–51 (omitting final verses); Kirkpatrick, *Book of Psalms,* 779; Calvin, *Commentary on the Book of Psalms,* trans. Anderson, V, 197.

imprisoned Spanish mystic Saint John of the Cross (1542–1591) and by Samuel Richardson. In his "Ballad on the Psalm 'By the Waters of Babylon,'" Saint John of the Cross construed the Old Testament stones as a type for "the rock that was Christ" and implied that the best vengeance upon the "Daughter of Babylon" would be the conversion of her children. Similarly, Richardson's fictional Pamela found the morals of 137:8–9 incongruent with her adaptation, so she "very kindly" turned the curse into a prayer:

> Yea, blessed shall the Man be call'd
> That shames thee of thy Evil,
> And saves me from thy vile Attempts,
> And thee, too, from the D—l.[29]

Perhaps because 137:8–9 is challenging to reconcile with the gospel of Christ, Cotton Mather does not address the conclusion in his commentary on Psalm 137 in *Biblia Americana*. Nor does he cite the psalm in what would seem a very likely referential context, his "Narrative of Hannah Dustan's Notable Deliverance from Captivity." Dustan's captors "dashed out the brains of [her] infant against a tree," and she "thought she was not forbidden by any law to take away the life of the murderers by whom her child had been butchered." She took her opportunity while they slept, making accomplices of two other captives in striking "such home-blows upon the heads of their sleeping oppressors that ere they could any of them struggle into any effectual resistance at the feet of those poor prisoners, 'They bowed, they fell, they lay down; at their feet they bowed, they fell where they bowed; there they fell down dead.'" Here Mather invokes, as a precedent for Dustan's violence, "the action of Jael upon Sisera." "The Song of Deborah" recounts how "Jael the wife of Heber" "smote" the sleeping Canaanite commander Sisera by driving a nail through his head with a hammer (Judges 5:24–26). Mather grafts the description of Sisera's death throes from Judges 5:27 ("he bowed, he fell, he lay down") onto the syntax of Dustan's narrative, changing only the plural for the singular third-person pronouns. In so doing, he subsumes the identities of Dustan's victims, who included six children, under the type of a single

---

29. "La piedra que era Cristo"; "hija de Babilonia" (Gerald Brenan, *St John of the Cross: His Life and Poetry*, trans. Lynda Nicholson [1973; rpt. London, 1975], 184–185; my understanding of the Spanish original disagrees somewhat with Nicholson's translation); Richardson, *Pamela*, 321.

biblical enemy combatant. The reference to the concluding verse of "The Song of Deborah" is implicit: "So let all thine enemies perish, O LORD" (Judges 5:31). Thus *Judges* furnished Mather with a more palatable parallel for Dustan's "action" than Psalm 137:8–9 would be. A more specific biblical warrant for Dustan's braining of native American children was available, but it was an ugly case to make.[30]

Indeed, the only considerations of Psalm 137:8–9 in reference to colonial conflicts illustrate its toxicity. In correspondence regarding the Massachusetts General Court's "disposition" of the captive wife and the nine-year-old son of Metacom (King Philip), the minister James Keith wrote to John Cotton in 1676, "I know there is some difficulty in Psalm 137. 8, 9, though I think it may be considered whether there be not some specialty and somewhat extraordinary in it." Thus Keith suggested that 137:8–9 could not be applied to present circumstances: it seemed to fit, but it was too outlandish to be considered an ethical precedent. Keith preferred Deuteronomy 26:6 ("The fathers shall not be put to death for the children, neither shall the children be put to death for the fathers") and the "commended Example" of King Amaziah, who applied this rule when he killed the men who had killed his father ("But he slew not their children" [2 Chron 25:4]). Acknowledging a verse that might justify executing Metacom's child, he instead chose one as the basis for a recommendation of clemency.[31]

Similarly, nearly a century later in Pennsylvania, one of the critics of the so-called Paxton Boys published a satirical dialogue in which one "Thomas Zealot" explained that his minister had offered the psalm as a

---

30. Mather, *Biblia Americana*, IV, *Ezra–Psalms*, 755; Cotton Mather, "A Narrative of Hannah Dustan's Notable Deliverance from Captivity," in Vaughan and Clark, eds., *Puritans among the Indians*, 163. Judges 5 does not mention that Sisera is sleeping, but in drawing the parallel to Dustan, Mather is also implicitly referring to Judges 4:21: "Then Jael Heber's wife took a nail of the tent, and took an hammer in her hand, and went softly unto him, and smote the nail into his temples, and fastened it into the ground: for he was fast asleep and weary. So he died." Teresa A. Toulouse describes Mather's use of Judges 5 "as a kind of orthodox representational replacement for the unorthodox Dustan's own act" (Toulouse, *The Captive's Position: Female Narrative, Male Identity, and Royal Authority in Colonial New England* [Philadelphia, 2007], 87. See also Ulrich, *Good Wives*, 167–170.

31. James Keith, "Letter to John Cotton, October 30 1676," Massachusetts Historical Society, *Collections*, 4th Ser., VIII (Boston, 1868), 690. Cattrell also notes that this is the only citation of Psalm 137:8–9 he has found in "colonial New England writing" ("Colonial New England Psalmody," 55). For an analysis of the discussion about the fate of Metacom's wife and son, see Jill Lepore, *The Name of War: King Philip's War and the Origins of American Identity* (New York, 1998), 150–154.

pretext for their slaughter of noncombatant Christian Indians, including women and children, at Conestoga and Lancaster: "The Night before,
he sung the 137 *Psalm,* where it says, 'happy surely shall he be, they *[sic]*
tender little ones, who shall lay hold upon, and them shall dash against
the Stones.'" The mangled citation is one indication of the perversity of
this rationale. "Andrew Trueman" responded: "I am afraid that you have
done amiss. Many Things were permitted to the Jews because of the Hard-
ness of their Hearts, which the Light of the Gospel has discovered to be
wrong." His commentary rejected Psalm 137:9, specifically, as too cruel to
be invoked as a precedent for Christian behavior.[32]

Given the general reticence concerning the famous psalm's harrowing
conclusion, the intertextual links to it from American captivity narratives
can only be approximate. Unlike the rivers and the requests for songs, the
dashing out of children's brains is not an explicit point of convergence
between the colonial and the biblical narratives. But verses 8–9 are subtly
implied by every citation of the other lines of the psalm, and in the narratives the citations from the psalm are juxtaposed with images that might
call these verses to mind. In Hanson's narrative, the murder of her two
children and her eldest daughter's reenactment of Psalm 137:1–3 are separated by five paragraphs and, within her chronology, one day. Perhaps the
psalm's further resonance with her experience contributed to making her
daughter's narrative "very affecting" and her heart "very full of trouble." In
Wadell's *Annals of Augusta County,* the account of the captive Mrs. Gilmore
singing the psalm is immediately preceded by horrific depictions of infanticide: "During the march westward the savages dashed out against a tree
the brains of a sick and fretful infant and threw the body over the shoul-
ders of a young girl, who was put to death the next day. On another day an
infant was sacrificed, by having a sharpened pole thrust through its body,
which was elevated in the air, and all the prisoners made to pass under it."
Especially with the privilege of historical hindsight, some of the audience
for this popular history would presumably have reflected that the psalm
specifically predicted the Indians' divinely enabled comeuppance for such
barbarities. If, possibly, Mrs. Gilmore did sing as depicted, one can imagine her fervency as she reached the concluding verses in the version by
Thomas Rous (the same version alluded to in the anti-Paxton pamphlet):

32. *A Dialogue, between Andrew Trueman, and Thomas Zealot: About the Killing the Indians at
Cannestogoe and Lancaster* (Philadelphia, 1764), 5–6.

"Yea, happy surely shall he be / that takes thy little ones; / And in his zeale to Sion shall / them dash against the stones."[33]

This last instance, in which a captive walked through a threshold formed by an impaled infant and subsequently responded to her captor's request for a song with the 137th psalm, exemplifies the complexity, volatility, and indeterminacy of the interaction between scripture and colonial encounters. One can never know what took place: there are so many variables at play in the encounters themselves and in the representations of those events, including the beliefs, practices, and stories of both European and native peoples. These were, not static traditions, but fluid systems interacting within dramatic, violent contingencies. When the colonists set out from Europe, especially the Protestants from England, they had a story in place (one of several) about how they were leaving Babylon to found the New Jerusalem in America. But they could not have anticipated how the literal reality of their conflict with native Americans would, at moments, override the figural operation through which their story of themselves tracked with an Old Testament narrative.

Conclusion

Diegetic references to Psalm 137 (136) in the accounts by Jogues, Rowlandson, Williams, and Hanson and in the popular histories by Baird and Waddell illustrate the literacy practice of turning to familiar texts as allegories for traumatically unfamiliar circumstances. This process has a similar rhetorical outcome but is different from the one wherein the allegory suggests the representation of circumstances. For example, in Richardson's *Pamela,* the heroine's composition of a version of the psalm is prompted when, "one *Sunday,*" her "Gaoler" Mrs. Jewkes "importuned" her "to sing a Psalm; but her Spirits not permitting, she declin'd it." Later, "she recollected, that the cxxxviith Psalm was applicable to her own Case; Mrs. *Jewkes* having often, on other Days, in vain, besought her to sing a Song." It seems as if Richardson invented the circumstance of Jewkes's requesting the psalm in order to contrive a further parallel to Psalm 137, then attempted to render the detail more credible by suggesting that Jewkes

---

33. Hanson, "God's Mercy Surmounting Man's Cruelty," in Vaughan and Clark, eds., *Puritans among the Indians,* 233; Waddell, *Annals of Augusta County,* 123–124; Fr[ancis] Rous, *The Booke of Psalmes in English Meeter* (London, 1641), 292.

regularly asked for songs. In this light, Williams's representation of his Mohawk captors' request for a psalm seems stranger than fiction; yet the practice of compelling captives to sing is one of the surprising parallels to the psalm that Christian captives encountered in Indian Country.[34]

Among colonial captivity narratives, similar circumstances and a shared allegorical text did not necessarily entail the same allegorical understanding: another variable was the Christian captive's interpretive tradition. For Rowlandson and Williams, the "Zion" of verses 1 and 3 was a type for New England, which in turn was a historical type for the millennial Kingdom of God. By contrast, when Jogues sang the "canticum Domini" from his retreat in the wilderness, "Sion" does not invoke the same historical-eschatological schema; it refers more directly to the heaven to which he wished to ascend as a martyr. The Jesuits were less disposed to identify with the justly chastised Jews of the Old Testament than with the suffering of Jesus and of the saints who had emulated him. The next chapter contrasts the accounts of Jogues's captivity with that of Williams, focusing on representations of literacy events via a pair of captive clerics.

34. Richardson, *Pamela*, 316–317; see also 140.

CHAPTER THREE

Captive Literacies in the Eastern Woodlands

On Christmas Day, 1643, the Jesuit Père Isaac Jogues (1607–1646), having escaped from captivity among Mohawks more than three months earlier, completed a circuitous journey back to France by way of New Netherland and England. "What happiness," he wrote of his arrival in Brittany, "after having dwelt so long among Savages, after having conversed with Calvinists, with Lutherans, with Anabaptists, and with Puritans, to see oneself among servants of God, in the Catholic Church! to see oneself in the society of Jesus!" Sixty-one years later, a French and Indian War party attacked the New England frontier town of Deerfield, Massachusetts, killing fifty English colonists and taking more than a hundred captives, including the minister Reverend John Williams (1664–1729). "Who can tell what sorrows pierced our souls," Williams later wrote, "when we saw ourselves carried away from God's sanctuary to go into a strange land exposed to so many trials: the journey being at least three hundred miles we were to travel; the snow up to the knees; we never inured to such hardships and fatigues; [and] the place we were to be carried to, a Popish country." For both colonists, Indian Country was a space between the true Church and the land of the heretics.[1]

Jogues's captivity is represented in various overlapping reports and testimonies in the *Jesuit Relations* of 1642–1647 and in a 1643 letter Jogues wrote in Latin. Williams's abduction and detainment in New France are recounted in his *Redeemed Captive Returning to Zion* (1707). In spite of these disparate dates and textual forms, the captivity accounts of Jogues and Williams are readily put into conversation with one another. Each is canonical within its cultural tradition, with the Jogues accounts exemplifying the colonial instantiation of Catholic hagiography and *The Redeemed*

---

1. "Quel bon-heur apres avoir demeuré si long-temps parmy des Sauvages, apres avoir converse des Calvinistes, des Lutheriens, des Anabaptistes, et des Puritains, de se vois parmy des seruiteurs des Dieu, dans l'Eglise Catholique! de se voir en la compagnie de Jesus!" (*JR*, XXV, 64–65). Williams: *CH*, 96.

Captive rivaling Mary Rowlandson's *Soveraignty and Goodness of God* as a "recurrent seller" in colonial New England. The Jogues accounts and the Williams narrative exhibit the contrasting literacy practices and discursive frameworks of a Jesuit priest and a Puritan minister in comparably extreme circumstances.[2]

Jogues and Williams each entered captivity as the pastors of captive folds, and they followed nearly inverse itineraries. Jogues was captured, along with Wendat (Huron) neophytes and French *donnés* (lay assistants), by Mohawks while canoeing upstream from Trois-Rivières on the Saint Lawrence River in 1642, on their return trip to the Jesuit mission in Wendat territory (Wendake). He was carried south into Mohawk territory and ultimately released into the hands of the Dutch at Fort Orange. Conversely, Williams was carried north; following the raid on Deerfield by the French and their Mohawk, Abenaki, and other Indian allies, Williams's Mohawk captors delivered him to New France. There, he was redeemed by the French governor and kept prisoner until he was repatriated to New England through a prisoner exchange, arriving in Boston in November 1706.[3]

This rough symmetry between the two stories highlights a contrast in

2. The letter was first published in Philippo Alegambe's *Mortes illustres et gesta eorum de Societate Jesu* (Rome, 1657), 616–642. A fairly imprecise English translation appears in John Gilmary Shea, *Perils of the Ocean and Wilderness; or, Narratives of Shipwreck and Indian Captivity, Gleaned from Early Missionary Annals* (Boston, 1857), 16–62. I'm using the edition of Shea's translation in *ACN*, 95–121. I include the Latin in footnotes. On the heterogeneous composition of the Jogues accounts in the *Jesuit Relations*, see Paul Perron, "Isaac Jogues: From Martyrdom to Sainthood," in Allan Greer and Jodi Bilinkoff, eds., *Colonial Saints: Discovering the Holy in the Americas, 1500–1800* (New York, 2003), 153–168. The only comparative study of Jogues and Williams I've found is Barbara Buchenau, "Prefiguring CanAmerica? White Man's Indians and Religious Typology in New England and New France," *Transnational American Studies* (Winter 2012), 179. Perron describes the Jogues accounts as a "founding text" in Jesuit martyrology ("From Martyrdom to Sainthood," 153). On Jogues as an epitome of "colonial hagiography," see Greer, "Colonial Saints: Gender, Race and Hagiography in New France," *WMQ*, 3d Ser., LVII (2000), 325–327, 331–333. According to Evan Haefeli and Kevin Sweeney, the Williams narrative became "a potent piece of propaganda"—especially against Catholics—that was "eventually inducted into the canon of early American literature" (Haefeli and Sweeney, "'The Redeemed Captive' as Recurrent Seller: Politics and Publication, 1707–1853," *New England Quarterly*, LXXVII [2004], 344, 356, 367). If Williams's narrative is second to Rowlandson's in the canon of New England captivity narratives, it has not received a proportionate share of scholarly attention. Important readings include those of the literary scholar Teresa Toulouse and the historians Haefeli and Sweeney, who pose different interpretations of the relation of *The Redeemed Captive* to the politics of its moment of publication, especially with regard to the controversial tenure of the royal governor Joseph Dudley, to whom the narrative is dedicated. It is also a principal primary source for John Demos, *The Unredeemed Captive: A Family Story from Early America* (New York, 1994).

3. *CH*, 89–91.

significance, because, from a hagiographic perspective, Jogues's redemption from captivity was a narrative detour: for the Jesuits, his story was not complete until 1646, when he returned to the Mohawks as a missionary and finally met his death, consummating his martyrdom. For Williams, the living allegory of captivity was completed with his redemption. His sermon preached in Boston in December 1706, printed as "Reports of Divine Kindness; or, Remarkable Mercies Should Bee Faithfully Published, for the Praise of God the Giver," followed by the publication of *The Redeemed Captive*, completed his discursive repatriation. Yet the story of the Deerfield captivity was not fully resolved, because some captives remained behind, including Williams's daughter Eunice, who was ten at the time of his writing.[4]

As with Rowlandson, allegory was an important element in the stories of Jogues's and Williams's captivities, not simply in the discourses relating them. The accounts suggest that correlations with sacred narratives informed their understanding of their situation as captives and inspired their actions. But the two clergymen operated within contrasting schemas. The *Jesuit Relations* and Jogues's own accounts indicate that the stories that informed his role as a captive priest include those of his Jesuit predecessors in the New World and Asia; of the order's founder, Saint Ignatius of Loyola, who in 1523 made a lame-footed pilgrimage from Spain to Jerusalem and suffered through illness while founding a religious order based on education, contemplation, and selflessness; of the early Christian martyrs; and, finally, of Jesus Christ. Williams had a more specifically Puritan identification with Old Testament types: although the collective captivity endured by the Deerfield congregation seemingly related to the Babylonian captivity, Williams also identified with Job, suggesting that his personal ordeal could be interpreted as a test of faith applied to a "perfect and upright" man (Job 1:1) who will be returned to his former prosperity after he has utterly relinquished his right to question God's will and has learned the lesson that it is God's righteousness, not his own, that matters.[5]

These intertexts intervened directly in the diegeses of the captivity accounts in representations of literacy events. The captive Jogues, like the

---

4. See Jon Parmenter's analysis of the political implications of Jogues's 1646 mission (Parmenter, *The Edge of the Woods: Iroquoia, 1534–1701* [East Lansing, Mich., 2010], 67–70).

5. Greer, "Colonial Saints," *WMQ*, 3d Ser., LVII (2000), 331–333; Buchenau, "Prefiguring CanAmerica?" *Transnational American Studies* (Winter 2012), 179. Haefeli and Sweeney note that Williams "was often compared to Job" by his contemporaries (*CH*, 89, 89n).

primordial missionary Saint Paul, wrote letters; he communicated with his peers and superiors in the Society of Jesus, participating in a rarefied discourse community from a contingent "locus of enunciation" he represented as degrading and his fellow Jesuits construed as paradoxically exalted. He also read from copies of books he acquired in captivity, the *Epistle of St. Paul to the Hebrews* and Thomas à Kempis's *De Imitatione Christi;* in the context of his Jesuit practice of performing his devotions in solitary retreats, he had dreams and visions involving texts. For Williams, literacy events are separated in two stages. During his passage from western Massachusetts to New France as a captive of Mohawks from the Jesuit mission town of Kahnawake, he read his plundered "piece of Bible" and held prayer meetings with his captive congregation, at which scriptures were "spoken from" and psalms (as discussed in the previous chapter) were sung. During his detainment in New France, he struggled to keep his estranged and scattered fold intact through writing—not only letters but also, remarkably, a poem.[6]

Williams's narrative, contrasting the Mohawks' toleration of Protestant literacy practices with the Jesuits' suppression and censorship, demonstrates how the colonial borderlands of eastern North America became the theater for an Old World conflict in language ideologies. Whereas, before the Protestant Reformation, the adjective "literate" signaled participation in a restricted circle of those able to read and write in Latin, with the diffusion of vernacular literacy it became a means of delimiting cultural identities against heathens and heretics alike. Jogues and other contributors to the *Jesuit Relations* repeatedly characterized the native Americans as without letters, but the benightedness this absence incurred was remediable, as it was in European society, through priestly mediation, and the attending cultural differences were of little spiritual consequence. Yet Jogues practiced literacy as an antidote to barbarism and to exercise his participation in an elite corps of communicators, the "masters of the written word." For Jogues himself, scripture was less a medium of communication with God than it was the symbol of an immediate communication that took place spirit to spirit, God's voice imprinting directly upon the human soul rather than speaking through the text. The Bible's presence facilitated such communication, even *"de medio Babylonis"* ("from the

6. *CH*, 102, 105. Walter Mignolo adapts the concept "locus of enunciation," the site "from which one 'speaks,'" from Michel Foucault (Mignolo, *The Darker Side of the Renaissance: Literacy, Territoriality and Colonization* [Ann Arbor, Mich., 1995], 5).

midst of this Babylon"); otherwise, away from the Church, estranged from all sacraments, and shrouded by paganism, Jogues felt cut off from communication with his God.[7]

Williams, appropriately to his doctrine, depended wholly on scripture as the basis for the literacy events that helped to define the collective identity of his captive church against the Indians. In his narration of his captivity among the French, however, the Bible became less a feature of his represented experience and more a point of reference: the "rule of faith" to assert the truth of his doctrine. He deplored the sort of direct revelation represented by accounts such as the ones about Jogues, the reports of miracles and trumpeting of superstition. For him, there was no bypassing scripture. His narrative's representation of literacy practices, before and during captivity, shows God communicating to Williams and his congregation through select Bible verses. After their arrival in New France, however, the representation is of a dysfunctional discourse community. As an estranged minister responsible for a disbanded congregation, Williams experienced the hazards of the medium of writing, the constant susceptibility to misrepresentation and imposture. In order to set himself apart from the French and the highly educated Jesuits, he had to establish a stylistic difference, recapitulating the best-known Puritan language ideology by implicitly contrasting the distortions, circumlocutions, and obfuscations imputed to Jesuit rhetoric with his own direct, "plain" truths.[8]

Whereas scholars have investigated the reports of Jesuit and Protestant missionaries as sources of information about indigenous responses to European literacy in the Eastern Woodlands, the comparison of Jogues

7. David D. Hall, "Readers and Writers in Early New England," in Hugh Amory and Hall, eds., *A History of the Book in America*, I, *The Colonial Book in the Atlantic World* (Cambridge, 2000), 121, 124; Michael Harbsmeier, "Writing and the Other: Travellers' Literacy, or, Towards an Archaeology of Orality," in Karen Schousboe and Mogens Trolle Larsen, eds., *Literacy and Society* (Copenhagen, 1989), 203. On Jesuits and literacy in missionary work, see Peter A. Dorsey, "Going to School with Savages: Authorship and Authority among the Jesuits of New France," *WMQ*, 3d Ser., LV (1998), 402–403; James Axtell, *The Invasion Within: The Contest of Cultures in Colonial North America* (New York, 1985), 59–61; Paul G. Monson, "Sacred Seeds: The French Jesuit Martyrs in American Catholic Historiography," *LOGOS: A Journal of Catholic Thought and Culture*, XVII, no. 4 (Fall 2014), 89; Allan Greer, ed., *The Jesuit Relations: Natives and Missionaries in Seventeenth-Century North America* (Boston, 2000), 3 ("masters"); *ACN*, 113; "P. Isaacus Jogues," in Alegambe, ed., *Mortes illustres*, 628.

8. *CH*, 113, 128. On Puritan "plain style," see Perry Miller, *The New England Mind: The Seventeenth Century* (1954; rpt. Cambridge, Mass., 1983), 331–364; Meredith Marie Neuman, *Jeremiah's Scribes: Creating Sermon Literature in Puritan New England* (Philadelphia, 2013), 13–21; Ezra Tawil, "Seduction, Sentiment, and the Transatlantic Plain Style," *EAL*, LI (2016), 254–264.

and Williams instead reveals the significance of native Americans within the ideological conflict between Christian sects. The Dutch-influenced Mohawks who burst in upon Jogues's spiritual retreat in the woods to attack him and his cross embodied the brutality underlying Protestant iconoclasm; two generations later, the Francophile Mohawk master who attempted to force Williams to kiss the cross, and dragged him to Mass, represented the lengths Catholics would go to compel belief. At stake in the outcome of their captivities, especially for Williams (who explicitly casts the Jesuits as antagonists), was the vindication of one Christian faith over its rival.[9]

"Recognize Me, though Unworthy, as One of Yours"

Isaac Jogues represents himself entering into captivity in 1642 voluntarily, compelled, not by his captors, but by his sacerdotal obligations. When the Mohawks attacked his party of French and Wendats, he was out of view, hidden in some bushes. He considered his options: "'Could I, indeed,' I said to myself, 'abandon our French and leave those good Neophytes and those poor Catechumens, without giving them the help which the Church of my God has entrusted to me?'" Jogues needed no ligatures on his journey to Mohawk territory other than his attachment to his congregation, and he repeatedly refused opportunities to escape or be ransomed. His contact with other captives exemplifies priestly mediation. A Wendat escapee, Joseph Taondechoren, is represented in the 1643–1644 *Relation* as declaring that Jogues's "discourse" ("discours") continually succored the other captives: "God had given them a man who was to them a father, a mother, a consoler, indeed all, in a place where all consolation failed them except what God gave them through his mouth." Jogues himself became a medium for God's word, which issued freely from his mouth despite torture and captivity.[10]

9. James Axtell, "The Power of Print in the Eastern Woodlands," *WMQ*, 3d Ser., XLIV (1987), 300–309; Peter Wogan, "Perceptions of European Literacy in Early Contact Situations," *Ethnohistory*, XLI (1994), 407–429.

10. "Pourrois-je bien, disois-je à par moy, abandonner nos François, et quitter ces bons Neophytes, et ces pauvres Catechumenes, sans leur donner le secours que L'Eglise de mon Dieu m'a confié"; "Dieu leur eust donné un homme qui leur servoit et de pere et de mere, de consolateur et de tout, en un lieu où toute consolation leur manquoit, sinon celle que Dieu leur donnoit par sa bouche," *JR*, XXIV, 261, XXVI, 189, 194, 196–197 ("consoler"), XXXI, 22–23 ("Could I"), XXXIX, 209.

As an apostle among the captive Wendats, Jogues was a latter-day Saint Paul. His superior, Jérôme Lalemant, writing about Jogues in the 1643–1644 *Relation,* expresses this identification through his integration of scripture within his account, melding the texts to an even greater degree than in Rowlandson's or Williams's narratives. According to Lalemant, Taondechoren related that Jogues "frequently went to confess and instruct them"; Lalemant commented, "In a word, he filled the office of an Apostle, and could say with St. Paul, *Verbum Dei non est alligatum, ideò omnia sustineo propter electos.*" Lalemant's French gloss on that citation from the Second Epistle of Paul to Timothy (2 Timothy 2:9–10) adapts to its rhetorical context by translating "alligatum" ("bound") as *"captive,"* reflecting Jogues's status among the Mohawks: "The word of God is not bound *[captive]*, therefore I endure all things for the sake of the elect *[ames predestines]* whom God has chosen, and has freed through me, in the midst of my bonds and of their chains." The first-person utterance extrapolates from the citation from the Vulgate, seemingly joining the voices of the apostolic saint and the colonial saint in the making.[11]

Playing the part of Saint Paul meant not only preaching to the unconverted but also writing epistles. Jogues's participation, through writing, in his own discourse community was a twofold mechanism for the real-time adaptation of his lived experience to the generic plotlines of a saintly life. First, his letters informed a public interpretation of his ordeal that was already pending upon his departure for the mission in Wendake and was quite established by the time of his redemption from captivity. Second, they reasserted his identity as a Jesuit. His abjection only made sense if it was in tension with his elite status. In the heathen wilderness, he was positioned for martyrdom but poorly stationed to advocate his own case. His letters could mobilize prayers up through the Church, and these, in turn,

---

11. "Il alloit souvent les confesser et les instruire, en un mot il faisoit l'office d'Apostre, et pouvoit dire après S. Paul, *Verbum Dei non est alligatum, ideò Omnia sustineo propter electos*"; "La parole de Dieu ne peut estre captive, et je souffre tout pour le salut des ames predestines, que Dieu a choisies et mises en liberté par mon moyen au milieu de mes liens et de leurs chaisnes," *JR,* XXVI, 196–197. Instead of translating Lalemant's translation of the Vulgate, Thwaites uses the Douay-Rheims Bible: "The word of God is not bound" *(CatholicBible.Online).* Thwaites uses quotation marks to demarcate Joseph Taondechoren's narrative from Lalemant's commentary, as well as the translation from the Vulgate, but these don't appear in the French, which is more ambiguous (L'Abbé J.-B Glaire, trans., *La Sainte Bible Polyglotte: Contenant le texte hébreu original, le texte grec des Septante, le texte latin de la Vulgate et la traduction francaise de M. L'Abbé Glaire* [Paris, 1900], 2847).

could promote his candidacy for martyrdom from afar, speeding his story toward its climax.[12]

The value of Jogues's letters was highlighted by their difficulty and rarity. The most emblematic of Jogues's mutilations was the loss of his left thumb, but fortunately, as he observed, the Mohawks spared his right one (although they crushed one of the fingers on that hand and pulled out all his nails), leaving him able to write. He showed an uncanny determination to do so. During his captivity, Jogues gave letters to warriors on their way "to hunt men upon the great stream of Saint Lawrence," instructing them to "fasten these letters to some poles on the banks of that great river." The *Relation* does not comment on the apparent willingness of these Mohawks to facilitate Jogues's communications.[13]

Unsurprisingly, Jogues's relay system was unsuccessful, but one letter that did reach its addressee signified a great deal more than its pragmatic content. In August 1643, a captive Wendat—"but an Iroquois by affection"—acting as an emissary for a party of Mohawks who approached Fort Richelieu "to treat of peace" presented a letter from Jogues addressed to the governor, Charles Hualt de Montmagny. "'Monsieur,'" the letter begins, "'here is the 4th that I have written since I am with the Iroquois. Time and paper fail me to repeat here what I have already conveyed to you at great length.'" He wrote "partly in French, partly in Latin, partly in the Savage tongue, so that, if it fell into the hands of some one else than the one to whom it was addressed," it would be opaque. The rationale for such caution is that the emphasis of the letter was more political and strategic than spiritual. It described Mohawk manpower ("seven hundred") and firepower ("nearly three hundred arquebuses"), their easy access to Trois–Rivières, and their apparent "design" to subsume Wendake into Iroquoia, "to make of them both but one people and only one land." Yet the letter also strikes a tone of self-sacrifice, warning of an impending raid and declaring, "Let not regard for us prevent from doing that which is to the glory of God" and reaffirming his commitment "not to go away, even though an opportunity should present itself." He explained: "My presence consoles the French, the Hurons, and the Algonquins. I have bap-

12. On Saint Paul as a model for Jesuit missionaries, see John W. O'Malley, *The First Jesuits* (Cambridge, Mass., 1993), 15, 73.

13. *ACN*, 102. Curiously, the statues of Jogues in Lake George Village and Auriesville, N.Y., get this detail wrong by amputating the thumb from the right hand. "Guerriers qui venoient à la chasse des hommes sur le grand fleuve de Sainct Laurent"; "attachassent ces lettres à des perches sur les rives de cette grande riviere": *JR*, XXXI, 88–89.

tized more than sixty persons, several of whom have arrived in Heaven. That is my single consolation, and the will of God, to which very gladly I unite my own." His concluding request for prayers on their behalf hints at the personal, eternal stakes: "I beg you to recommend that prayers be said, and that masses be offered for us, and above all for the one who desires to be forever." The superior in Quebec, Barthélemy Vimont, sang the letter's praises, declaring, "This letter contains more substance than words; its construction is excellent, although the hand which formed its characters is all torn; it is composed in a style more sublime than that which proceeds from the most pompous schools of Rhetoric; but in order better to understand the riches of him who traced it, one must consider his poverty." The "substance" of Jogues's writing was put into relief by the circumstances of its production. As Alexander Pope was to write of Longinus, for Vimont, Jogues was "himself that great Sublime he draws."[14]

Jogues similarly emphasizes the adverse circumstances of his authorship in the opening of a second letter, which he sent in 1643 to his father provincial in France from the colony of Rensselaerswijck, on the Hudson near Fort Orange (present-day Albany), during a brief reprieve from his captivity. His stylistic disclaimers and choice of language are instructive about his present subjectivity as a writer. This time, he was evidently more assured that the letter would reach its addressee, his *"Reverend Father in Christ,"* and he tried discursively to rise to the occasion. Jogues explains that he hesitated over whether to write in French or Latin, "almost equally forgetful of both," before choosing "the less common idiom." One reason

14. "Mais Iroquois d'affection"; "traiter de paix"; "Monsieur, voicy la 4. que j'escris depuis que je suis aux Iroquois. Le temps et le papier me manquent, pour repeter icy ce que je vous ay desia mandé tout au long"; "sept cent Iroquois"; "pres de trois cents arquebuses"; "ne faire des deux qu'un sel people et une seule terre"; "Ma presence console les François Hurons et Algonquins. J'ay baptisé plus de soixante personnes, plusieurs desquels sont arrivez au Ciel. C'est mon unique consolation et la volonté de Dieu, à laquelle tres volontiers je conioicts la mienne. Je vous supplie de recommender qu'on fasse des prieres, et qu'on dise des messes pour nous, et sur tout pour celuy qui desire ester à jamais." Thwaites's English translation places a comma instead of a period after "forever" ("jamais"), running it into the subscription: "Monsieur, Your very humble servant, Isaac Jogues, of the Society of Jesus." "Cette lettre a plus de suc que de parolles, la tissure en est excellente quoy que la main qui en a formé les charactere, soit toute dechirée, elle est composée d'un stile plus sublime que celuy qui fort des plus pompeuses écoles de la Rhetorique: mais pour mieux cognoistre les richesses de celuy qui la tracées, il en faut considerer la pauvreté." As published in the *Jesuit Relations*, the polylingual letter is transcribed and translated into French (*JR*, XXIV, 292–299, 305). See also Alexander Pope, *Poetical Works*, ed. Herbert Davis (London, 1966), 83. Parmenter describes Jogues's letter as "one of the clearest assessments of contemporary Iroquois objectives to appear in documentary sources" (*Edge of the Woods*, 60).

for this choice is because he "wished this letter to be less open to all." He asked his honorable addressee to "excuse, in a man for eight years a companion and associate of savages, nay, a savage now himself in form and dress, whatever may be wanting in decorum or correctness." The letter repeatedly attests to Jogues's sense of alienation from a community in which he was only able to participate ideationally, and intermittently and falteringly through discourse.[15]

Another reason for choosing Latin, Jogues indicated, was to enable the integration of scripture, as he demonstrated with an exemplary citation from Psalm 45 from the Vulgate: "I shall be better able to use the words of Holy Scripture, which have been, at all times, my greatest consolation: 'Amid the tribulations which have found us exceedingly.' (Ps. 45.2.)" The confluence between his Latin prose and the Vulgate is more apparent in the Latin, which was first published in Philippo Alegambe's *Mortes Illustres* (1657), than in John Gilmary Shea's nineteenth-century English translation. The phrases from the Vulgate appear without quotation marks or verse identifications, or any demarcation: "Quod liberius Sacrae Scripturae verba usurpare potero, quae mihi maximo solatio semper fuerunt in tribulationibus quae inuenerunt me nimis." Here, Jogues adapts the verse "tribulationibus inventus es validum" to his context, changing the conjugation of the verb *invenio* (to come upon), changing the object from first person plural (us) to first person (me), and amplifying the adverb from "strongly" *(validum)* to "exceedingly" *(nimis)*. Possibly, the change in grammatical object was deliberate, and the substitution of adverbs was a happenstance of memory—because Jogues did not have a complete Bible but only an edition of the *Epistle of St. Paul to the Hebrews*. He explained that, of the cache of books his party had been bringing back from Quebec to the Wendat mission "for the use of the Frenchmen living there," this book was the only one that had "fallen into my hands." In his letter, he described how he supplemented this book with scriptures "which my memory had retained," attempting to imbibe the lesson that he must live by faith alone. "I searched them; I followed their stream, and sought, as if were, to quench

15. *JR*, XXIV, 304–305; *ACN*, 95. According to Alexis Lussier, by writing to his father provincial, Jogues was complying with the "epistolary requirements of the mission" (Lussier, "Une scène imaginaire en Nouvelle-France: Isaac Jogues et le martyre," *Voix et images*, XXXII, no. 3 [Spring 2007], paragraph 7 [my translation]). "Afin que si elle tomboit entre les mains de quelque autre, que de celuy auquel elle s'adressoit."; "Reverende in Christo Pater"; "si quid sit ab homine iam ab annis octo usu, consuetudine, imo nunc habitu et vestitutu Barbaro aliquid contra leges officii aut sermonis peccatum": "P. Isaacus Jogues," in Alegambe, ed., *Mortes illustres*, 619.

my daily thirst." Jogues created his own stream, commingling verses from the Vulgate with his Latin syntax to a greater degree than Protestant authors did with their vernacular languages and the Bible.[16]

One passage fluidly recontextualizes and adapts verses, demonstrating, despite his exile and debasement, his status as an insider in his discourse community. Jogues blended verses from Psalms 1 and 118 into a single sentence, to the effect that if he had not "meditated on the law of God night and day" (Psal. 1:2), he would have "perished in my abjection" (Psal. 118:92). A citation from Psalm 124:5–6 swept from the figurative — "And my soul had passed through a water unsupportable" — to the starkly literal: "But, blessed be God, who did not give us a prey to the teeth of our enemies." This last verse was "suitable" in the sense used by Rowlandson: Jogues had described how his captors had bitten "almost all my nails, and crunched my two fore-fingers with their teeth, giving me intense pain." The ascendancy of the Mohawks was such, Jogues indicated through citations from Luke and Second Corinthians, that he "was weary of life, and could say with Job, though in a different meaning, 'Although he should *[not]* kill me, I will trust in him.'" That is, unlike Job, who declares his intent to confront God and justify his ways, even at the risk of death, Jogues declares his willingness to continue to suffer indefinitely, without losing faith, even at the risk of not consummating his martyrdom. Here, his rhetorical play with scripture evinces what may be an ironic sensibility about his situation. The passage, much more syntactically fluid in its Latin original than in the English translation, is a virtuosic display of Bible literacy, as an addressee with comparable "discoursal expertise" would have readily appreciated.[17]

16. *ACN,* 95, 111, 114. "Omnibus libris quos in usum Gallorum"; "venerate in manus meas Epistola Beati Pauli ad Hebraeos"; "quorum loca memoriter tenebam"; "Scrutabar eas, rimabar rivulos earum, quasi diuturnam sitim explore cupiens": "P. Isaacus Jogues," in Alegambe, ed., *Mortes illustres,* 619, 627, 629.

17. *ACN,* 98, 114. "Et in lege Dei meditabar die ac nocte, quae quidem Dei lex nisi fuisset meditatio mea, forte perijssem in humilitate mea, et pertransijsset anima nostra aquam intolerabilem. Sed benedictus Deus qui non ddedit nos incaptionem dentibus inimicorum nostrorum"; "cum alij advenientes mihi etiam ungues pene omnes mordicus avulserunt, indices duos dentibus mihi contriverunt ingenti doloris sensu"; "Ita ut nos taederet vivere, diceremque cum Job contrario sensu: Etiamsi me non occiderit, sperabo in eo": "P. Isaacus Jogues," in Alegambe, ed., *Mortes illustres,* 620, 629. Jogues altered the Latin of Job 13:15: "Etiam si occiderit me in ipso sperabo" ("Although he should kill me, I will trust in him.") Shea's translation overlooks the negation before "occiderit" ("kill") and doesn't convey Jogues's "different meaning" ("contrario sensu"). See *CatholicBible.Online*; John M. Swales, *Genre Analysis: English in Academic and Research Settings* (New York, 1990), 24–27.

The closing of the letter demonstrates its performative function. He exhorts his father provincial to "recognize me, though unworthy, as one of yours; for, though a savage in dress and manner, and almost without God in so tossed a life, yet, as I have ever lived a son of the most holy Church of Rome, and of the Society, so do I wish to die." Jogues, shrouded in the "dense darkness of paganism," amid "constant nakedness" and promiscuity, apart from "all the Sacraments," found his way to a remote Dutch outpost. The visit to Rensselaer brought him into communication networks that could carry his letter to his father provincial in France, much more reliably than the system involving Mohawk warriors and poles on the riverbank, but no closer to his God. He had stepped out from the Mohawk woods into the distortions of heresy governing the Dutch settlement. Thus Jogues used the medium of writing and the cooperation of his discourse community to raise up prayers through clearer channels than those his circumstances afforded him. He wrote in order to be recognized by one of the men who had inducted him into his discourse community and thereby to mobilize the "prayers of the pious" so that he could be strong enough in his faith to be incorporated into the community of Saints: "so that, when that good Shepherd shall come, 'who will gather together the dispersed of Israel,' (Ps. 147.2), he may gather us from among the nations to bless his holy name. Amen! Amen! (Ps. 106.47)." His citations from the psalms illustrate the contrast to the typologies of the Puritan captives like Rowlandson and Williams—instead of wishing for a physical repatriation as a sign of spiritual redemption, he, as a Jesuit, sought a direct spiritual repatriation to the celestial "Sion." Relative to a Puritan captive, then, Jogues's participation in his discourse community was less of an end and more of a means.[18]

The contrasting significances of captivity for Jogues and Williams are encapsulated by their different understandings of Zion. Jogues's "entrance to the holy Sion" came, at long last, via the "blow from a hatchet" he received when he left the security of Old France to return to Mohawk country as a missionary. For Williams, his spiritual return to Zion, through re-

18. *ACN*, 95, 121. "Rogo igitur ex animo R. V. ut me indignum licet semper ut suum agnoscat: lecet enim habitu, et vestitu Barbarus, imo et pene in tam tumultuosa vita sine Deo meo, semper tamen et Sanctissimae Romanae Ecclesiae, et Societatis filius ut vixi semper, ita et moricupio"; "Fides quidem in tam spissis infidelitatis tenebris; spes in tam longis, et duris sane probationibus, charitas in tanta carnalitate, et Sacramentorum omnium carentia"; "ut cum venerit bonus ille Pastor, qui dispersions Israelis congregabit, congreget nos de nationibus ad benedicendum nomini sancto suo. fiat, fiat."; "piorum virorum precibus": "P. Isaacus Jogues," in Alegambe, ed., *Mortes illustres*, 619, 632.

pentance, was a precondition for his return to New England, a historical fulfillment of the promised land of the Old Testament, which in turn was a type for the Kingdom of Christ; that is, his physical captivity and redemption became a nonfictional allegory, like John Bunyan's fictional one in *The Pilgrim's Progress* (1678), for the soul's journey. Williams's account is paradigmatic of the captivity genre, in which temporal "redemption" is an essential feature of the narrative formula.[19]

"Communications avec Dieu"

Like Rowlandson's or Williams's, Jogues's physical captivity was allegorized as a spiritual one, and his soul needed to be prepared for redemption. However, "redemption" had a different meaning, one that was ultimately deferred until the sequel to the story of his captivity, when he daringly returned to Mohawk country as a missionary and met his death. His preparation for that eventual martyrdom during his initial captivity similarly involved literacy events, but the printed word was less a medium of divine communication than a symbol of it. This figurative value is apparent in the beginning of the account of Jogues's captivity by Lalemant, the provincial superior of Canada, in the 1647 *Jesuit Relations*. According to Lalemant, sometime before setting out from the mission of Sainte-Marie in Wendake (he would be captured on the return trip), Jogues, "finding himself alone before the Blessed Sacrament . . . prostrated himself to the ground, beseeching our Lord to grant him the favor and grace of suffering for his glory." God's response to Jogues's ecstatic prayer was "engraved in the depth of his soul, with a certainty similar to that which Faith gives us: *Exaudita est oratio tua; fiet tibi sicut à me petisti. Confortare et esto robustus,*— 'Thy prayer is heard; what thou hast asked of me is granted thee. Be courageous and steadfast.'" While the Jesuits, like other Christian missionaries, insisted on the superiority of writing over speech as a medium for the preservation of God's truth, words issued by such an author and engraved on such a substrate as Jogues's soul acquired the mystical substantiality of holy scripture. This sort of spiritual imprimatur represents the metaphysical resolution of act and significance. "The results which followed," according to Lalemant, "have shown that these words, which were always

19. "L'entrée de la Saincte Sion"; "un coup de hache": *JR*, XXXI, 68–69; Alden T. Vaughan and Edward W. Clark, eds., *Puritans among the Indians: Accounts of Captivity and Redemption, 1676–1724* (Cambridge, Mass., 1981), 1.

very present with him in all his sufferings, were verily substantial, —words issuing from the lips of him with whom saying and doing are only one and the same thing." This complete identification between word and deed, "le dire et le faire," is the telos of Jogues's colonial hagiography; it was consummated by a hatchet stroke.[20]

This process of "assimilation to types," of the accommodation of a historical actor into the literary paradigm of the saintly martyr, is the project not only of the hagiographer but also of the would-be saint. That is, as a protagonist, Jogues was also an author of his own hagiography, fulfilling words through his deeds: "mindful of his meekness 'who was led like a lamb to slaughter' (Acts 8.32), I went to my death, begging the Lord with David 'to turn away evil from my enemies and scatter them in his truth.' (Ps. 53.7)." But his imitation of Christ was a struggle: he needed instruction. This instruction came through experience, certainly, but also through contemplative reading, and finally through visions.[21]

Through experience, in Jogues's representation, Jesus taught him that any fortitude he displayed "came not from myself, but from him who gives strength to the weary." As he hung by his arms from two poles, Jogues "groaned aloud" and "begged my torturers to ease me some little from

20. Perron describes this "most complete and final account of the life and death of Isaac Jogues" as the founding narrative of his martyrdom that led not only to his canonization but also to that of the seven other missionaries ("From Martyrdom to Sainthood," in Greer and Bilinkoff, eds., *Colonial Saints*, 157–158). "Se trouvant seul devant le Saint Sacrement, ils se prosterna par terre, suppliant Nostre Seigneur de luy accorder la faveur et la grace de souffrir pour sa gloire"; "Cette responce luy fut gravée au fond de l'ame avec une certitude semblable à celle que nous donne la Foy, *Exaudita est oratorio tua, fiet tibi sicut à me petisti, confortare et esto robustus.* Ta priere est exaucée, ce que tu m'as demandé t'est accordé, sois courageux et constant"; "Les effets qui se sont ensuivis ont fait voir que ces paroles qui luy ont toûjours esté tres-presantes dans toutes ses souffrances estoient veritablement substantielles, paroles sorties de la bouche de celuy à qui le dire et le faire ne font qu'une mesme chose": *JR*, XXXI, 16–19. On the Jesuits' "privileging of written over oral texts," see Dorsey, "Going to School with Savages," *WMQ*, 3d Ser., LV (1998), 416.

21. Greer, "Colonial Saints," *WMQ*, 3d Ser., LVII (2000), 325; Richard Kieckhefer, "Imitators of Christ: Sainthood in the Christian Tradition," in Kieckhefer and George D. Bond, eds., *Sainthood: Its Manifestations in World Religions* (Berkeley, Calif., 1988), 32; *ACN*, 111. "Sed memor illius mansuetudinis qui tanquam ovis ad occisionem ductus est, ibam ad mortem rogans Dominum cum Davide, ut averteret mala inimicis meis, et in vertate sua illos disperderet": "P. Isaacus Jogues," in Alegambe, ed., *Mortes illustres*, 627. If Shea's translation of Jogues's citation from Psalm 53 (54) in the Vulgate is correct, then it implies a New Testament revision of an Old Testament verse. He translates "averteret mala inimicis meis" as "turn away evils from my enemies," which is technically possible, but the Douay-Rheims Bible renders that verse "turn back the evils upon my enemies," which is more coherent within the context of the psalm *(Catholic-Bible.Online)*.

those hard, rough ropes." Instead, they tightened them, bringing him to the "point of fainting." Jogues attributed their actions to Jesus, who thereby intimated to Jogues the difference in degree between his suffering and the Passion: "I have been allowed to learn, by some slight experience, how much thou didst deign to suffer on the cross for me, when the whole weight of thy most sacred body hung not by ropes, but by thy hands and feet pierced by hardest nails!" In other words, he learned more about the story of the Passion than he could through reading or ritual. To obtain martyrdom, Jogues had to learn to resist the desire for any abatement in his divinely wrought suffering.[22]

Jogues's particular struggle was that the ultimate moment of relief from suffering was constantly imminent but repeatedly deferred. Each reprieve from death was also a letdown. The Mohawks beat, tortured, and mutilated him but held off from a finishing blow. They killed his "dear companion," the donnée René Goupil, as he walked by Jogues's side, making him the first, seemingly overdue, North American martyr. Jogues "knelt down on the spot, and, uncovering my head, awaited a like blow"; but it did not come. Jogues praised Goupil "as a martyr—martyr to obedience, and still more, a martyr to faith and to the cross." Such a death was a sign of great worth. Jogues was careful to indicate that his own expectation of a like fate did not betoken pride: "Not I alone, but the other Iroquois, every moment expected to see me tomahawked." When the blow did not come, the reason must have been that "my sins still rendered me unworthy." The physical suffering enabled the identification with Jesus, but Jogues could not complete this identification, through death, until he had eliminated his stubborn remnant of sinfulness.[23]

22. "Si quid patienter hactenus sustinuissem, id non a me, sed ab eo esse profectum, qui dat fortitudinem lassis"; "ingemui"; "tortores meos rogavi, paululum de vinculorum asperitate remitterent"; "me brevi deliquium passurum animi"; "quod aliquâ levi experientiâl didici quantum pro me in Cruce pati dignatus es, cum non in funes, sed in manus pedesque tuos durissimis clavis perforatos totius tui Sacratissimi corporis pondus incumberet": "P. Isaacus Jogues," in Alegambe, ed., *Mortes illustres*, 624.

23. *ACN*, 108–109, 111. "Cher compagnon": *JR*, XXXI, 68–69. "The French Jesuits' missionary zeal was so fervent," according to Monson, "that by 1639 the Jesuit superior lamented that no missionary had yet died for the faith" ("Sacred Seeds," *LOGOS*, XVII, no. 4 [Fall 2014], 89). "Ego vero sanguineam illam securim conspicatus in eo ubi eram loco positis humi genibus, Deo meo me commendans similem ictum praestolabar"; "Sed ut Martyrem *(ita illi piè loqui tunc placuit)* non obedientiae tantùm, sed et fidei, et Crucis, amo et veneror"; "ibi me singulis momentis securi percutiendum, et ego credebam, et eaeteri sibi persuadebant Irokei"; "Sed nec dum illud peccata mea meruerant": "P. Isaacus Jogues," in Alegambe, ed., *Mortes illustres*, 626–627.

His immersion in Mohawk culture mitigated against such purification. Jogues felt cut off from God in the Mohawk village of Andagoron, which, to him, epitomized worldliness to an extreme that even the most depraved European society did not approach. This circumstance lent an urgency to the Jesuit practice of repairing to spiritual retreats, as prescribed by Ignatius of Loyola's *Spiritual Exercises.* Jogues recounts how he would leave the village and resort to the "wild wood, where I begged the Lord not to disdain to speak to his servant"; there, "I had recourse to the Holy Scriptures, my only refuge in the tribulations, which had found me exceedingly: these did I venerate; with these I wished to die." It was only in his retreat that Jogues could find conditions that were propitious to his eligibility for martyrdom.[24]

Like Williams, while he was a Mohawk captive, Jogues did not have a complete Bible but only the aforementioned *Epistle of St. Paul to the Hebrews.* For Jogues, this edition—which included a popular paraphrase by Anthony Godeau, bishop of Gratz, and "a picture of St. Bruno, the illustrious founder of the Carthusian Order," and to which "some indulgences were attached"—was a sacred synecdoche, a holy object that he constantly carried, along with a "rude wooden cross" he had fashioned. When the moment came, "I could most cheerfully die with the Holy Scriptures which had ever been my greatest consolation, with the graces and indulgences of my most holy Mother the Church, whom I had always greatly, but now most tenderly, loved, and with the cross of my Lord and Savior." With this equipment, Jogues was able to create a channel to God from the midst of the wilderness.[25]

24. "Introduction," in George E. Ganss, trans., *The Spiritual Exercises of Saint Ignatius* (St. Louis, 1992), 4; Louis L. Martz, *The Poetry of Meditation: A Study in English Religious Literature of the Seventeenth Century* ([1962]; rpt. New Haven, Conn., 1965), 25–26; *ACN*, 111. "Amabam solitudines, in quibus rogabam Dominum ne dedignaretur loqui ad servum suum"; "Recurrebam ad praesidia sacrarum scripturarum"; "unicum meum refugium in tribulationibus, quae invenerant me nimis: has venerabar, cum his volebam mori": "P. Isaacus Jogues," in Alegambe, ed., *Mortes illustres,* 627. He refers to the village's name in "Novum Belgium" (*ACN*, 105).

25. *ACN*, 111–112. "Imagine Beati Brunonis illustrissimi Carthusianorum ordinis Fundatoris"; "cui applicatae errant Induulgentiae"; "Crucem quam mihi ex lingo utcunque"; "Ferebam semper mecum, ut ubicunque me mors, quam praesentissimam semper ante oculos habebam, oppresssisset, cum Scriptura Sacra, quae mihi maximo semper solation fuerat, cum donis, et Indulgentijs Sanctissimae matris meae Ecclesiae, quam cum maxime semper, tunc tenerrime diligebam, et cum Cruce Domini mei libentissime morerer": "P. Isaacus Jogues," in Alegambe, ed., *Mortes illustres,* 627–628. According to O'Malley, "The Jesuits believed in and defended this hotly contested practice" of indulgences, or remissions of temporal punishment (O'Malley, *First Jesuits,* 271).

Jogues's spiritual practice enacted parallels with the Old and New Testaments and emulated his order's founder. In his letter from Rensselaer, he compares the Mohawk's winter hunting camp both to Babylon and Sodom, evoking Lot's flight in Genesis 19: "I went forth every morning from the midst of this Babylon, that is, our hut where constant worship was paid to the devil and to dreams, and 'saved myself in the mountain' (Gen. 19.17), a neighboring hill." At the foot of a "majestic tree," on which he had made a "large cross" by "stripping off the bark," Jogues "spent the whole day with my God, whom, almost alone in those vast regions, I worshipped and loved"; he prayed, meditated, and read Thomas à Kempis's *De Imitatione Christi,* "which I had just before recovered." This was the same book that Saint Ignatius had meditated upon during an eleven-month retreat in a cave in Manresa in 1522, in what became the prototype for Jesuit spiritual retreats. Jogues does not give any explanation of how the book came into his possession, but it must have passed through Mohawk hands. By reading it during his spiritual retreat, he was imitating Ignatius's imitation of Christ.[26]

While Jogues studied for his role, his Mohawk persecutors fulfilled theirs, attacking him, as he described in his 1643 letter, "most violently" while he was at prayer, "saying that they hated the cross; that it was a sign that they and their friends the neighbors, (Europeans), knew not, alluding to the Dutch Protestants." This was a period when the Iroquois were the dominant power in the region. Jogues was captured during a war of extermination against the Wendats, in which the Mohawks' ascendancy was enabled in large measure by guns acquired from the Dutch. Neither European power was an effective threat to Haudenosaunee dominance. The Mohawks were historically positioned to be allegorical persecutors.[27]

26. O'Malley, *First Jesuits,* 25; Avery Dulles, "Preface," in Louis J. Puhl, trans., *The Spiritual Exercises of St. Ignatius* (New York, 2015), xv; Robert S. Miola, ed., *Early Modern Catholicism: An Anthology of Primary Sources* (New York, 2007), 285. On Jogues's enslavement, see Roland Viau, *Femmes de personne: Sexes, genres, et pouvoirs en Iroquoise ancienne* (Quebec, 2000), 116–117; *ACN,* 113. "Singulis igitur diebus mane exibam de medio Babylonis, tugurio nimirum ubi perpetuus ferè cultus Daemoni, et somniis exhibebatur, et saluabar in monte, colle nimirum vicino"; "ibi in ingenti arbore ingentem Crucem, detracto cortice mihi efformaveram, ad cuius pedem, quà meditando, et orando, quà librum de imitatione Christi, quem paulo ante receperam legendo, totos pene dies cum Deo meo, quem solus pene in tam vastis Regionibus et colebam, et amabam, transfigebam": "P. Isaacus Jogues," in Alegambe, ed., *Mortes illustres,* 628.

27. *ACN,* 113; Parmenter, *The Edge of the Woods,* 41–76. As Greer writes, the good Wendat and Algonquian neophytes and the malevolent Iroquois were necessary stock figures in "colonial hagiography" ("Colonial Saints," *WMQ,* 3d Ser., LVII [2000], 326, 341).

According to Lalemant, Jogues's transformation into a saint was further abetted and encouraged by remarkable, visionary "communications with God"; these featured written language as a hallmark of his metaphysical passage. The first was a dream that he had while still based in Andagoron, after René Goupil was killed, "when my soul was filled with anguish." His account of the dream, which he wrote in a Latin "memoir" that Lalemant translates and cites in the 1647 *Relation*, renders it as a journey to an allegorical dimension that paralleled his own, one with more transparent significations. Jogues returned from the woods to find the village transformed into an ancient city with "towers, bulwarks, and walls of an illustrious beauty." The gates of this city were adorned with the engraved letters *L* and *N* and the picture of "a little lamb, slaughtered." While Jogues pondered "how Barbarians who have no knowledge of our letters could have engraved those characters," he saw a scroll above him, containing the Latin phrase *"Laudent nomen ejus,"* or "let them praise his name." The representation of the dream vision incidentally expresses the language ideology whereby "want of Letters" is a definitive sign of barbarity. However, although "some Hiroquois" who came out of the ancient city assured him "that in truth it was our village," Jogues does not construe its inhabitants as savage—they are designated by their offices: "a sentinel" sent him to appear before "our Judge and our Captain" to be chastised for his "temerity," because he entered the city without heeding the sentinel's command to halt. The judge, "an old man, full of majesty, like to the Ancient of days," beat him with a switch, causing him pain tantamount to the beating he took on his first arrival in a Mohawk village. Jogues "suffered with pain all that was applied to me, finding patience in view of my own baseness"; he had not been worthy of martyrdom because he had not completely owned his "baseness." Now, his judge, "falling on my neck, embraced me; and, in banishing my griefs, he filled me with a consolation wholly divine and entirely inexplicable." It was a dream of wish fulfillment.[28]

28. "Communications avec Dieu"; "que mon ame estoit remplie d'angoisse"; "memoire"; "en des tours, en des bouleurs, et en des murailles, d'une insigne beauté"; "un petit agneau massacré"; "comme des Barbares qui n'ont aucune connoissance de nos lettres auroient pû graver ces characters"; "quelques Hiroquois"; "qu'en effet c'estoit nostre bourgade"; "une sentinelle"; "nostre Juge et devant nostre Capitaine"; "un viellard tout plein de majesté semblable à l'Ancien des jours"; "souffrois avec douleur tout ce qui m'estoit appliqué, trouuvant de la patience dans la veuë de ma bassesse"; "seittant à mon col, il m'enbrassa et en bannissant mes ennuys, il me remplit d'une consolation toute divine et entierement inexplicable" (*JR*, XXXI, 62–67, 74–75). "Want of Letters": Samuel Purchas, *Hakluytus Posthumus; or, Purchas His Pilgrimes: Contayning a*

The dream narrative's value as prognostication depended on its construal as allegory. Like Rowlandson's reading of Deuteronomy 28–30, it enabled a look ahead on a parallel track. Accordingly, Jogues awoke feeling transformed and believing that, although his "death was delayed," like Goupil he would be "received into blessedness." Lalemant comments that Jogues "did not understand" that his dream symbolized his actual death, that the judge's blows presaged the "blow from a hatchet" he would receive when he returned to Mohawk country in 1646, after his present captivity. More prosaically, in Jogues's own narrative, the blows seem to represent the punishment he received from the Mohawks, and the dream offered a resolution to his spiritual dilemma, correcting the presumptuousness and pride he evinced through his paradoxical candidacy for martyrdom. The importance Jogues and Lalemant accord to the dream also evinces a sort of "blockage," a blindness to cultural parallels, because they readily condemned the Indians for being directed by dreams. In a fascinating counterpoint to Jogues's dream, he recounted that a sick Mohawk dreamed that Jogues must participate in a healing ceremony, "holding his book in his hand and behaving as the French do when they pray to God." Jogues "rebukes the vanity of their dreams," refusing to have his rituals, including literacy practices, subsumed by Iroquois spirituality.[29]

For Jesuits, a more orthodox discourse genre than the dream was the vision, an optimal outcome of spiritual exercises. In his retreat from the Mohawks' winter hunting camp, Jogues experienced ascetic conditions that were conducive to the sort of vivid, ecstatic visualizations prescribed by Saint Ignatius: he was fasting, because he abstained from eating game that, in his view, "had been offered to the devil," and he was exposed to

---

History of the World in Sea Voyages and Lande Travells by Englishmen and Others (Glasgow, 1905), I, 486. According to Lussier, Jogues's "dream of the Holy City" warrants "a place in all anthologies of writings from New France" ("Une scène imaginaire en Nouvelle-France," *Voix et images*, XXXII, no. 3 [Spring 2007], paragraph 19 [my translation]). Its Christian, Old World symbolism might be contrasted to that of another dream represented in the *Jesuit Relations*: that of Paul le Jeune, which "seems to orient itself within northeastern woodland cosmologies." See Drew Lopenzina, "Le Jeune Dreams of Moose: Altered States among the Montagnais in the *Jesuit Relations* of 1634," *Early American Studies*, XIII (2015), 30–31.

29. Stephen Greenblatt, *Marvelous Possessions: The Wonder of the New World* (Chicago, 1991), 121 ("blockage"); Ann Marie Plane and Leslie Tuttle, "Introduction: The Literatures of Dreaming," in Plane and Tuttle, eds., *Dreams, Dreamers, and Visions: The Early Modern Atlantic World* (Philadelphia, 2013), 13, 25–26; Tuttle, "French Jesuits and Indian Dreams in Seventeenth-Century New France," ibid., 167. "Mort estoit retardée"; "receu dās la beatitude"; "ne comprenoit pas"; "un coup de hache"; "tenant son livre en main, et se comportant comme sont les François quand ils prient Dieu"; "rebutte la vanité de leurs songes": *JR*, III, 68–69, 130–133.

extreme cold and snow. He was, accordingly, again transported to another dimension.[30]

Jogues's vision was a sort of meta-allegory: a story about conforming the story of one's life to a textual script. Its locale was even more imbricated with literacy than was the ancient city of which he had dreamed. He found himself in the company of several Jesuit fathers, whom he "begged . . . with all the strength of my heart, to commend me to the Cross." He then found himself in "the shop of a Bookseller stationed in the Holy Cross Cloister, in the city where I had my birth." Jogues asked the proprietor "if he had not some Book of piety and edification; he answered that he had one, on which he placed great value. At the same time when it was put into my hands, I heard this voice: 'This Book contains *Illustres pietate viros et fortia bello pectora,*—the acts and deeds of men Illustrious in piety and of hearts brave in war.' These are the very words which I heard, which stamped this truth upon my soul, that we must enter into the Kingdom of Heaven through many tribulations." Through this vision, two seemingly antithetical settings were conflated: Jogues was simultaneously in a winter wilderness in Canada and in a bookshop in his hometown of Orléans. The bookseller presented him with a book of types, or exemplars, and the authority of the voice that proclaimed its "truth," like the response to Jogues's prayer before his captivity, is made manifest by the metaphor of printing: it is an immediate or unmediated communication in that it was printed directly on his soul.[31]

Following the protocol of the Jesuit founder, Jogues was finally re-

---

30. Martz, *Poetry of Meditation*, 27–30; *ACN*, 113; Buchenau, "Prefiguring CanAmerica?" *Transnational American Studies* (Winter 2012), 171. According to Tuttle, "Ignatian spirituality cultivated vivid, internal visioning and relied on the profound emotional reactions this sight might elicit, and yet it was silent about dreaming, the quasi-universal human experience of such sight" ("French Jesuits and Indian Dreams in Seventeenth-Century New France," in Plane and Tuttle, eds., *Dreams, Dreamers, and Visions*, 175).

31. "Les priois de toutes les forces de mon coeur, de me recommander à la Croix"; "la boutique d'un Libraire, placé dans le Cloistre de Sainte Croix, en la ville où j'ay pris naissance"; "s'il n'avoit point quelque Livre de pieté et d'edification, il me repart qu'il en avoit un, dont il saisoit grand estat, à mesme temps qu'on me l'eust mis entre les mains, j'entendis cette voix. Ce Livre contient *Illustres pietate viros et fortia bello pectora*, les faits et les gestes des hommes Illustres en pisté et des coeurs genereux dans la guerre, ce sont les propres paroles que j'entendis, lesquelles imprimerent cette verité dans mon ame, qu'il nous faut entrer dans le Royaume des Cieux, par beaucoup de tribulations": *JR*, III, 74–77. The location in Holy Cross Cloister is significant because, in his dream, Jogues claimed to the other Jesuits "that I was a fellow-citizen of the Cross, since I had been born in a City whose principal and Metropolitan Church was dedicated to the Holy Cross."

warded with illumination. The last in Jogues's series of spiritual instructions came when he "found myself half dead in hunger, in cold, and in nakedness" and amid "mortal anguish in my soul," in view of his past sins and the imminent "pains of death." A "voice condemned the pusillanimity of my heart" and urged him to "fix my thoughts upon the goodness of my God, and cast myself entirely upon his bosom." This admonition was seconded by another voice, which he believed was that of Saint Bernard. According to Jogues, these spoken words were transformative. He himself "pronounced" "words of saint Bernard," offering himself to Jesus just as Jesus offered himself to Saint Bernard, and with a soul "full of joy," he returned to the village and the death he believed awaited him there. Jogues had undergone a sequence of meditation, self-deprivation, penitence, and eventual rejection of self-centered consideration of his sins for a complete subjection to God, all of which corresponded to the religious experience of Ignatius of Loyola during his penitence in Manresa; the illumination he received and the resulting joy similarly corresponded to Saint Ignatius's illumination by the banks of the River Cardoner.[32]

Jogues carried this protocol, which he had rehearsed in his training, into his captivity among the Mohawks, who fantastically embodied the antagonists in the literary genre of the lives of saints. Just as Indian captivity reified the Puritans' identification with the Israelites, so it viscerally enabled the Jesuits' imitation of Christ. The difference, though, was in the Jesuits' tendency towards apotheosis—not analogy or even metaphor but incarnation, word made flesh: "'Not without reason does he ask our life, who has given up his own for us.'" As opposed to the Puritan belief, exemplified in Rowlandson and Williams, that God communicated by directing the reader to relevant places in scripture, Jogues's narrative fulfills the Ignatian ideal by having God write directly upon his soul. In terms of language ideology, the correlative of this incarnation was the experience of direct revelation.[33]

32. Joseph A. Tetlow, "Introduction," in Tetlow, ed., *Spiritual Exercises of Ignatius Loyola, with Commentary* (New York, 1992), 15, 21–22; O'Malley, *First Jesuits*, 25. "Je me trouvay demy mort dans la faim, dans la froid, dans la nudité"; "des angoisses mortelles dans mon ame"; "les douleurs de la mort"; "une voix qui condamnoit la pusillanimité de mon coeur"; "j'arestasse ma pensée sur la bonté de mon Dieu, et que je me jettasse entierement dans son sein"; "prononçay"; "mots de saint Bernard"; "plein de joye": *JR*, XXXI, 77–79.

33. "Ce n'est pas sans raison que celuy-là demande nostre vie, qui a livré la sienne pour nous" (*JR*, XXXI, 78–79). According to O'Malley, "The immediate action of God on the individual is the fundamental premise of the *Exercises*" (*First Jesuits*, 43).

"A Piece of Bible"

The opening sentence of *The Redeemed Captive Returning to Zion* implies an image of John Williams, the season after his return from New France, having been urged by Cotton Mather to "'show how great things God had done unto him'" and having already expounded on the lessons of his captivity from the pulpit in Boston, sitting down at his desk with blank pages before him. "The history I am going to write," he begins, "proves that days of fasting and prayer, without reformation, will not avail to turn away the anger of God from a professing people." There was no way to preempt righteous judgment, but like Rowlandson, Williams suggests a distinction between afflicted sinners and afflicted saints: "Yet witness how very advantageous gracious supplications are to prepare particular Christians patiently to suffer the will of God in very trying public calamities!" Like Lalemant's account of Jogues, then, Williams's story of captivity begins with a preparatory prayer. Appropriately to their doctrinal differences, however, instead of an individual, metaphysical literacy event in which God's word was "engraved in the depth of his soul," it was a communal one in which the boundary between matter and spirit was mediated by scripture. The first incident he recounts is a "day of prayer" in early 1704 that prepared his congregation for captivity.[34]

According to Williams, during the period when the town had been alarmed by warnings of an imminent attack, and perhaps some had settled into complacency as winter set in and the raid failed to materialize, "some of us moved with Fear," decided to hold a prayer day. As represented through Williams's indirect discourse, their supplications were voiced using an either / or formula that was careful not to presume to tell God what to do. They asked him "*either* to spare and save us from the hands of our enemies *or* to prepare us to sanctify and honor Him in what way soever He should come forth towards us." These alternatives, in turn, correlated to the two "places of Scripture from whence we were entertained": "Genesis 32:10–11: 'I am not worthy of the least of all the mercies and of

34. Mather citation in Teresa A. Toulouse, *The Captive's Position: Female Narrative, Male Identity, and Royal Authority in Colonial New England* (Philadelphia, 2007), 126. See also *CH*, 90, 94 (emphasis added). Williams left Quebec on October 25, 1706, arriving in Boston on November 21. He delivered his sermon, "Reports of Divine Kindness," on December 5. The dateline on the first page of the *Redeemed Captive* is March 3, 1707 (*CH*, 94, 156). The sermon is not reprinted in modern editions but is available in the 1758 edition: John Williams, *The Redeemed Captive, Returning to Zion . . .*, 3d ed. (Boston, 1758), 80–94.

all the truth which thou hast showed unto thy servant. Deliver me, I pray thee, from the hand of my brother, from the hand of Esau, for I fear him, lest he will come and smite me, and the mother with the children.' And [in the afternoon], Genesis 32:26. 'And he said, "Let me go, for the day breaketh." And he said, "I will not let thee go, except thou bless me."'" Whereas the first verse calls for immediate deliverance, the second suggests the rewards of perseverance. Which story would theirs be?[35]

The selection of Genesis 32 aptly identified the situation of the vulnerable settlement, awaiting the rumored approach of "'300 Indians with some French,'" with that of Jacob's people as they awaited the encounter with his vengeful brother Esau "and four hundred men with him" (Genesis 32:6). Jacob's plea in Genesis 32:10–11 almost perfectly scripts the Puritans' rhetorical position by calling for mercy while declaring their unworthiness. In his narrative, although perhaps not in the prayer meeting, Williams accentuates the parallel by omitting the second part of 32:10, where Jacob explains the basis of his unworthiness ("for with my staff I passed over this Jordan; and now I am become two bands"). Although the elided details about the staff, the river crossing, and the division of Jacob's company have no specific relevance to the plight of the Deerfield congregation, the conflict between Jacob (about to become Israel) and his brother Esau, the hunter, was readily analogous to the conflict between English and Indians.[36]

Unlike Jacob, who managed to appease Esau and induce a reconciliation, Williams's congregation was not saved "from the hands of our enemies"; so the afternoon scripture proved more prescient. The story of Jacob's wrestling match with the angel illustrated "how it becomes us with an undeniable importunity to be following God with earnest prayers for His blessing in every condition." Williams presents the day of prayer as a two-paragraph prologue to the narrative account of his captivity, which gets under way in the third paragraph: "On the twenty-ninth of February, 1703/4, not long before the break of day." This is the same sort of adver-

35. *CH*, 94 (emphasis added). Williams doesn't specify the date of the prayer day. On the "warnings" of the imminent raid, see Evan Haefeli and Kevin Sweeney, *Captors and Captives: The 1704 French and Indian Raid on Deerfield*, Native Americans of the Northeast (Amherst, Mass., 2003), 95–111. On this "prefatory material," see Toulouse, *Captive's Position*, 133.

36. Haefeli and Sweeney, *Captors and Captives*, 97. This analogy carried through from the seventeenth century, when New England was typologically associated with Canaan, through to the nineteenth. See Michael Paul Rogin, *Fathers and Children: Andrew Jackson and the Subjugation of the American Indian* (New Brunswick, N.J., 1995), 126–128.

bial phrase that opens Rowlandson's 1682 narrative, indicating a similar experience of a typologically suggestive "sudden violence," evocative of the unforeseen onset of Judgment Day.[37]

Thus *The Redeemed Captive* starts out as a story of a community, told from the perspective of its leader. The first part of the narrative recounts the Deerfield congregation's subjection to a collective ordeal and remarks as various individuals egress from the main plotline superintended by Williams's point of view, as they are sorted into the various outcomes of Indian captivity—assimilation, death, redemption—until Williams's solitary arrival in Canada. From that point of separation, his concern was how to be the minister of a dispersed discourse community under hostile conditions.

En route to Canada, Williams continued to facilitate his captive congregation's communications with God; he held a Sabbath prayer meeting on March 5. "The place of Scripture spoken from was Lamentations 1:18: 'The Lord is righteous, for I have rebelled against his commandment. Hear, I pray you, all people, and behold my sorrow. My virgins and young men are gone into captivity.'" That scripture, and presumably the psalm they sang on that day, as well as the one they sang at a prayer meeting on March 9, just before the company disbanded, emphasized the jeremiad interpretation of their experience. They were sinful, proving themselves unworthy "of all the mercies and of all the truth" that God had shared with their community, and therefore God had swept them up into his hands; now, as Genesis 32:26 had instructed them, they must hold on for God's blessing.[38]

But Williams's great concern was for the steadfastness of the "'virgins and young men,'" his own children among them. While they had their books and their minister, their spiritual prospects were relatively secure; Williams noted that their Indian captors not only permitted the English to "join together in the worship of God" but even furnished them with devotional texts: "My master gave me a piece of Bible, never disturbed me in reading the Scriptures, or in praying to God. Many of my neighbors also found that mercy in their journey to have Bibles, psalm books, catechisms, and good books put into their hands with liberty to use them."

37. *CH*, 94. "On the tenth of February, 1675, Came the *Indians* with great numbers upon *Lancaster*" (*SGG*, 68). Richard Slotkin observes the structural and thematic parallels between Rowlandson's narrative and Michael Wigglesworth's poem "Day of Doom" (1662) (Slotkin, *Regeneration through Violence: The Mythology of the American Frontier, 1600–1860* [Middletown, Conn., 1973], 103, 105).

38. *CH*, 94, 102–103.

Williams's acknowledgment of the Indians for tolerating and even foster-ing the practice of their faith marks a turning point in the development of the captivity narrative genre, in that his representation of the Indians is subordinated to the ulterior rhetorical purpose of defaming the Catholics. Whereas Mary Rowlandson elides her native benefactor's agency in the provision of a Bible, Williams highlights the contrast between the Indians and the "French priests" they encountered "after their arrival at Canada," who forbade the Puritans from assembling in prayer and, "to their great grief and sorrow," took away their holy books.[39]

The Deerfield congregation's native captors were perhaps sufficiently exposed to Christianity to recognize the value of holy books to their Prot-estant captives, without being so invested in doctrinal differences as to wish to suppress their literacy practices. To the frustration of the Catho-lic missionaries, the Mohawks from Kahnawake, who formed the largest contingent in the Deerfield raid, had retained many of their cultural tradi-tions, incorporating Catholicism into a syncretic community of practice. By 1704, the most intense period of Catholic devotion was three decades behind them, and their alliance with the French had been tested by the Second French-Iroquois War (1683–1701), which in principle had pitted them against their kin. They had no such ambivalence about joining a raid against New England, but they would not have shared their French allies' animus against Protestantism. And although Jogues's Mohawk captors, more than a half century earlier, had recognized that his devotion to the cross violated the tenets of their Calvinist neighbors in Fort Orange, Wil-liams's captors would not necessarily have known that, from the Jesuits' perspective, the Puritans' manner of reading, preaching, and singing were heretical.[40]

Accordingly, whereas the New Englanders' lives were in constant jeop-ardy on the way to Canada, their cultural identities were given safe pas-sage. However, upon arrival, they were like foreign nationals who have had their passports confiscated. On the first Sabbath after "God had . . . separated me from the congregation of His people," as the raiding party separated into "smaller companies," Williams reflected despairingly on his

39. Ibid., 102, 105. In eighteenth-century captivity narratives, Indian barbarity often became less an aspersion of the Indians themselves than of the whites who supposedly instigated it, whether French, British, or Anglo-American. See Roy Harvey Pearce, "The Significances of the Captivity Narrative," *American Literature*, XIX (1947), 1–20.

40. On the Kahnawakes and their participation in the Deerfield raid, see Haefeli and Sweeney, *Captors and Captives*, 67–73; see also Parmenter, *Edge of the Woods*, 155.

and their situation; typically, he found solace in scripture. "God spoke those words," he recounted, "with a greater efficacy than man could speak them for my strengthening and support." Williams was reassured by the same scripture that Mary Rowlandson shared with her son Joseph, Psalm 118:17 ("I shall not die but live"); furthermore, Psalm 42 exhorted him to "'Hope thou in God,'" and Nehemiah 1:8–9 gave him hopeful foresight: "'Remember, I beseech thee, the word that thou commandest thy servant Moses, saying, "If ye transgress, I will scatter you abroad among the nations; but if ye turn unto me, and keep my commandments and do them, though there were of you cast out unto the uttermost part of the heavens, yet will I gather them from thence and will bring them unto the place that I have chosen, to set my name there."'" As with Rowlandson, scripture delivered the components of a jeremiadic understanding of captivity: righteous affliction, reform, redemption.[41]

Williams might have discerned providential design not only in his receipt of a "piece of Bible" but in the selection of that particular, viscerally material excerpt, which comprised some of the familiar Old Testament signposts for the Puritan captive. They were conducive to an allegorical reading of his experience as a jeremiad, assuring Williams that he would live through affliction to restoration. In his readings, Williams moved backward, with the two psalms and the verse from Nehemiah appearing to him in reverse of their sequence in the Bible: "Those three places of Scripture, one after another by the grace of God, strengthened my hopes that God would so far restrain the wrath of the adversary that the greatest number of us left alive should be carried through so tedious a journey." Williams began to see these scriptures partially fulfilled by the Indians' apparent care to safeguard the lives of his surviving children as they carried them to New France.[42]

Indeed, it was the children who faced the greater spiritual hazards, although these varied according to the child's age, gender, and the degree of the host community's devotion to Catholicism. Ten-year-old Stephen Williams, adopted by a Pennacook family that was relatively diffident towards the Jesuit mission, was more secure in his cultural identity than his seven-year-old sister, Eunice, who was headed for the Mohawk mission town

41. *CH*, 103–104.

42. Ibid., 104, 105. In addition to Psalms and Nehemiah, Williams also cites Lamentations, the scripture he read from the prayer meeting. So possibly his fragment comprised at least the 16th through the 25th books of the Old Testament.

of Kahnawake. Her transformation was foreshadowed by Williams's encounter with two women at the Fort of Saint Francis soon after his arrival
in New France.[43]

These women seemed to showcase the disadvantage of Williams's Puritan faith in the competition for souls. One was a former acquaintance:
"a certain savagess" named Ruth, who had been a prisoner during King
Philip's War and had lived, presumably as a servant, at the house of Ger-
shom Bulkeley, the minister in Wethersfield, Connecticut. She also, according to Williams, "had been often at my house." She retained her English education without any remaining adherence to the Protestant faith
that had been its purpose; having been "proselyted to the Romish faith,"
she was apparently among those Praying Indians who took to "comparison shopping" and preferred the Catholic faith. Ruth "could speak English
very well," and apparently she could read; contesting Williams's refusal to
follow his master's orders to make the sign of the cross, she cited scripture: "Ruth said, 'Mr. Williams, you know the Scripture, and therefore act
against your own light, for you know the Scripture saith, "Servants, obey
your masters." He is your master and you his servant.'" Although in Williams's representation Ruth evinces the same sort of facile engagement
with scripture that Rowlandson attributes to the Praying Indians in her
narrative, his depiction of her discourse fluency is still remarkable, especially in juxtaposition to the stereotypical broken English he attributes
to his "master": "'No good minister, no love God, as bad as the devil.'" His
narration tacitly recognizes her education.[44]

As an Indian woman who retained her acquired language and "knowledge of Puritan scripturalism," Ruth posed an "ironic contrast" to the English children who quickly lost both. As if to demonstrate to Williams the
tenuousness of any English person's culture and faith, Ruth brought to her
meeting with him "an English maid" who had been captured during the
previous decade, "who was dressed up in Indian apparel, could not speak
one word of English," and "could neither tell her own name or the name
of the place from when she was taken." Although this girl was presumably
captured at a younger age than Eunice, Williams's daughter would also be
numbered among "outcasts ready to perish," who, "having lost the English
tongue, will be lost and turn savages in a little time unless something ex-

43. Haefeli and Sweeney, *Captors and Captives*, 155.

44. *CH*, 113–114; Neal Salisbury, "Embracing Ambiguity: Native Peoples and Christianity in
Seventeenth-Century North America," *Ethnohistory*, L (2003), 251 ("comparison shopping").

traordinary prevent" it. From his perspective, this outcome represented a worst-case scenario for Indian captivity—not just turning savage but turning into a Papist savage.[45]

In this regard, the Deerfield captives whom the Indians killed during the long march to Canada were in better stead, spiritually, than the ones they safeguarded. Williams recounts that the Indians killed a number of captives, including his wife, as their infirmities retarded the northward journey. He refers to his wife as "one whose spirit [God] had taken to dwell with Him in glory" and notes that his English neighbors, pursuing the retreating war party, carried her corpse back to town for a Christian burial. He describes another congregant, a "pious young woman," who came to him and explained that she was prepared for her imminent slaughter: "'God has (praised be His name) by His spirit with His word strengthened me to my last encounter with death.' And [she] mentioned me some places of Scripture so seasonably sent in for her support." Williams presents her to his readers as an exemplar to "stir up all in their young days to improve the death of Christ by faith to give them a holy boldness in the day of death." In contrast, the "English maid"–turned-savage and, eventually, his own daughter became counterexamples.[46]

As he sought to shore up the faith of his captive congregants, Williams also ministered to himself, necessarily through the same channel: commenting on the death of his wife, he describes how "That Scripture, Job 1:21, 'Naked came I out of my mother's womb, and naked shall I return thither. The Lord gave, and the Lord hath taken away; blessed be the name of the Lord,' was brought to my mind and from it that an afflicting God was to be glorified, with some other places of Scripture, to persuade to a patient bearing [of] my afflictions." Like the diegetic appearances of scriptures in Rowlandson, this reference to Job 1:21 is not an allusion but part of a series of events.[47]

Williams's rhetorical purpose, in recounting his own and other captives' engagements with scriptures, was didactic. He sought to provide a devotional model that others could follow: if he had been able to maintain a Joblike "patient bearing" under such afflictions, then surely his readers could do so in New England. By contrast, the accounts of Jogues's captivity were intended to inspire devotion. Lay readers would not be ex-

---

45. Toulouse, *Captive's Position*, 149; *CH*, 113, 156.
46. *CH*, 100, 102, 103, 113.
47. Ibid., 100.

pected to follow him on his spiritual journey, and very few of his fellow Jesuits might be expected to undergo such a course of suffering. Accordingly, his divine instructions were intended only for him.[48]

Williams, as the Mohawks carried him to New France, followed orthodox practice by seeking comfort in scripture, for his congregants and for himself, from reading and from memory. Notably, however, such references to scriptural communications from God cease after Williams changes hands from the Mohawks to the French. References to scripture shift from Williams's personal account of a spiritual trial to his polemical exchanges with the Jesuits or the internally cited written exhortations to his captive son to remain steadfast in his faith. It is not that Williams did not have access to an English Bible; he was given one by a French naval officer in Quebec. But it seems that recourse to the Bible was more essential to his psychological well-being during the severe emotional and physical stress of the Indian phase of his captivity than it was during the relative security of his stay in Canada. Presumably, he continued to read the Bible when he had opportunity, but these events were no longer sufficiently noteworthy to be recorded in his narrative.[49]

At one point on the march to New France, Williams's "patient bearing" faltered, and he begged God for physical relief, implying that he would not be satisfied by a verse "seasonably sent in" or by the secondary remediation of being strengthened to better bear his affliction. In recounting his passage across the frozen Winooski River and Lake Champlain on bloody, swollen feet (his matter-of-fact description of wringing "blood out of my stockings" each night refuses the sort of allusions to the Passion that pervade Jogues's narratives), Williams reports that he "lifted up my cry to God in ejaculatory requests that He would take notice of my state and some way or other relieve me." In that instance, his direct appeal was granted. God made fall a "very soft" snow to blanket the hard ice: "wonderful favors in the midst of trying afflictions!" Williams's "ejaculatory requests" and God's apparent response circumvented the mediation of scripture, but in a way that contrasts with Jogues's lesson that the desire for relief was unworthy of a candidate for martyrdom.[50]

48. See Greer, "Colonial Saints," *WMQ*, 3d Ser., LVII (2000), 327.
49. *CH*, 125.
50. Ibid., 102, 103, 105–106; and see Toulouse, *Captive's Position*, 134–135.

"I Took My Pen and Wrote a Letter"

Whereas Jogues used letters to maintain contact with his Jesuit fellows, Williams, as a prisoner of war in New France, attempted to use them to keep his scattered church intact. But he struggled with what he saw as Jesuit communicative practices. Whereas the use of alphabetic literacy presented a counterpoint to what he perceived as the radical cultural difference of the Indians, it was his particular practice of it that, in his mind, distinguished him from the erudite Jesuits. Once in Canada, the difference to establish was, not between barbarity and literacy, but rather between a discourse community characterized by purity of expression and interpretation and one characterized by censorship, deception, and sophistry. "Can that religion be true," he urged in a letter addressed to his vulnerable son Samuel, "that can't bear an examination from the Scriptures that are a perfect rule in matters of faith?" Williams's doctrine of *sola scriptura* extended to writing more broadly; it should be allowed to speak for itself, to deliver its truth without human embellishment or interference. In his portrayal, the Jesuits blasphemed the medium by using it to promote falsehoods and by dismissing the unadorned truth as heresy. A great deal of *The Redeemed Captive* is devoted to highlighting the contrast between Puritan best practices and Jesuit discursive misconduct.[51]

According to Williams, the Jesuits' suppression of unmediated reading extended not only to scripture but to other texts: "When I used their own authors to confute some of their positions, my books, borrowed of them, were taken away from me, for they said I made an ill use of them." In his view, the Catholics used their own writings not to communicate truth but to propagate distortions and outright falsehoods. Just as the Jesuits circulated "a compendium of the Romish Catholic faith" substantiated "by Scriptures horribly perverted and abused," so they circulated false representations, including a letter purportedly seized from an English ship in which Queen Anne "approved . . . designs to ensnare and deceitfully seize on the Indians." This letter had contributed to inciting the reluctant Abenakis to join what would become known as Queen Anne's War and thus was indirectly responsible for the raid on Deerfield and Williams's capture. Williams retorted that "the letter was a lie forged by the French." Presumably, to Williams, the Indians were especially susceptible to being

51. *CH*, 148.

taken in by such a "pretense" because they were reliant on just the sort of mediation practiced by priests, who translated and paraphrased scriptures for their illiterate congregations. They had no way of verifying the origin or authenticity of the letter. In Canada, his scattered congregants found themselves in much the same position as the Abenakis; although they could read, they were cut off from their interpretive community and especially from their minister's authority, leaving them vulnerable to misrepresentations.[52]

In his portrayal of the Jesuits' culture of communication, Williams explores the dark flip side of a language ideology in which the authority of writing derives from the authority of scripture, in which the ultimate model for literacy is a sacred book written and underwritten by an omnipotent and omnipresent Author. The "rule of faith" that Williams invokes is paradoxically dependent upon faith, but in absence of faith in the truthfulness and even the identity of the author, writing becomes an epistemological "funhouse"—a condition familiar enough to postmodern theorists but perhaps distressingly baffling to early modern Christians with a deep-seated belief in the presence of the word. Williams was understandably concerned that, without his skeptical guidance, some of his congregants would not be able to find their way out.[53]

For example, Williams devotes a lot of space to an incident in which the Jesuits circulated letters touting the deathbed conversions of two captive English women. The women themselves were obviously unable to confirm or deny this report, and there were no English or independent witnesses to their great change. Therefore, Williams was unable to disprove the Jesuits' claim that they had renounced Protestantism; he could only enumerate "the just grounds we have to think these things were falsehoods." He pointed to a similar case in which the Jesuits prematurely trumpeted the conversion of a seemingly dying man; he recovered and disavowed any inclination toward Catholicism. "There is no reason to think that these two women were any more papists than he, but they are dead and cannot

52. Ibid., 111, 126–128. According the Haefeli and Sweeney, the governor of Acadia "did in fact attempt to embroil the Eastern Abenakis and Pennacooks in a war with the English by various subterfuges, including the forged letter" Williams refers to (*CH*, 111n). See *Captors and Captives*, 90–91.

53. *CH*, 113. I'm referring to John Barth's iconic short story, "Lost in the Funhouse" (in Barth, *Lost in the Funhouse: Fiction for Print, Tape, Live Voice* [Garden City, N.Y., 1968]), and to Walter J. Ong's *Presence of the Word: Some Prolegomena for Cultural and Religious History* (New Haven, Conn., 1967).

speak." Even if true, Williams suggested, responding to a letter that was purportedly composed by his son Samuel, the words of a dying woman, "'distempered with a very high fever, if not distracted,'" could hardly be evidence of the truth of Catholicism: "'An argument to be sent from Dan to Beersheba, everywhere, where any English captives are, to gain their belief of a pope.'" Always, his avowed contrast is about the quality of evidence: God's word versus a priest's supposed representation of the words of a mentally disabled woman.[54]

Against the ideal of the word made flesh, the ultimate identity between text and person, Williams experienced the affronts of forgery and impersonation. Even handwriting was not a reliable proxy for the person. Thus he was aggrieved—"grief and sorrow that I want words to utter"—by the representation of Samuel's apostasy, yet he suspected that Samuel's handwriting actually conveyed the words of "the priest, Mr. Meriel." Through a "faithful hand," Williams circumvented the Jesuit censors and got an alarmed and admonishing letter to Samuel, receiving a brief but reassuring response that confirmed his suspicions: "As for that letter you had from me, it was a letter I transcribed for Mr. Meriel." The implication is that a written utterance is reliable only if it is consistent with one's intimate knowledge of the utterer and is conveyed through a trustworthy chain of custody.[55]

Yet Williams's own handwriting continued to represent his personhood. He was generally frustrated in his efforts to defuse the "crafty endeavors" of the Jesuits because his letters were so often "intercepted and burned." Upon learning that they were propagating the story of how one Joseph Edgerly had been persuaded to attend Mass after a dead English captive had appeared to him "in flaming fire, telling him he was damned for refusing to embrace the Romish religion," Williams "took my pen and wrote a letter" to two English captives "to make a discovery of this lying plot," but the letter "fell into the hands of the priests and was never delivered." Literacy was central to Williams's self-conception as a purveyor of truth against falsehoods: "Sometimes notice would be given to the English that there were letters written, but they were burned, so that their writing was somewhat useful though never perused by the English because they judged those letters condemned popery." The burning of his letters and

54. *CH*, 133, 145, 151.
55. Ibid., 135, 150.

of other letters with Christian content transformed their words into rhe-torical martyrs, in that their very demise made them into advertisements for the true faith.⁵⁶

Because Williams was largely cut off from his flock, he was greatly con-cerned that the Jesuits would speak for him as they did for others: "They would tell the English that I was turned that they might gain them to change their religion." The fear was most "exercising," and perhaps in re-sponse to it, Williams engaged in some unusual discursive behavior. He wrote a poem — "(though unused to and unskillful in poetry)" — to share with captives on their "secret visits" to him. He offers the disclaimer that he included "Some Contemplations of the Poor and Desolate State of the Church at Deerfield" in his published narrative only at the urging of some of the former captives. The poem, with its "plain style," is an evident counterpoint to some opprobrious Latin "distichs" that had been com-posed by a Jesuit, who "gave them to his scholars to translate into French. ... The import of them was that the king of France's grandson had sent out his huntsmen, and that they had taken a wolf, who was shut up, and now he hopes the sheep would be in safety." Williams's own poem reasserts his status as a shepherd, or a servant of the holy Shepherd, and not a "wolf." The Jesuits and the Indians are the wolves who have ravaged his "fold" with "popish rage and heathennish cruelty." The poem concludes:

Oh Lord! Mine eyes on Thee shall waiting be
Till Thou again turn our captivity
Their Romish plots Thou canst confound, and save
This little flock, this mercy I do crave.
Save us from all our sins and yet again
Deliver us from them who truth disdain.
Lord! For Thy mercy sake Thy covenant mind,
And in Thy house again rest let us find.
So we Thy praises forth will show, and speak
Of all Thy wondrous works, yea we will seek
The advancement of Thy great and glorious name;
Thy rich and sovereign grace we will proclaim.

In exchange for this double redemption from captivity and sin, Williams offers God what a Puritan humbly can give: praise. Indeed, as he argues in

56. Ibid., 132–133, 152–153, 155.

his homecoming sermon, God's own "Glorification" had been God's "Design" all along; and Williams has a sacred obligation to promote it.[57]

Williams's poem is reminiscent of one by his more accomplished contemporary and fellow minister, Edward Taylor. In his Preparatory Meditation II.43, Taylor presents a hierarchy of communicative modes, in which he ranks "Words Writ" above "Words Orall" and "Mentall." Even so, his "Goose quill-slabbred draughts, / Although the fairest blossoms of the minde" are hardly adequate to the subject of the Almighty. His hope is that justification by Christ would elevate his poetic prowess, and on this basis, he offers God a deal:

> Be though my God, and make mee thine Elect
> To kiss thy feet, and worship give to thee:
> Accept of mee, and make me thee accept.
> So I'st be safe, and thou shalt served bee.
> I'le bring thee praise, busk't up in Songs perfum'de,
> When thou with grace my Soule hast sweetly tun'de.

The deal is similar to the one proposed by Williams—save me, and I'll glorify you—and illustrates how Williams's captivity, like Rowlandson's, functions as a worldly allegory for the spiritual plight of every Protestant Christian. Because Taylor's verses were "Preparatory" to the Lord's Supper (which Williams insists is merely "figurative"), it highlights the contrast with Jogues, whose literalism demanded the sacrifice of his own life.[58]

Conclusion

The narrative accounts of the captivities of Jogues and Williams exemplify two functions of captive literacy practices: communication and allegoresis. Whether or not Jogues's letters reached their destination, his reading and writing were central to his identity as a member of that elite brotherhood that carried God's Word into the wilderness. The very conditions that made communication so difficult also augmented the value of those letters that did reach his fellow Jesuits. Similarly, the significance of his divine communications from God was augmented by his physical estrangement from the Church and the absence of sacraments. God

---

57. *CH*, 123, 128–129.

58. Donald E. Stanford, ed., *The Poems of Edward Taylor* (New Haven, Conn., 1960), 159–160; *CH*, 147.

prepared him for his role through devotional reading, certainly, but also through more immediate forms of communication in which writing was less a medium and more a symbol. In this story, the Mohawks fulfilled the function of Counter-Reformation antagonists: mutilating his fingers, breaking up his retreat as the agents of heretics. Jogues's dream of the lettered city and vision of the bookseller interpreted these antagonists allegorically as necessary auxiliaries, helping to bring his story in line with the plot of martyrdom. His literacy lent meaning to his abjection.

Decades later, the story of the Deerfield community was coherent so long as they were able to read, tell, and sing it together; their shared scriptures explained their captivity. In the first stage, it was a familiar explanation: the Indians were the allegorical counterparts to the Old Testament Babylonians. Yet many captives transitioned from one allegorical captivity to another. The raid on Deerfield was almost like a concatenation of the sackings of the First and Second Temples, by a typologically confederated Babylonian and "Romish" army, with a resulting dispersal of captives throughout both Indian Country and a "Popish Country." For Williams, the Indians were bad, but the Papists were worse; moreover, the Indians' misdeeds were laid to the account of the French, especially the Jesuits, whom Williams portrayed as his primary antagonists.[59]

Williams faced nearly the opposite discursive situation as Jogues: so long as he had his Bible, his line of communication with his God was the same as it ever was; but he found writing to be a fundamentally flawed means of interpersonal communication, uncertain of reaching its addressee, subject to distortion, misrepresentation, and imposture. Dispersed in New France, some of the Deerfield captives found their story changed. Would they be redeemed from captivity, or was their captivity itself a means of redemption from heresy? At least, Williams struggled to retain control over the meaning of their collective experience, even after his restoration to his position of authority. For Williams, restoration from captivity meant a return to a closed circuit of communication, within which he could acclaim the power of God and, in jeremiad style, urge "reformation." Wil-

---

59. *CH*, 96. Since Puritan historians associated the founding of New England with the building of the Second Temple in 516 BCE after the restoration from the Babylonian captivity, its destruction by Rome in 70 CE was a likely correlate for French and Indian Wars and their captivities. See Cecelia Tichi, "The Puritan Historians and Their New Jerusalem," *EAL*, VI (1971), 143; David A. Boruchoff, "New Spain, New England, and the New Jerusalem: The 'Translation' of Empire, Faith, and Learning (Translatio Imperii, Fidei Ac Scientiae) in the Colonial Missionary Project," ibid., XLIII (2008), 20–21; Toulouse, *Captive's Position*, 79–80, 84–85.

liams begins to fulfill his obligation in his sermon on Luke 8:39, which his poem had anticipated with its reference to the Lord's "House": "Return to thine own House, and shew how great Things GOD hath done unto thee." Williams finally had a captive audience, as it were, free from the interference of his "crafty Adversaries." *The Redeemed Captive* disseminated his message more broadly, in a triumphant "plain style."[60]

Thus Williams had a last word in the contest for the souls of the majority of the Deerfield captives; but some of the lambs from the fold remained "unredeemed." Whereas Jogues had written to his father provincial in order to elicit the "prayers of the pious" so that God "may gather us from among the nations to bless his holy name," Williams calls for his readers' "compassion and prayers to God to gather" those who were left behind, including his by-now ten-year-old daughter Eunice. He was hoping for a worldly repatriation. Besides the medium of prayers to God, they were beyond his reach as a minister.[61]

Eunice became by far the most famous of these unredeemed captives. As an adoptee in the Mohawk mission town of Kahnawake, she was cut off from the discourse community of her first education and acculturated into a new one. Whereas, following the 1704 raid on Deerfield, her father's life experience had tracked with the Old Testament narratives of Job and the exiled Israelites, his daughter entered into a different set of discursive relations, especially with the medieval saint and the Mohawk woman who became her namesakes. The next chapter, the second part of this comparatist diptych, puts Eunice Williams's story in dialogue with that of the most celebrated Catholic Mohawk: the first native American saint, Kateri Tekakwitha.

---

60. *CH*, 90; Williams, *Redeemed Captive*, 81, 90.
61. *CH*, 156.

CHAPTER FOUR

Fulfilling the Name

Daughters of Kahnawake

Kateri Tekakwitha (1656–1680) and Marguerite Kanenstenhawi (1696–1785) are two of the most famous women of colonial North America. Both women were the children of captives taken by Mohawks: Tekakwitha's mother was a Christian Algonquin whose name is unrecorded; Kanenstenhawi's father was John Williams, the Deerfield minister. As Catholic Mohawks, both became the spiritual progeny of Isaac Jogues, whose "blood must have been the seed of Christianity in that heathen land," according to Pierre Cholenec, the priest who had been Kateri Tekakwitha's confessor and had officiated at the marriage of Marguerite Kanenstenhawi in 1713. Insofar as the events of their lives took place beyond the scope of the first-person captivity narrative, this chapter is a counterpoint to the preceding one. Instead of representations of literacy events and practices, its comparative focus is a different sort of discursive intersection: the name.[1]

Kateri Tekakwitha and Marguerite Kanenstenhawi were both products of the same cultural crucible: the Iroquois-Jesuit mission village of Kahnawake, which was founded in 1676 when a predominantly Mohawk group of converts and the mission connected with them relocated from slightly downriver to the site the French called the Sault-St.-Louis, across the Saint Lawrence River from Montreal. Kahnawake burgeoned during the 1680s and soon had the largest native populace in New France, becoming the center of "Iroquois Catholicism." This site may offer a productively un-

---

1. "Son sang devoit être la semence du christianisme dans cette terre infidèle": "Lettre du Père Cholenec, missionnaire de la Compagnie de Jèsus, au père Augustin le Blanc, de la même compagnie, procureur des missions du Canada, 1715," in *Lettres édifiantes et curieuses, écrites des missions étrangères*, IV, *Mémoires d'Amérique* (Lyon, 1819), 28. Unless otherwise indicated, translations from the French in this chapter are my own. According to Ellen Hardin Walworth, "Ten years after Ondessonk [Jogues] had shed the last drop of his blood to make these Mohawks Christians," Tekakwitha "was born among the people who had seen the blackgown die, in the Village of the Turtles,—some say in the 'cabin at the door of which the tomahawked priest had fallen'" (Walworth, *The Life and Times of Kateri Tekakwitha: The Lily of the Mohawks, 1656–1680* [Buffalo, N.Y., 1893], 5).

familiar vantage point for onomastics, or the study of names and naming. Specifically, the collision between European and Iroquoian initiations and naming practices, especially baptism and requickening, challenges western notions of the relation of name to identity. (*Requickening* is an Iroquois naming practice that places an adoptee into a family by giving her / him the name of a deceased family member.) Each woman successively experienced both forms of initiation and renaming. Each transition exemplifies how individual selves "become entangled — through the name — in the life histories of others." Each name the women bore represented a different set of entanglements, a distinct, contingent personhood. These interconnections spanned not only synchronically, to form "a social matrix," but also through time, linking a seventeenth-century Mohawk woman with a fourteenth-century Italian ascetic mystic and embedding an English girl within a Mohawk lineage.[2]

Kateri Tekakwitha migrated to Kahnawake from her natal village of Gandaouagué in 1677. Kahnawake itself was transforming during this period. Kateri's brief life and death there epitomized a phase of "intense new female religiosity." After her death in 1680, she was credited with exceptional chastity, as well as several posthumous cures and other intercessions. Two Jesuit priests who had worked with her, Cholenec and Claude Chauchetière, composed hagiographic accounts that made the case for

2. Allan Greer suggests that "Iroquois Catholicism" be considered, not as an example of syncretism, but rather as a "local religion," a concept that "focuses attention on performance rather than belief, on specific settings among people with particular experiences and traditions rather than on theological systems with pretentions to universality" (Greer, "Conversion and Identity: Iroquois Christianity in Seventeenth-Century New France," in Kenneth Mills and Anthony Grafton, eds., *Conversion: Old Worlds and New* [Rochester, N.Y., 2003], 178). See Gerald F. Reid, *Kahnawàke: Factionalism, Traditionalism, and Nationalism in a Mohawk Community*, The Iroquoians and Their World (Lincoln, Neb., 2004), 7; Evan Haefeli and Kevin Sweeney, *Captors and Captives: The 1704 French and Indian Raid on Deerfield*, Native Americans of the Northeast (Amherst, Mass., 2003), 67, 73; Greer, *Mohawk Saint: Catherine Tekakwitha and the Jesuits* (Oxford, 2005), 89–110; Daniel K. Richter, *The Ordeal of the Longhouse: The Peoples of the Iroquois League in the Era of European Colonization* (Williamsburg, Va., and Chapel Hill, N.C., 1992), 32–33; Barbara Bodenhorn and Gabrielle vom Bruck, "'Entangled in Histories': An Introduction to the Anthropology of Names and Naming," in vom Bruck and Bodenhorn, eds., *The Anthropology of Names and Naming* (New York, 2006), 3 ("entangled," "matrix"). Richard H. White discusses a distinction in studies of identity between "self and person, with self . . . understood as a self-conscious subject and person understood as a socially constructed identity." See White, "'Although I Am Dead, I Am Not Entirely Dead, I Have Left a Second of Myself': Constructing Self and Persons on the Middle Ground of Early America," in Ronald Hoffman, Mechal Sobel, and Fredrika J. Teute, eds., *Through a Glass Darkly: Reflections on Personal Identity in Early America* (Williamsburg, Va., and Chapel Hill, N.C., 1997), 405.

her holiness, and thereafter she was the subject of several derivative hagiographies. Her cult was established by the early decades of the eighteenth
century. Beginning in the late nineteenth century, her prospective canonization became a point of pride for American Catholics; in 1980, the ter-
centennial of her death, Pope John Paul II made her the first native American to be beatified, and finally in 2012, Pope Benedict XVI made her the
first to be canonized. Saint Kateri Tekakwitha is the "symbolic figurehead"
of native American Catholics, whose membership organization is called
the Tekakwitha Conference. As a remarkable figure at the intersection of
ethnohistory, women's studies, and religious history, in recent decades Tekakwitha has increasingly attracted the attention of scholars.[3]

Eunice Williams was brought to Kahnawake in 1704 as one of the captives taken in the infamous French and Indian raid on Deerfield, Massachusetts, during Queen Anne's War. As the "unredeemed captive," she was
forever the foil to her biological father, John Williams. A series of names—
Waongote, Marguerite, and Kanenstenhawi—marked her egress from an
existence that had been circumscribed by literacy. Her final interview with
her father, during his visit to Kahnawake while he was still a detainee in
New France, was perhaps her last English-language literacy event as a person who identified as *Eunice Williams.* He "told her she must be careful she
did not forget her catechism and the Scriptures she had learned by heart,"
but he later heard from others that "she was much afraid she should forget her catechism, having none to instruct her." Ultimately, she was among
those captives who "lost the English tongue" altogether. She became an
object of morbid fascination to generations of New Englanders, who saw
her conversion to Catholicism and marriage to a Mohawk warrior as fates
worse than death because of their implications for her soul. Whereas Kateri Tekakwitha was the subject of hagiographies, the minister's daughter became a model for "cautionary" representations of white savages in

3. Haefeli and Sweeney, *Captors and Captives,* 69; Paula Elizabeth Holmes, "The Narrative
Repatriation of Blessed Kateri Tekakwitha," *Anthropologica,* XLIII (2001), 87–88. The most
comprehensive scholarly work on Tekakwitha is Greer, *Mohawk Saint.* Other studies include
Susan R. Dauria, "Kateri Tekakwitha: Gender and Ethnic Symbolism in the Process of Making
an American Saint," *New York Folklore,* XX, nos. 3–4 (1994), 55–73; K. I. Koppedrayer, "The
Making of the First Iroquois Virgin: Early Jesuit Biographies of the Blessed Kateri Tekakwitha,"
Ethnohistory, XL (1993), 277–306; Daniel K. Richter, *Facing East from Indian Country: A Native
History of Early America* (Cambridge, Mass., 2001), 79–90; Nancy Shoemaker, "Kateri Tekakwi-
tha's Tortuous Path to Sainthood," in Shoemaker, ed., *Negotiators of Change: Historical Perspectives on Native American Women* (New York, 1995).

nineteenth-century American fiction, including Faith, the younger sister of the heroine of Catherine Maria Sedgwick's *Hope Leslie* (1827), and Ruth in James Fenimore Cooper's *Wept of Wish-Ton-Wish* (1829). Marguerite Kanenstenhawi has also been the subject of scholarship, but to a lesser extent than Tekakwitha, at least in part because of the relative scarcity of sources.[4]

As a young adult, Tekakwitha, through her conversion to Catholicism, entered the discursive frame of "colonial hagiography." As a child, Eunice Williams, through her adoption, exited the discursive frame of the captivity narrative, going where only fiction could follow. Accordingly, the two women have posed complementary methodological challenges for scholars. Tekakwitha's brief life may be "more fully and richly documented than that of any other indigenous person of North or South America in the colonial period," yet the hagiographic discourse may obscure as much as it reveals: it is impossible to determine the "truth about the historical individual behind the religious narrative." By contrast, from the moment her biological father's captivity narrative takes leave of her with the words, "I have yet a daughter of ten years of age," the historical record contains only "a very few, very bare facts" pertaining to the impressively long life of Marguerite Kanenstenhawi. Since the information about one historical figure is unreliable and that about the other is scarce, scholarship on both has emphasized cross-references with contextual information. For Tekakwitha, the Jesuit biographies need to be read within the discursive context of "Counter-Reformation French culture"; for both, their lives at Kahnawake can be speculatively elaborated through ethnohistorical research.[5]

4. *CH*, 118–119, 156. In light of "the uneven preparation in reading and writing and the unequal treatment of boys and girls," Eunice Williams's literacy might have been more susceptible to lapsing than if she had been a boy. See E. Jennifer Monaghan, *Learning to Read and Write in Colonial America*, Studies in Print Culture and the History of the Book (Amherst, Mass., 2005), 21; June Namias, *White Captives: Gender and Ethnicity on the American Frontier* (Chapel Hill, N.C., 1993), 97; John Demos, *The Unredeemed Captive: A Family Story from Early America* (New York, 1994). See also Alexander Medlicott, Jr., "Return to This Land of Light: A Plea to an Unredeemed Captive," *New England Quarterly*, XXXVIII (1965), 202–216; Audra Simpson, "Captivating Eunice: Membership, Colonialism, and Gendered Citizenships of Grief," *Wicazo Sa Review*, XXIV, no. 2 (Fall 2009), 105–129.

5. Greer, *Mohawk Saint*, vii–viii ("richly documented"); Richter, *Facing East from Indian Country*, 83 ("truth"); *CH*, 156 ("daughter"); Demos, *Unredeemed Captive*, 140 ("facts"); Greer, "Savage / Saint: The Lives of Kateri Tekakwitha," in Sylvie Dépatie et al., eds., *Habitants et Marchands, Twenty Years Later: Reading the History of Seventeenth- and Eighteenth-Century Canada* (Montreal, Que., 1998), 139. Alden T. Vaughan and Edward W. Clark propose four categories of

This collision between European religious history and ethnohistory is effectively encapsulated by the names *Kateri Tekakwitha* and *Marguerite Kanenstenhawi*. This chapter proposes that the lives of the two women were shaped, at least in part, by the stories of their namesakes. Christian and Iroquoian naming practices are apparent analogues, but they had very different valences. In Christian belief, the bestowal of a baptismal name links the newborn or convert to ancestors and other predecessors with the same name and also, especially, to her or his patron saint. As the *Rituel du Diocèse du Québec* (1703) attests, the Church "commands that the child be given the name of a male or female saint, depending on their sex, so that he or she can emulate the virtues and feel the effects of the Saint's protection before God." In Iroquois practice, the bestowal of a name inducts an adolescent or a captive-adoptee into a persona that had been previously inhabited by a deceased namesake. In other words, it resuscitates, or re-quickens, a persona that has lapsed into dormancy. Iroquoian requickening might have more closely resembled exceptional cases, such as Isaac Jogues's emulation of the lives of saintly predecessors and his incarnation of the language of scripture, than the Catholic layperson's relation to his or her baptismal namesake.[6]

Kateri Tekakwitha and Marguerite Kanenstenhawi may illustrate two different outcomes to the encounter between Christian and Iroquoian baptism and requickening. In the first case, insofar as Tekakwitha applied the logic of requickening to her baptism, she might have understood the story of Catherine of Siena, her patron saint, less as a source of inspiration and more as a template for her new identity. Kateri Tekakwitha lived in

captivity narratives: 1) those in which the authors betray limited or no alteration in their cultural identity as a result of their experience, 2) those in which the authors "gained empathetic insight into Indian culture," 3) those written by former captives "who had difficulty adjusting to their natal culture after long exposure to Indian life," and 4) a "hypothetical" category that "could have been written by those who never returned to their natal culture" (*Puritans among the Indians: Accounts of Captivity and Redemption, 1676-1724* [Cambridge, Mass., 1981], 14–16).

6. The *Oxford English Dictionary* defines "namesake" simply as "a person who or thing which has the same name as another." It can refer to either a person named after another or to the person he or she is named after. "Elle commande qu'on lui donne le nom d'un Saint ou d'une Sainte, selon son sexe, afin qu'il enpuisse imiter les vertus et ressentir les effets de sa protection aupres de Dieu": *Rituel du Diocèse de Québec* (Paris, 1703), 23–24, cited in Brett Rushforth, *Bonds of Alliance: Indigenous and Atlantic Slaveries in New France* (Williamsburg, Va., and Chapel Hill, N.C., 2012), 267, 267n. I translate the French somewhat differently. See Thomas W. Sheehan, *Dictionary of Patron Saints' Names* (Huntington, Ind., 2001), 7. On requickening: Richter, *Ordeal of the Longhouse*, 32; see also José António Brandão, *Your Fyre Shall Burn No More: Iroquois Policy towards New France and Its Native Allies to 1701* (Lincoln, Neb., 1997), 41.

Kahnawake when the Mohawks' fervor for the new faith was at its apex; even so, she was extraordinary in her devotions. John Williams's biological daughter, in contrast, would have ceased to be *Eunice* upon her adoption, yet her new baptismal name would not have displaced her Mohawk identity. The Jesuits' choice of a new Christian name for her, however, might have been motivated by parallels between the stories of Eunice Williams of Deerfield and Saint Margaret of Antioch.[7]

We can gain further insight about Kateri Tekakwitha and Marguerite Kanenstenhawi through comparison. In particular, an analysis of the representations of Tekakwitha's transformation into a saint sheds some light on Eunice Williams's transformation into a Mohawk woman. Whereas comparative analyses typically juxtapose figures from disparate contexts, this one has the additional warrant of a genuine historical convergence. In the nearly quarter of a century between Kateri Tekakwitha's death in Kahnawake and Eunice Williams's arrival there as a captive, Kateri's reputation as an intercessor had waxed, so that her spiritual presence suffused the region. One of Eunice Williams's fellow captives, Joseph Kellogg, reported being offered "relicks of the Rotten wood of the coffin" of "Saint Katherine" as an inducement to a sickbed conversion. The newly arrived Eunice Williams would have encountered "Saint Katherine" in the mission church. According to her great-grandson Eleazer Williams, when Eunice-turned-Marguerite was undergoing her spiritual instruction, "Catharine Tekawitawa [sic] a Mohawk convert who was sainted by the Jesuits, was held up to her view, more than any of the scripture saints, or even the perfect pattern of her savior." Eleazer Williams's biography of "The Fair Captive," written under the pseudonym Charles B. de Saileville, is a fanciful, apparently unreliable account, but this detail seems plausible. Since the superior of the Mission at Kahnawake was none other than Pierre Cholenec, who had completed his manuscript "La vie de Catherine Tegakouita" six years before Eunice Williams's arrival, Kateri Tekakwitha was probably showcased to all the converts at Kahnawake.[8]

7. As Jon Parmenter points out, "historians must not assume that the Jesuits' lengthy descriptions of the extreme Christians devotions of a few individuals like Catherine Tekakwitha necessarily represented mainstream Iroquois behavior at these settlements" (Parmenter, *The Edge of the Woods: Iroquoia, 1534–1701* [East Lansing, Mich., 2010], 155).

8. Greer, *Mohawk Saint*, 148; Charles B. de Saileville [Eleazer Williams], "A History of the Life and Captivity of Miss Eunice Williams, Alias, Madam De Roguers, Who Was Styled 'The Fair Captive'" (1842), 243, microfilm, reel 7, 27–29, State Historical Society of Wisconsin, Area Research Center, Green Bay. The first three chapters of this biography are included in *CH*,

It seems likely that the visual connotation—"held up to her view"— was literal. In *La Vie de la B. Catherine Tegakoüita dite à présent la Saincte Sauvagesse,* which Chauchetière, for his part, had begun writing around 1685, he explains that Kateri appeared to him in a vision and requested him "to make paintings for the instruction of the savages and to serve me in exhorting those she wished to attract to heaven after her." At the time of his writing, his "portrait de Catherine"—*"cette grande image"*—was on display in the church at the Sault-St.-Louis, "serving to instruct the Savages in the life and manners of Catherine." The oil painting hangs today in the Church of Saint Francis Xavier in Kahnawake (Figure 4). It is perhaps the most significant material artifact pertaining to the life of either woman: a posthumous portrait by an artist who had known Kateri Tekakwitha personally and a noteworthy exhibit in the religious instruction of Marguerite Kanenstenhawi.[9]

The scholar's decisions as to how to designate each of these two polynomial historical figures carry implications. The woman referred to by her eighteenth-century biographers as *Catherine Tekakwitha* (or similar transliterations of the Mohawk name) was canonized in 2012 as "St. *Kateri,* Protectress of Canada and the first native American saint." Like most modern scholars, I refer to her as *Kateri* Tekakwitha, employing the Mohawk version of the French *Catherine.* An 1876 Mohawk-language translation of Cholenec's *Vie de Catherine Tekakouita* (1696) attests to this practice, using *Kateri* throughout. For example, the clause "il la baptisa et lui donna le nom de Catherine" [he baptized her and gave her the name Catherine] is rendered, "8asakonek8aheste, Kateri 8asakonatonk8e" [they baptized her, and named her Catherine]. The translator, Joseph Marcoux, a Jesuit who spent forty-two years among the Iroquois at St. Regis and Kahnawake and "acquired such proficiency in the Iroquois tongue as to attain a high rank

---

227–243. As they explain, Saileville is apparently a pseudonym for Marguerite Kanenstenhawi's great-grandson Eleazer Williams, in whose papers the manuscript appears (ibid., 222). Among other discrediting details, Eleazer Williams claimed to be the exiled dauphin of France. For more information, see Demos, *Unredeemed Captive,* 242–246.

9. Pierre Cholenec specifies that Chauchetière was inspired to make the painting after two "apparitions" from Kateri, on September 1, 1681, and April 21, 1682. See Cholenec, "La vie de Catherine Tegakouita première vierge irokoise," in William Lonc, ed., *Catherine Tekakwitha: Her Life,* Early Jesuit Missions in Canada, VII (Halifax, N.S., 2002), 51. Greer identifies this painting as "the one that still hangs in the church at Kahnawake" (*Mohawk Saint,* 19). Other sources suggest that the painting at Saint Francis Xavier Church is not the original but a copy made by Chauchetière in the 1690s (J. Russell Harper, *Painting in Canada: A History* [Toronto, Ont., 1977], 8).

Figure 4 Oil painting of Kateri Tekakwitha. By Claude
Chauchetière. Ca. 1683. Photograph by Anne M. Scheuerman.
Department of Special Collections and University Archives,
Marquette University Libraries

among philologists," would have adjusted the French *Catherine* to Mohawk phonology, which did not allow the final *ine. Tekakwitha*, after her
baptism, most likely referred to herself as *Kateri.*[10]

10. Holy See Press Office, "Sanctity Arises from the Well-Spring of Redemption," *Vatican Information Service,* Oct. 22, 2012 (emphasis added); Cholenec, "La vie de Catherine," in Lonc,
ed., *Catherine Tekakwitha,* 4; Pierre Cholenec, *Vie de Catherine Tekakouita: (Traduction iroquoise),*
trans. Joseph Marcoux ([Montreal, Que.], 1876), 12; Florence Rudge McGahan, "Joseph Mar-

Conversely, the woman identified in the Jesuit notice of her death, at age eighty-nine, as "Marguerite, mother-in-law of Annasetegen," would have referred to herself as *Eunice Williams* for only a small fraction of her life. The prevalent use of that name in scholarship tacitly assumes the perspective of her natal community and has an infantilizing connotation. "Many little girls were left behind," wrote Emma Coleman in her 1925 history of New England captives brought to Canada, "some to marry Indians, more to marry Frenchmen and a few to become nuns; but no other captive-child caused so much trouble to the two Governments as little Eunice, and the name of no other is so well known to later generations." This chapter recognizes her cultural conversion by employing the name *Marguerite Kanenstenhawi*.[11]

The Lily of the Mohawks

Kateri Tekakwitha's common sobriquet, "The Lily of the Mohawks," may have a racial implication, suggesting that her virtue made her more white than other Mohawks. It probably originates with Chauchetière's allusion to the Song of Solomon 2:2, in which the husband (in Christian exegesis, understood to be Christ) declares that his spouse (the "true Church") is like a "lily among thorns." Whereas Kateri Tekakwitha at Gandaouagué was "like a lily among thorns," God "transplanted this beautiful lily and placed it in a garden full of flowers, I mean in the mission of the Sault which has been, is and will be full with very beautiful flowers, which are the virtuous persons that are still seen there shining in virtue." Within the

---

coux," *Catholic Encyclopedia (1913)*, IX, *Wikisource*. Greer advocates the use of *Catherine*, claiming that the introduction of the name *Kateri* was a successful "gambit" perpetrated by the biographer Ellen Hardin Walworth in 1893, "in an atmosphere of fin de siècle primitivism." That is, Walworth condescendingly perpetuated a Mohawk mispronunciation of *Catherine*. See *Mohawk Saint*, xi, 197. Yet the Marcoux translation, which predates Walworth's biography, demonstrates that she was quite correct in describing *Kateri* (pronounced with the emphasis on the final syllable) as "the Iroquois form of the Christian name *Katherine*." See *The Life and Times of Kateri Tekakwitha*, 1n. *Kateri* is no more a mispronunciation of the French than is the English version, which articulates the *th* phoneme. In an earlier published version of this chapter, before I was aware of the 1876 translation and had consulted with the late Mohawk linguist Roy Wright (who described the transformation of Catherine into Kateri as "perfectly regular"), I recommended that "scholars should now follow Greer's lead in referring to her as Catherine Tekakwitha" (Andrew Newman, "Fulfilling the Name: Catherine Tekakwitha and Marguerite Kanenstenhawi [Eunice Williams]," *Legacy*, XXVIII [2011], 250).

11. Demos, *Unredeemed Captive*, 237; Emma Lewis Coleman, *New England Captives Carried to Canada, between 1677 and 1760 during the French and Indian Wars*, II (Portland, Me., 1925), 54.

multihued flower garden cultivated by the Jesuit fathers, the lily had a special status, symbolizing betrothal to Christ. It was likewise the emblem—"the sceptre of her virginity"—of Saint Catherine of Siena, who would be the "patron saint of Kateri's band" at Kahnawake.[12]

Before the Mohawk girl could become the American version of Saint Catherine, however, she had to become Tekakwitha. Each Iroquois clan had a proprietary pool of personal names, each of which could be "in use" by only one individual at a time. The newborn would receive an available "baby name," which it would eventually relinquish, to receive an available "adult name." Kateri Tekakwitha's childhood name is unrecorded; *Tekakwitha* was the name she would have received after her first menses, "a new and distinct adult identity." The two most widely cited translations for *Tekakwitha,* both furnished by Ellen Hardin Walworth, her Victorian-era biographer, are the following: "One who approaches moving something before her" and "One who puts things in order." If the second, for which the ultimate source is Marcoux, the aforementioned translator and "the author of a complete Iroquois dictionary," is correct, it might correspond to Tekakwitha's role within her natal village of Gandaouagué as a maker of handicrafts, especially the belts of wampum that were used in diplomacy.[13]

12. "Catholic Bible: Douay-Rheims Bible Online," http://www.drbo.org/. "Comme un lis entre les epines"; "Dieu a transplanté ce beau lis et la mis dans un jardin rempli de fleurs je veux dire dans la mission du Sault qui a esté est et sera remplie de tres belles fleurs qui sont les personnes vertueuses qu'on y voit encore reluire en vertu" (Claude Chauchetière, *La vie de la B. Catherine Tegakoüita, dite a present la saincte sauvagesse* [Manate, (N.Y.), 1887], 58). Walworth suggests that "Lily of the Mohawks" is "altogether foreign to the Iroquois language, as they have no distinctive word for *Lily* (nothing more definite than 'white flower'); and *Mohawks* is a name they dislike, because it was first given to them by their enemies; they prefer, therefore, their own term, *Caniengas" (Life and Times of Kateri Tekakwitha,* 283–284). The phrase "a lily among thorns" sounds counterintuitive in English, but it was idiomatic enough in early modern French; for example, a 1701 treatise declares, "The Church is like a lily among thorns" ("l'Église est comme un lis entre les épines"). See P. Louis Thomassin, *Traité dogmatique et historique des edits et des autres moiens spirituels et temporels . . . pour établir, et pour maintenir l'unite de l'Eglise catholique. . . .* (Paris, 1703), 268; Raymond of Capua, *Life of Saint Catharine of Sienna,* trans. Regis Hamilton (New York, 1862), 432; David Blanchard, ". . .To the Other Side of the Sky: Catholicism at Kahnawake, 1667–1700," *Anthropologica,* XXIV (1982), 97.

13. Elizabeth Tooker, "Women in Iroquois Society," in Michael K. Foster, Jack Campisi, and Marianne Mithun, eds., *Extending the Rafters: Interdisciplinary Approaches to Iroquoian Studies* (Albany, N.Y., 1984), 112; Greer, *Mohawk Saint,* 47, 217n; Walworth, *Life and Times of Kateri Tekakwitha,* 36. Greer describes Gandaouagué, the name of Tekakwitha's natal village, as "a cognate name" to Kahnawake, the name the mission village took on when it relocated in 1676 from La Prairie to the Sault-St.-Louis (*Mohawk Saint,* 28). *Kahnawake* means "at the rapids" (Reid, *Kahnawàke,* 7). Both names were also commonly rendered as *Caughnawaga;* each was used as an ethnonym as well as a toponym. Tooker points out that adult names can be "associated with particular obligations (in effect, roles) in the society" ("Women in Iroquois Society," 112).

Tekakwitha was baptized as *Catherine* on Easter Sunday, 1677, in Gandaouagué. Catherine was apparently a common name for Indian converts. In recounting her baptism, Chauchetière writes, "Many savages have borne that name before and since her, but none has fulfilled it like the Blessed Catherine Tekakwitha." In other words, the appropriateness of the name became apparent retroactively. It was not chosen because it suited her; rather, she chose to fulfill it. To do so, she would have had to learn the life story of her namesake from the Jesuits. It became her story—the history of *Kateri*.[14]

Although Christian and Iroquoian initiations had similarities, they were not analogous. Through baptism, the individual self became regenerated, or *regeneratus*—separated from a state of sinfulness and incorporated into one of purity. Chauchetière speaks of "the horror of the new Christians [in Kahnawake] at the life they had led among the Iroquois before their baptism." By contrast, through Iroquoian initiations, the captive undergoing adoption or the adolescent transitioning into adulthood became incorporated into a new identity altogether. It was not the initiate who was regenerated but rather the preexisting persona that had been dormant since the death of the initiate's namesake. In that sense, rather than being reborn, Tekakwitha would have become a regenerated Catherine.[15]

The observations of outsiders such as the Jesuit Joseph-François Lafitau illustrate this distinction between Christian rebirth and Haudenosaunee requickening. As a missionary at Kahnawake in the early eighteenth century, he would have had the opportunity to observe several adoptees, including Marguerite Kanenstenhawi. He wrote that, whereas captives,

Although Tooker uses the present tense, she cites colonial-era sources. For a synthesis of the anthropological literature on native American naming practices, see David H. French and Kathrine S. French, "Personal Names," in William C. Sturtevant et al., eds., *Handbook of North American Indians*, XVII, *Languages* (Washington, D.C., 1978), 200–221. On Kateri Tekakwitha's handicrafts, see Greer, *Mohawk Saint*, 34–42.

14. "Plusieurs sauvagesses ont porte ce nom avant et apres elle mais il ny en a eu aucune qui lait rempli comme a fait la B. Catherine tegak8ita" (Chauchetière, *La vie*, 46). According to Greer, "We may be sure that she would have listened attentively when the Jesuits told her of the life of that great fourteenth-century mystic-ascetic saint." He speculates that the French name Catherine might have been favored by Mohawk proselytes because it was "easier for Iroquois speakers to approximate than other saints' names" (*Mohawk Saint*, 52–53).

15. Arnold van Gennep, *The Rites of Passage*, trans. Monika B. Vizedom and Gabrielle L. Caffee (Chicago, 1960), 93–96. Greer suggests that baptism "may have made sense to Mohawks" in light of their own rituals of "adoption, requickening, and initiation" (*Mohawk Saint*, 52). "Lhorreur que les nouveaux chrestiens du sault avoint de la vie quils avoint mené aux Iroquois avant leur baptesme": Chauchetière, *La vie*, 129.

or *"esclaves"* (slaves), were liable to meet with cruel deaths among both Iroquois and "les Nations Algonquines," those whose lives were spared could consider themselves fortunate to be adopted by Iroquois (Algonquian peoples also adopted captives, but requickening was a specifically Iroquoian practice). Upon adoption, according to Lafitau, the whole Iroquois village would feast to celebrate the captive's assumption of "the name of the person whom he is resurrecting." The "friends and allies of the dead man also give a feast to do him honour, and from that moment he enters upon all his rights." When a female adoptee replaced a departed matriarch, it was "good fortune for this household and for her. All hope of the family is placed in this captive who becomes the mistress of this family and the branches dependent on it." Similarly, when a man "requickens an Ancient, a man of consequence he becomes important himself, and has authority in the village if he can sustain by his own merit the name he takes." The good treatment was conditional upon the captive's embrace of his or her social role and Iroquois identity.[16]

The account of Colonel James Smith—who, as an adolescent during the Seven Years' War, had been adopted by a band of Kahnawake migrants in the Ohio Country—instantiates Lafitau's description, especially with regard to the expectations accompanying the assumption of a preexisting persona. Smith describes a ceremony in which he was ritually cleansed of his past identity and initiated into another, and he also conveys a sense of the accompanying expectations. The ceremony included an "Indian baptism," during which three "young ladies" led him into a stream, "plunged me under water, and washed and rubbed me severely." According to Smith's representation of a subsequent oration, "one of the chiefs" told him, "By the ceremony which was performed this day, every drop of white blood was washed out of your veins; you are taken into the Caughnewago nation, and initiated into a warlike tribe; you are adopted into a great family, and now received with great seriousness and solemnity in the room

16. Joseph-François Lafitau, *Customs of the American Indians Compared with the Customs of Primitive Times*, trans. William N. Fenton and Elizabeth L. Moore (Toronto, 1977), 171–172. "Le nom de la personne qu'ill releve"; "les amis et les allies du défunt font aussi festin en son nom pour lui faire honneur: et dès ce moment il entre dans tous ses droits"; "C'est une fortune pour cette Cabane-là, et pour elle. Toute l'esperance de là famille est fondée sur cette Esclave, qui deviant la maîtresse de cette famille, et des branches qui en dependent"; "Ressuscite un Ancien, un Considerable; il deviant considerable lui-même, et il a de l'autorité dans le Village, s'il scait soùtenir par son merite personnel le nom qu'il prend" (Lafitau, *Moeurs des sauvages amériquains, comparées aux moeurs des premiers temps* [Paris, 1724], 308).

and place of a great man." Smith's adoptive elders scolded him when he failed to live up to this role and commended him when he succeeded. In one instance, after he had taken a turn with a hoe, as he had presumably done in his former life as a member of a farming community in Pennsylvania, "The old men hearing of what I had done, chid me, and said that I was adopted in the place of a great man, and must not hoe corn like a squaw." In another, after demonstrating his resourcefulness by surviving a night alone in a snowstorm, his elder brother announced, "We are glad to see the prospect of your filling the place of a great man, in whose room you were adopted." Smith's narrative represents an experience on a European-Mohawk "gender frontier," insofar as his natal and adoptive cultures had different notions of "a great man."[17]

The Catholic-Iroquois community at Kahnawake would have similarly presented women with paradigms for identity that were distinct from those available to women in the surrounding native villages, the neighboring French settlement, and the English colonies to the south. One understanding of the hagiographic accounts by Chauchetière and Cholenec is that, just as Smith understood his charge to fill "the room and place of a great man," the girl formerly known as Tekakwitha sought to occupy the persona of her namesake, Catherine of Siena, especially through exceptional chastity. Chauchetière suggests a practice of emulation that greatly exceeded the logic of baptism in his observation that the "spirit of Catherine of Sienna, and other Saints of that name, was renewed in her by a particular conduct of God, who sometimes revealed to her the secrets of spiritual life." The priest's knowledge of Catherine of Siena might have influenced his depiction of Kateri Tekakwitha, but it is also possible that he simply recognized her efforts to fulfill her name by practicing physical penance and extreme self-deprivation, participating in a circle of female ascetics, and resisting familial pressures to marry. The story of Catherine

17. James Axtell, "The White Indians of Colonial America," *WMQ*, 3d Ser., XXXII (1975), 72 ("Indian baptism"); *An Account of the Remarkable Occurrences in the Life and Travels of Col. James Smith (Now a Citizen of Bourbon County, Kentucky), during His Captivity with the Indians, in the Years 1755, '56, '57, '58, and '59* (Lexington, Ky., 1799), 15–16, 39, 45, 66. Smith mentions his "Indian name," Scoouwa, only once (ibid., 39). Haefeli and Sweeney suggest, "Most likely the name Smith remembered was a mishearing of *skoha*, a Mohawk word that literally means, 'Go get it'" (*Captors and Captives*, 153). This interpretation may be correct, but it conflicts with Smith's professed fluency in the language and with the supposed prestige of his namesake. On the concept of the "gender frontier," see Kathleen M. Brown, *Good Wives, Nasty Wenches, and Anxious Patriarchs: Gender, Race, and Power in Colonial Virginia* (Williamsburg, Va., and Chapel Hill, N.C., 1996), 13–106.

of Siena might not only have guided Kateri Tekakwitha's hagiographers in writing her life but also Kateri herself in living it. Kateri Tekakwitha might have interacted with the story of Catherine of Siena directly and not just on the page.[18]

If Kateri Tekakwitha fully applied the principle of requickening to her baptism, then it seems plausible that she renounced Tekakwitha to devote her being to Kateri. In the hagiographic representations, however, there is a basic continuity of self—the anomalously virtuous girl was always destined to become Kateri. Cholenec, in a 1715 letter to the procurer of missions, describes how the catechumen "Tegahkouita" manifested "a saintly impatience" to become baptized. Upon receiving her baptism, she became a neophyte: "She was named Catherine; and so I shall call her for the rest of this letter." Chauchetière recounts how her natal community in Gandaouagué recognized her renunciation by ceasing to address her "by her Indian name." Instead, they "called her 'Christian' in derision as one would speak to a dog." Eventually, "her name was forgotten." Kateri "felt herself happy to have lost her name." Possibly, what Chauchetière construed as antagonism may have more simply reflected a shared understanding of the significance of her baptism: Kateri was no longer Tekakwitha.[19]

Accordingly, once she moved from Gandaouagué to Kahnawake to join a community of Christian converts, her "Indian name" might have been more functional than significant. That is, the Jesuits might have used it to distinguish her from other Catherines, in the same way that teachers

18. Mónica Díaz observes that "colonial spaces" such as Kahnawake "allowed women in general and native American women in particular to exercise agency in new ways" ("Native American Women and Religion in the American Colonies: Textual and Visual Traces of an Imagined Community," *Legacy*, XXVIII [2011], 206). See also Haefeli and Sweeney, *Captors and Captives*, 69. "Lesprit de ste Catherine de Sienne et des autres saintes de ce nom a este renouvellée en elle par une conduitte particuliere de Dieu qui luy a decouvert quelquefois les secrets de la vie spirituelle": Chauchetiere, *La vie*, 102. Greer suggests this comment indicates that Chauchetière "began to adopt something of an Iroquoian attitude toward names and identities" (*Mohawk Saint*, 52–53). For a brief summation of Catherine of Siena's biography, see Gerald Parsons, *The Cult of Saint Catherine of Siena: A Study in Civil Religion* (Aldershot, U.K., 2008), 6–9. On her association with the *mantellate*, a group of female penitents, see F. Thomas Luongo, *The Saintly Politics of Catherine of Siena* (Ithaca, N.Y., 2006), 34–42.

19. "Une sainte impatience"; "elle fut nommée Catherine; c'est ainsi que je l'appellerai dans la suite de cette lettre": "Lettre du Père Cholenec," in *Lettres édifiantes et curieuses*, 33. "On ne l'appelloit plus par son nom sauvage; mais qu'on lappelloit par le nom de Chrestienne en derision comme qui auroit voulu dire une chienne ce qui dura si long temps qu'on sestoit oublié de-son nom ne luy en donnant point dautre que la chrestienne parcequil ny avoit quelle de baptisée dans sa cabane, bien loing de saffliger de ces mepris quon faisoit d'elle elle sestimoit heureuse davoir perdu son nom" (Chauchetière, *La vie*, 52).

now use family names or initials to distinguish students with the same first name from one another. The Jesuit father Jacques Bigot, writing at the Abenaki mission in Sillery a few years after Kateri Tekakwitha's death, observed that the Jesuits were "obliged to give two names to many" of their neophytes "in order to avoid Confusion in a great number"; the neophytes, however, "do not wish, for the most part, to be called by anything but their baptismal names—insomuch that I lately had all the difficulty in the world in drawing from some persons their family names; one answered me that they had no other name here than that of their baptism." Bigot wrote that the converts "manifest a great eagerness to know the lives of their individual Patron Saints; and some have extremely taken to Heart to imitate the most Important traits of their Patron, and have Thereby actually arrived at a high Degree of virtue—either of purity, or of deep humility and self-contempt, or of great Charity, etc." Bigot's description expresses an orthodox sensibility: the patron saint served to inspire the neophyte to be a better person, but there necessarily remained a difference in "Degree."[20]

Chauchetière's claim that "the life that the Blessed Catherine led during her two years" at Kahnawake "could serve as an example to the most fervent Christians in Europe" illustrates how her self-patterning after Catherine of Siena transcended the sort of imitation of saints that Bigot recognized in Sillery. She made herself into a counterpart to the Jesuit saints, who achieved an identification with canonical saints through their seemingly superhuman submission to martyrdom. Requickening pointed toward this sort of emulation through action and experience. Just as Isaac

20. "Obliges de donner deux noms a plusieurs pour eviter La Confusion dans le grand nombre"; "ils ne veulent ester appellez la pluspart que par leur nom to baptesme, tellement que Jeus dernierement toutes les peines du monde a tirer de quelques personnes leurs noms de famille, une me repondit quils nauoient point icy dautre nom que celuy de leur baptesme"; "ils tesmoignent un gd empressement de scavoir la vie particulaire de leur St Patron et quelques uns ont extremement pris a Coeur dimiter ce qu'il y a de plus Considerable dans leur Patron et font veritablement arrivez par La a un haut Degré de vertu soit de pureté soit dune profonde humilité et mespris de soy mesme, soit dune gde. Charité etc": *JR*, LXIII, 34–35. Bigot also figures in the story of the Williams family; he is "the Jesuit" who whips Eunice's brother Stephen (Haefeli and Sweeney, *Captors and Captives*, 153). As the example of Stephen shows, although adoption and requickening were more prevalent among the Iroquois, the Abenakis and other Algonquians also attempted to incorporate captives to replace lost family members (Colin G. Calloway, *The Western Abenakis of Vermont, 1600–1800: War, Migration, and the Survival of an Indian People* [Norman, Okla., 1994], 29). According to Greer, the Jesuit missionaries gave "instruction in Christian lore through the use of pictures, especially depictions of the torments of hell, and through stories of saints and of the life of Jesus" ("Conversion and Identity," in Mills and Grafton, eds., *Conversion*, 182).

Jogues, in his vision, was presented with a book exhibiting *"'the acts and deeds of men Illustrious in piety and of hearts brave in war,'"* so James Smith's elder adoptive brother exhorted him to "do great actions, as it is only great actions that can make a great man." A contemporary of Smith's on the French side of the war explained that the captive-adoptee was "continually reminded" of the room he was expected to fill, "of the dead man's conduct and good deeds." Kateri, similarly, would have understood the story of Catherine of Siena's life as a script for her own transformation.[21]

In the Jesuits' representation, she greatly exceeded expectations, and even propriety, in her fulfillment of her name. According to Chauchetière, "the Father was totally surprised" when her sisters in penance, fearing for her life, divulged to Cholenec that Kateri had been practicing intense mortifications, including fasting, exposing herself to intense cold, and scourging herself with rods and with "a belt of iron with spikes." "But without revealing his astonishment he strongly condemned the indiscretion, which he also judged forgivable in such new Christians. He henceforth instructed and regulated their devotion." However, he moderately acceded to Kateri's requests to be allowed to resume her mortifications "so that her body didn't have the victory." Yet even such excess and "indiscretion" corresponded to Catherine of Siena, who likewise practiced surreptitious mortifications and had to demonstrate that her chastity and hatred of her body were not self-authorized but rather inspired by the Holy Spirit.[22]

Saint Catherine of Siena's *Life* was more imitable than that of a "virgin martyr" like Saint Margaret of Antioch, who was Marguerite Kanenstenawi's baptismal namesake. Yet it is impossible to sort out actions from literary constructions in understanding the correspondences between Catherine of Siena and Kateri of Kahnawake. Some may be attributable to neither. The plagues that provide grim backdrops for the accounts written of both their lives are historical as well as literary parallels: the Black Death "struck Siena with brutal and devastating force" in 1348; a small-

21. "La vie que la B. Catherine a mené pendant deux ans peut server dexemple aux plus fervents chrestiens de leurope": Chauchetière, *La vie*, 102. See Allan Greer, "Colonial Saints: Gender, Race and Hagiography in New France," *WMQ*, LVII (2000), 323–348; Smith, *Account*, 66; J.-C. B., *Travels in New France*, ed. Sylvester Kirby Stevens et al. (Harrisburg, Pa., 1941), 73.

22. "Une ceinture de fer qui avoit de longues pointes"; "le pere fut tout surpris; mais sans tesmoigner son etonnement blasma fort lindiscretion qui fut pourtant jugée bien pardonnable dans de nouvelles chrestiennes on les instruisit et on regla toute cette devotion"; "que son corps neust pas la victoire": Chauchetière, *La vie*, 127, 134.

pox epidemic wracked Gandaouagué in 1661–1663. Then, too, in the narrative sequences, some of the similarities occur before Tekakwitha would have even heard of Saint Catherine; both girls enraged their families by refusing to take a husband, and as a result each was treated, in Cholenec's phrase, "like a slave" (esclave). It may be tempting to think that such a concurrence must derive from the Jesuit authors' attempts to reconcile the two stories, but not all of the details in the episode can be explained so easily. For example, Cholenec writes of Tekakwitha, "She was constantly reproached for her lack of attachment to her relatives," and "she was accused of harboring a secret hatred for the Iroquois nation, because she was of Algonquin descent." The implication, quite unrelated to European hagiography, was that her mother, who had been a Christian Algonquin captive, had undergone an incomplete incorporation—she had never assimilated herself to the Mohawk persona she had requickened, and her daughter had inherited this sense of dissociation. In this view, Tekakwitha's conversion was an act of allegiance with the former identity of her mother, who had died from smallpox when Tekakwitha was about six. The precedent of Tekakwitha's mother illustrates the complexity of the interpersonal relations involved in identity formation and the challenges of speculation about subjective motivations. Tekakwitha's conversion to Christianity and emulation of Catherine of Siena can be understood either as a recursion to her mother's former identity as a Christian or as a fulfillment of the same transformative process her mother had undergone, albeit in a different community. Just as her mother's marriage to a Mohawk "confirmed and solidified her new status," Kateri's refusal of such a marriage and apparent choice of Jesus as her only spouse would have cemented her Christian identity.[23]

The Heresiarch's Daughter

Eunice Williams, like Kateri Tekakwitha, lost her biological mother as a young girl. Eunice Mather Williams was one of the casualties of the raid on

23. Wendy R. Larson, "Who Is the Master of This Narrative? Maternal Patronage of the Cult of St. Margaret," in Mary Carpenter Erler and Maryanne Kowaleski, eds., *Gendering the Master Narrative: Women and Power in the Middle Ages* (Ithaca, N.Y., 2003), 96; Parsons, *Cult of Saint Catherine of Siena*, 6; Greer, *Mohawk Saint*, 27–28. "On lui reprochoit sans cesse son peu d'attachement pour ses parens"; "on l'atribuoit à une haine secrete qu'elle portoit à la nation iroquoise, parce qu'elle étoit de race algonquine": "Lettre du Père Cholenec," in *Lettres édifiantes et curieuses*, 31.

Deerfield. Already enfeebled from having recently lain in, she fell into an icy stream on the journey north; her captors killed her, as they did others who were unable to keep pace. The young Eunice, apparently marked for adoption at the outset, was never in such danger. According to her father, she "was carried all the journey, and looked after with a great deal of tenderness." The Christian name Eunice is Greek for "The Happy, Victorious One." In the Bible, Eunice is the mother of Timothy (2 Tim. 1:5). Yet Eunice Williams was not named directly after the biblical Eunice but rather after her mother, the niece of Increase Mather of "the colony's premier line of religious leaders." For John Williams, this woman had been "the desire of my eyes and companion in many mercies and afflictions." He recounts their final farewell, as she resigned herself to dying en route to Canada. "After our being parted from one another, she spent the few remaining minutes of her stay in reading the holy Scriptures, which she was wont personally every day to delight her soul in reading, praying, meditating of and over, by herself in her closet, over and above what she heard out of them in our family worship." Fulfilling the name *Eunice Williams,* then, would have meant emulating such a model of female piety through devotional literacy practices, as well as realizing the social trajectory of a well-born New England woman by marrying within her caste, perhaps to a minister, like her father, and raising children. Instead, as Marguerite Kanenstenhawi, she assumed a corresponding place in Kahnawake society; both she and her daughters (Catherine Gassinontie and Marie Skentsiese) married well. (She would have pronounced her eldest daughter's baptismal name *Kateri.*)[24]

In Kahnawake, Eunice Williams was adopted and raised to fulfill a different name or names. According to Eleazer Williams, two years before the 1704 raid, the woman who became Eunice's mother had "lost an only child (daughter) on account of which she became inconsolable." She accompanied the expedition in order to "place one in the room of that which she had lost." Eleazer's claim that Eunice's adoptive mother participated in her adoptive daughter's capture is doubtful, if not impossible, but it does seem plausible that Eunice was marked for such a place from the

---

24. Demos, *Unredeemed Captive,* 8, 28–29, 164 (emphasis added); *CH,* 104; Sheehan, *Dictionary of Patron Saints' Names,* 105; *CH,* 99–100. On the contrast between Eunice Williams and her mother, "the one named for the other," see Teresa A. Toulouse, *The Captive's Position: Female Narrative, Male Identity, and Royal Authority in Colonial New England* (Philadelphia, 2007), 147.

beginning, which would explain the apparently solicitous treatment she received from her captors, as noted by her father. Presumably, like James Smith, she underwent an adoption ceremony. However, Eunice's first recorded Mohawk name, Waongote—"she has been planted as a person"—seems to refer to her status as an adoptee rather than to her assumption of a preexisting identity.[25]

Early in her life at Kahnawake (it remained a "captivity" only from the perspective of her natal community), Waongote was baptized *Marguerite*. The choice of *Marguerite* as a baptismal name for *Waongote* might have been deliberate and significant, unlike that of *Catherine* for *Tekakwitha*, which was probably somewhat arbitrary (the name Catherine prescribed the resemblance, instead of vice versa). Indeed, the names Waongote and Marguerite are almost cognate in their connotations, because Margaret of Antioch was someone who had been planted as a person—an adoptee who had undergone a religious conversion. The Jesuits' rebaptism of Protestant captives was controversial, because it denied their former status as Christians. However, the opportunity to rebaptize the daughter of a Puritan minister—a man the Jesuits styled an egregious heretic, a "wolf" in shepherd's clothing, whose flock they had captivated for the safety of their souls—was especially noteworthy. The Jesuits seemed to make a statement by rebaptizing Eunice as *Marguerite*.[26]

According to the medieval *Golden Legend* by Jacobus de Voragine, Saint Margaret of Antioch was the "daughter of Theodosius, patriarch of the pagans. As a child she was entrusted to a nurse, and when she reached the age of reason she was baptized, and so incurred the bitter hatred of her father." That is the allegorical donnée of the story, casting John Williams as Theodosius, the enemy of the true faith, Eunice's adoptive mother as the virtuous nurse, and Eunice herself as the virgin martyr. The Jesuits would not, however, have intended the *Life of Saint Margaret of Antioch* as a template for Waongote's life; they would not have expected Waongote to fulfill her baptismal name in the way they credited Kateri Tekakwitha with having done. If they had, she would have found Saint Margaret's per-

25. *CH,* 229n, 235; Demos, *Unredeemed Captive,* 97–98, 142. I use the spellings provided by Haefeli and Sweeney rather than Demos, who renders Eunice's Mohawk names as A'ongote and Gannen-stenhawi. See *Captors and Captives,* 152–53; *Unredeemed Captive,* 141, 162. A literal translation of Waongote, according to the linguist Roy Wright, would be "she is stood upright," meaning "established" or "planted" (personal communication).

26. Demos, *Unredeemed Captive,* 78–79, 151; *CH,* 123.

secutions and triumphs more difficult to emulate than Tekakwitha found those of Catherine of Siena.[27]

Much of the legend of Margaret of Antioch would have lent itself only to figurative parallels with the lives of her namesakes. Margaret was abducted by a Roman prefect, Olibrius, whom she steadfastly refused to marry, "declaring herself a bride of Christ." Subjected to torture and imprisonment, Margaret split open a dragon that had appeared in her cell and, in some versions, swallowed her alive. Jacobus himself considered this detail "apocryphal and of no historical value"; it was a figurative representation of Margaret's pitched combat with the devil, whom she finally threw to the ground, stepping triumphantly on his neck and declaring, "'Lie there, proud demon, prostrate beneath a woman's foot!' 'O blessed Margaret,' the demon cried, 'I admit defeat! If a young man had beaten me, I would not have minded; but to be beaten by a young girl—! And it hurts me all the more because your father and mother were friends of mine!'" Margaret's death was a glorious martyrdom: Olibrius had her publicly beheaded. If Waongote, like the Abenaki converts in Sillery and, presumably, like Kateri Tekakwitha, had been eager to know about the life of her patron saint, she would have heard the story of a girl who had been able to achieve a spiritual triumph over the circumstances of her birth.[28]

Marguerite was not Eunice Williams's ultimate identity, although this, her second baptismal name, pertained to her until the end of her life. It is the name that appears in the mission records' notice of her death. In these same records, she is listed as a godparent in notices of four baptisms, and she gave her own name, *Marguerite,* to a baby, an adult captive, and to an Iroquois woman who had previously been "baptized by the English." Since the record of Eunice's rebaptism is not extant, the identity of her own godmother is not known. Another Marguerite? The bestowal of the name *Marguerite* did not necessarily imply such a spiritual coup as the conversion of a heresiarch's daughter. The only evidence that the Jesuits

27. Jacobus de Voragine, *The Golden Legend: Selections,* ed. Richard Hamer, trans. Christopher Stace (London, 1998), 162. According to Wendy R. Larson, "The *Golden Legend* was eventually translated from the original Latin into every known western European language, and was, after the Bible, the most popular book in the late medieval West (in the early days of printing, it was *the* most popular book)" (Larson, "Three Thirteenth-Century Lives of St. Margaret of Antioch," in Thomas Head, ed., *Medieval Hagiography: An Anthology* [London, 2001], 177).

28. Larson, "Who Is the Master?" in Erler and Kowaleski, eds., *Gendering the Master Narrative,* 96; Voragine, *Golden Legend,* ed. Hamer, trans. Stace, 163.

intended such an allusion is the striking parallel between the stories of Eunice Williams and Margaret of Antioch.[29]

Whereas Kateri Tekakwitha arrived at Kahnawake during a period of intense Catholic fervor, at the time of Eunice Williams's arrival and acculturation, Catholicism had been largely subsumed within a new "Kahnawake Mohawk" cultural identity. Upon her initiation into adulthood in Kahnawake, Marguerite Waongote became Marguerite *Kanenstenhawi*, or "she brings in corn"—a name, and her ultimate identity, that she could fulfill simply by being a functional member of her adoptive society.[30]

Separation and Incorporation

In the classic study *The Rites of Passage*, Arnold van Gennep distinguishes between rites of separation and incorporation. Funerals typically embody the former, whereas marriages embody the latter. The tendency of the story of Kateri Tekakwitha, as told by her hagiographers, is toward separation from the same culture into which Eunice Williams was incorporated through marriage.[31]

In the Jesuits' accounts, Kateri increasingly withdrew from the communal lifestyle of Gandaouagué and then Kahnawake. According to Chauchetière, "By a kind of miracle, she alone escaped from the floodwaters of impurity that inundated the entire land of the savages." For the Jesuits, Tekakwitha's natal culture is a metaphor for corporeality. By contrast, Eunice's eventual Mohawk name signified her participation in communal activities. For both women, the bridge-burning steps in their divergent trajectories lay in their choice of a spouse. On the one hand, Kateri's chastity, her refusal to marry an eligible Mohawk, and her exclusive commitment to "her Divine Spouse" (son Divin Espoux) were key points of identification with her namesake and, in the view of her hagiographers, underpinnings of her posthumous success as a saintly intercessor. On the other hand, Marguerite Kanenstenhawi's marriage to the Christian Mohawk warrior François Xavier Arosen completed her integration into

---

29. Demos, *Unredeemed Captive*, 162, 237. "In their role as godmothers," notes Rushforth, "both Native and French women chose names for slaves in their charge, extending fictive kinship to a broader set of cultural forbears" (*Bonds of Alliance*, 267).

30. Haefeli and Sweeney, *Captors and Captives*, 145, 153; Demos, *Unredeemed Captive*, 162.

31. Van Gennep, *Rites of Passage*, trans. Vizedom and Caffee, 10–11.

Kahnawake society. To her family in New England, it meant she was lost. Had Marguerite chosen instead to emulate her virginal patron saint by preserving her chastity, she would, in a sense, have stopped short of "becoming Indian." Kateri's choice fulfilled her name, just as Marguerite Kanenstenhawi's fulfilled hers.[32]

Apparently, the gatekeeper for both unions was Pierre Cholenec, Kateri's confessor and the superior of the mission at Kahnawake during Marguerite Kanenstenhawi's youth. According to the 1715 letter that Cholenec sent to the procurer of missions about Kateri Tekakwitha, she overrode his objections to her taking a vow of chastity with her determination to live in holiness. She had come to him complaining about her relatives' attempts to force her to marry and insisting that she wanted no other man than Jesus. Cholenec counseled patience and restraint, advising her that if, after three days, she "persisted in her resolution, I promised her I would put an end to her relatives' importunities." She returned to him fifteen minutes later, declaring, "It is done. . . . It is no longer a matter for deliberation; my choice was made long ago; no, my father, I will not have any other spouse than Jesus Christ." The priest wrote: "I believed I must no longer oppose a resolution that seemed to me to be inspired by none other than the Holy Spirit; accordingly, I praised her persistence, and assured her that I would defend her against all those who troubled her on this account." Here his representation verges suspiciously close to the story of Catherine of Siena, who was also subjected to "the importunate concerns of her relatives," who wished her to marry. Catherine of Siena's parents similarly appealed to a "Friar Preacher" for support, and, like Cholenec, this cleric became persuaded that the girl's choice was divinely inspired.[33]

32. Salomon de Priezac, *La vie de Sainte Catherine de Sienne* (Paris, 1665), 98. "Cest une espece de miracle de la voir echappée des eaux du deluge de limpurete qui inonde toute la terre qhabitent les sauvages": Chauchetière, *La vie*, 177. On the reactions in New England to the news of Eunice Williams's marriage, see Demos, *Unredeemed Captive*, 98–99. As Haefeli and Sweeney point out, "Intermarriage and religion were the primary ties that bound captives to Native communities. At Kahnawake, captives married Mohawks, not other captives" (*Captors and Captives*, 223). Audra Simpson argues, "The story of Eunice Williams's captivity" contributes to "the gendered structure and imaginary of contemporary colonial settler society of North America"; it is a preliminary to the Indian Act of 1876, which in Canada provided that white women, but not men, could become Indian through marriage. See "Captivating Eunice," *Wicazo Sa Review*, XXIV (2009), 106, 125.

33. "Persistoit dans sa résolution, je lui promis de mettre fin aux importunités de ses parentes"; "C'en est fait. . . . [I]l n'est plus question de délibérer, mon parti est pris depuis longtemps; non, mon père, je n'aurai jamais d'autre époux que Jésus-Christ"; "Je ne crus pas devoir m'opposer davantage à une résolution qui me paroissoit ne lui être inspirée que par le Saint-

If these parallels between the hagiographies of the two Catherines cast doubt on Cholenec's representation, his credibility is further undermined by a discrepancy with Chauchetière. Although, in his 1715 letter, he does not quite say that he allowed Kateri to consecrate her virginity with a vow, Cholenec presented precise details of the supposed ceremony in his undated *La vie de Catherine Tegakouita première vierge irokoise,* explaining that Kateri's "grand and glorious title of virgin" exalted her above "all the other savages in New France who have embraced the faith." It was on the traditional Lady Day, the Feast of Annunciation, March 25, 1679 (the attributed date of Catherine of Siena's birth), "at eight in the morning that Catherine Takakwitha, a moment after Jesus Christ had given himself to her through the Communion, gave herself wholly to him, renouncing marriage forever, and promising him perpetual virginity." Chauchetière contradicts his colleague's account. While concurring with encomiums of Kateri's chastity, calling it "the most beautiful jewel in her crown," he also explicitly states that Cholenec never had her make a vow: "If one had thought to have her make a vow, a vow of chastity would not have been misplaced, since she did not fall short of living up to such a vow, which makes me believe that she had the merit of one. The priest was sorry after her death not to have had her make one." The implication that "she had the merit of one" might be that she, like Catherine of Siena, had made a vow privately — that it had been between her and Christ. Cholenec's embellishment might have been intended to cover up his oversight and to aggrandize his own role — establishing him, perhaps, as the counterpart to Catherine of Siena's saintly confessor and biographer, Raymond of Capua — rather than to promote Kateri's candidacy for sainthood. The discrepancy between the hagiographers actually lends credit to their corresponding claims to have become fully persuaded of Kateri's chastity.[34]

Esprit: je l'exhortai donc à la persévérance, et je l'assurai que je prendrois sa défense contre tous ceux qui voudroient désormais l'inquiéter sur cet article": "Lettre du Père Cholenec," in *Lettres édifiantes et curieuses,* 49. "Des soins importuns de ses Parens": de Priezac, *La vie de Sainte Catherine de Sienne,* 100. Greer argues, "Everything we know about Iroquoian respect for personal autonomy, especially in the areas of sex and marriage, suggests that the pressure exerted on Tekakwitha would not have gone beyond advice and gentle persuasion" ("Savage / Saint," in Dépatie et al., eds., *Habitants et Marchands, Twenty Years Later,* 144). See also Raymond of Capua, *Life of Saint Catharine of Sienna,* trans. Hamilton, 37.

34. "Ce grand et glorieux titre de vierge"; "tous les sauvages qui ont embrassé la foi dans toute la France septentrionale"; "Sur les huit heures du matin que Catherine Tegakoüita un moment après que Jésus-Christ se fut donné à elle dans la Communion, se donna aussi tout à lui, et que renonçant pour toujours au mariage, elle lui promit virginité perpétuelle" (Cholenec, "La vie

Cholenec's 1715 account of Kateri Tekakwitha's petition to wed Jesus finds indirect corroboration in a 1713 letter by the Albany agent John Schuyler, reporting the marriage of "Margarett Williams" and François Xavier Arosen. Schuyler, on a frustrated mission to redeem John Williams's daughter, recounts that he approached "the priest" and "proposed to know the Reason why this poor Captive should be Married to an Indian, being a Christian Born (tho neerly taken from the Mother's Breast and such like Instances etc)." Schuyler represents the unnamed priest's response as quoted speech: "(First, sd he they came to me to Marry them) very often wch I always refus'd with good words and persuasions to the Contrary." The priest declared that they were so persistent, he sought to get away from them, "But both continuing in their former resolution to Such a Degree that I was constrained to be absent from the fort three Severall times, because not Satisfyed mySelf in their Marriage." Finally, the priest could only consent to a fait accompli: "at last after Some days past they both came to me, and sd that they were Joined together, And if he would not marry them they matter'd not, for they were resolved never to leave one the other. But live together heathen like; Upon wch I thought proper to Join them in Matrimony." Schuyler, however disapproving of their marriage, realized that he could not blame the priest for it. Schuyler's rendition of the priest's language concerning Marguerite Kanenstenhawi and Arosen—"continuing in their former resolution"—would be a serviceable translation of Cholenec's phrasing in his letter concerning Kateri Tekakwitha, who "persistoit dans sa résolution." This echo supports the identification of the priest who married François and Marguerite with Kateri's confessor. The consistency in language, at least, supports the idea of a repetition of behavior. In Cholenec's account, Kateri overcame his

---

de Catherine," in Lonc, ed., *Catherine Tekakwitha*, 33–34). "Le plus beau fleuron de sa coronne"; "si on eust eu la pensee de luy en faire le voeu le voeu de chasteté ne luy auroit pas manque quoy quelle naye pas manque ace voeu ce qui me fait croire quelle en a eu le merite, le pere fut mari apres sa mort de ne luy avoir pas fait faire": Chauchetière, *La vie*, 177–178. Greer's somewhat different translation implies that Cholenec forbade her vow: "If it had occurred to anyone to have her take a vow, the vow of chastity would not have been wanting, though she did not fail to live up to such a vow, which makes me believe that she received the merit of it. The priest was sorry after her death not to have let her make it" (*Mohawk Saint*, 178). My translation is more literal. Greer worked directly with Chauchetière's manuscript; I use the 1887 Cramoisy edition, which is based on it. Greer concludes that Cholenec "had declined to administer the vow of chastity while Catherine was alive, and, regretting his decision afterward, he revised the record of events." The story of the vow, according to Greer, "seems designed both to bring the larger narrative into closer conformity with standard hagiographic plots for women saints and to shore up the claim to virginal status" (*Mohawk Saint*, 178).

objections by presenting her vow as a fait accompli; in Schuyler's account, Marguerite and François overrode the priest's objections with their determination to live in sin if necessary.[35]

Kateri's marriage positioned her to lead an extremely successful afterlife. Cholenec reported in 1715, "God did not delay in honoring the memory of this virtuous girl, with an infinite number of miraculous cures, that were done after her death, and are still accomplished daily by her intercession." By then, her cult had spread beyond the Catholic Mohawks to the colonists in Quebec and Montreal, "who came frequently to her tomb to realize their wishes, or to thank her for the good graces that she had obtained for them in Heaven." Her credits continued to accumulate over centuries, culminating in her canonization in 2012.[36]

Conclusion

Kateri Tekakwitha's short life, her death "in odor of sanctity," and her afterlife as an intercessor mapped perfectly onto the template of the *Life* of her namesake. Marguerite Kanenstenhawi's exceptionally long life, marriage, children, and grandchildren testify to her successful incorporation into her adoptive society, an integration tested and reaffirmed by four visits to her biological family in New England. Whereas devotees throughout New France, and eventually beyond, prayed to Kateri Tekakwitha to intercede with her husband on their behalf, in 1741 Marguerite Kanenstenhawi's biological cousin, Solomon Williams, bore witness to the "numberless prayers" that "have been put up to God" by her family and former neighbors. The occasion was a sermon he delivered in Mansfield, attended by the former Eunice Williams herself, on her second visit to New England. Solomon considered her visits to be evidence of God's attention to their prayers, "dawnings towards her deliverance," yet he used her presence as an object lesson for his congregants. Her supposedly captive state was a metaphor for the even more perilous condition of the unregenerate among them. It must have been galling to New Englanders that, despite their worldly enticements, including an offer of land, she refused to stay, "saying 'it would endanger her soul.'" Perhaps the perspective of her natal

35. The letter is reproduced in its entirety in Charlotte Alice Baker, *True Stories of New England Captives Carried to Canada during the Old French and Indian Wars* (Cambridge, Mass., 1897), 144–146.

36. "Lettre du Père Cholenec," in *Lettres édifiantes et curieuses,* 59–60.

community mirrors that of Mohawk traditionalists like Kateri Tekakwitha's maternal uncle, who resisted and resented the defections to Kahnawake and is accordingly vilified in the hagiographies.[37]

The scholarship on the two women, following the documentary sources, has involved opposing points of view. On the one hand, the "family story" of Marguerite Kanenstenhawi has centered on the Williamses and New England. On the other hand, Kateri Tekakwitha's transformation was documented from the perspective of her adoptive culture, although ethnohistorians have explicitly generated correctives to the colonialist bias of the Jesuit sources, attempting to reconstruct her experience as a native woman in a contact zone. It is partly for this reason, as I suggested above, that the comparison does more to illuminate the story of Marguerite Kanenstenhawi than that of Kateri Tekakwitha. The Iroquoian concept of requickening can help bridge the gap between native life and European writing. We may think of the story of Catherine of Siena as one that Kateri Tekakwitha embodied or enacted, as well as one that shaped Cholenec's and Chauchetière's compositions. In turn, the discussion of how Kateri Tekakwitha fulfilled her Christian name may suggest how Marguerite Kanenstenhawi fulfilled her Mohawk one.

There is no evidence that Kateri Tekakawitha or Marguerite Kanenstenhawi (who, as Eunice Williams, could read English) learned to read Latin or French. Unlike Isaac Jogues and John Williams, then, they did not directly participate in their respective communities through literacy. Because literacy practices often leave records, they are more conducive to historical analysis than other modes of communication. With Jogues and John Williams, the written representations of their reading reveal how sacred texts furnished them with models for their captivities and, in turn, for the composition of their accounts. A similar process might have played out with the two Kahnawake women, except with mediation on all sides. Their knowledge of their Christian namesakes might have been indirectly sourced from texts such as Raymond of Capua's *Life of Saint Catherine of Sienna* and *The Golden Legend,* but there is no record of Jesuits' relating these stories. The written *Lives* of saints themselves functioned within the

---

37. Demos, *Unredeemed Captive,* 201–206; Solomon Williams, "Extract from a Sermon, Preached at Mansfield, August 4, 1741 . . . ," in Stephen W. Williams, ed., *The Redeemed Captive Returning to Zion; or, A Faithful History of Remarkable Occurrences in the Captivity and Deliverance of Mr. John Williams . . .* (1853; rpt. Bedford, Mass., 1993), 170–171; Coleman, *New England Captives,* II, 63. "Morte en odeur de saincteté": Cholenec, *La vie,* iii.

more comprehensive discursive domain of oral tradition. The names *Kateri Tekakwitha* and *Marguerite Kanenstenhawi* are themselves the succinct records of the named individuals' positions at the confluence of traditions. Whereas one lived out her brief term as a Catholic under the purview of literate observers, the other only intermittently came into contact with the producers of written representations. We may infer, however, that for her, bringing in corn was as much a performance of cultural identity and communal affiliation as reading the Bible had been for her biological father.

CHAPTER FIVE

Silent Books, Talking Leaves

A Narrative of the Lord's Wonderful Dealings with John Marrant, a Black (1785) is the minister William Aldridge's written version of an oral account that Marrant performed in Bath on the occasion of his own ordination in the Methodist-Calvinist "Connexion" of Selina, the countess of Huntingdon. This ceremony, and the publication of Marrant's *Narrative* that same year, completed a trajectory that had begun in 1769 with his characteristically forceful, involuntary induction into this discourse community. The fourteen-year-old Marrant had dropped in on a church meeting led by the itinerant preacher George Whitefield, on his final tour of America; Marrant intended to play a prank by blowing upon his French horn. He recounts, "Mr. Whitefield was naming his text, and looking around, and, as I thought, directly upon me, and pointing with his finger, he uttered these words, 'PREPARE TO MEET THY GOD, O ISRAEL.' The Lord accompanied the word with such power, that I was struck to the ground, and lay both speechless and senseless near half an hour." Marrant's subjective representation of his own conversion is entirely consonant with prevalent representations of the Calvinist Whitefield's power, seemingly, to draw the Holy Spirit through scripture (in this case, Amos 4:12) and to channel it through his speech, exciting prescribed somatic effects upon individual auditors. Marrant reported, "Every word I heard from the minister was like a parcel of swords thrust into me, and what added to my distress, I thought I saw the devil on every side of me." This account of his conversion sounds a keynote for the narrative, particularly with regard to the representation of literacy, inspired speech, and the workings of the Holy Spirit.[1]

According to his account, shortly after his conversion, pronounced "crazy" by his unregenerate family, Marrant "took up a small pocket Bible

---

1. *UV*, 113, 129n. In a meta-sermon on "How to Hear Sermons" (1740), Whitefield exhorted auditors to "find the Word preached sharper than a two edged Sword, and mighty through GOD, to the pulling down of the Devil's strong Holds!" (*Directions How to Hear Sermons, Preach'd by the Reverend Mr. George Whitefield, A.B.* . . . [Boston, 1740], 13).

and one of Dr. Watts's hymnbooks" and left his home in the South Carolina backcountry. He went "over the fence, about a half mile from our house, which divided the inhabited and cultivated parts of the country from the wilderness." His account of the events that followed, especially the literacy events that took place during his captivity among the Cherokees—which transitioned into a two-year sojourn—would burnish his credentials to serve as a minister in the mold of Whitefield, attesting to a comparable power to mobilize the Holy Spirit. Marrant discovers this power by unintentionally wielding "the sword of God's word" against his would-be "executioner," against the "eldest daughter" of the Cherokee "king," and finally against the king himself, until "a great change took place among the people; the king's house became God's house; the soldiers were ordered away, and the poor condemned prisoner had perfect liberty, and was treated like a prince." This passage from abjection to exaltation anticipates Marrant's 1790 depiction, in a published journal, of his ministry among black loyalists in Nova Scotia. This, in turn, shows how Marrant emulated Whitefield's practice, catalyzing conversions in the form of enthusiastic responses to God's word, spoken or read.[2]

This chapter focuses on Marrant's depictions of literacy events during his captivity, arguing that, despite warranted skepticism about his *Narrative* as a record of colonial encounter, his representations originate in the Cherokees' responses to his evangelical practices. This reading contests the "foundational" one by Henry Louis Gates, Jr. In recent decades, Marrant's *Narrative* has been read largely through Gates's critical frame around Marrant's representation of his Bible-reading performance at the court of the Cherokee "king." Because the king's eldest daughter kissed the Bible "but said, with much sorrow, the book would not speak to her," Gates groups this episode with other instances in Anglo-African narratives that represent persons previously unfamiliar with alphabetic literacy attributing the power to speak, and therefore to refuse to speak, to European books (especially Bibles). Gates designates this topos "the trope of the Talking Book" and identifies Marrant's instance as the second link in a "signifyin(g) chain" connecting works by five Anglo-African writers:

---

2. *UV*, 115, 119, 120; John Marrant, *A Journal of the Rev. John Marrant from August the 18th, 1785, to the 16th of March, 1790* . . . (London, 1790); *The Works of the Reverend George Whitefield, M.A., Late of Pembroke-College, Oxford, and Chaplain to the Rt. Hon. the Countess of Huntingdon* . . . , VI (London, 1772), 124 ("sword"); and see Joanna Brooks, *American Lazarus: Religion and the Rise of African-American and Native American Literatures* (New York, 2003), 105–112.

Albert Ukasaw Gronniosaw (1772), Marrant, Quobna Ottobah Cugoano (1787), Olaudah Equiano (1789), and John Jea (likely 1812). According to Gates, Gronniosaw used the "trope" to figure his own passage from naïveté into knowledge; Marrant "revised" it by transferring the naïveté to the Cherokee "princess," and each successive writer in the chain innovated it anew. "The trope of the Talking Book," Gates declares, "is the ur-trope of the Anglo-African tradition." This influential argument brought renewed attention to Marrant's *Narrative* and the other four works and illuminated the theme of the relationship between spoken and written language within them.[3]

Following Gates, most commentators on Marrant have been literary scholars, and most of these, even where they query aspects of his analysis, accept the classification of Marrant's climactic representation of a literacy event as a "trope" pertaining to the Anglo-African tradition. This somewhat idiosyncratic application of a literary studies term that usually refers to figures of speech such as metaphors presumes that Marrant's representation of the Cherokees' response is not a literal depiction of "quaint experience." In other words, Gates asserts that the presentation of the book and the declaration that it would not speak definitively did not happen, in Marrant's experience or that of any of his counterparts.[4]

Yet confining Marrant's Talking Book to a narrow sequence of influence and innovation comprising eighteenth-century black writers disregards three explanatory frameworks for its occurrence: the rhetorical context of Marrant's *Narrative,* the historical context of eighteenth-century evangelical Christianity, and the ethnohistorical context of late-eighteenth-

3. *UV*, 119; Elizabeth Maddock Dillon, "Atlantic Aesthesis: Books and *Sensus Communis* in the New World," *EAL*, LI (2016), 377; Henry Louis Gates, Jr., *The Signifying Monkey: A Theory of African-American Literary Criticism* (New York, 1988), 131, 142–146. Tiya Miles credits Gates with recovering "Marrant's text from obscurity in 1988, identifying it as a key work in early African American literature" (Miles, "'His Kingdom for a Kiss': Indians and Intimacy in the Narrative of John Marrant," in Ann Laura Stoler, ed., *Haunted by Empire: Geographies of Intimacy in North American History,* American Encounters / Global Interactions [Durham, N.C., 2006], 180).
4. Sandra M. Gustafson, *Eloquence Is Power: Oratory and Performance in Early America* (Williamsburg, Va., and Chapel Hill, N.C., 2000), 104; Miles, "'His Kingdom for a Kiss,'" in Stoler, ed., *Haunted by Empire,* 180–181; April Langley, "Early American Slave Narratives," in Kevin J. Hayes, ed., *The Oxford Handbook of Early American Literature* (Oxford, 2008), 425; Elizabeth Maddock Dillon, "John Marrant Blows the French Horn: Print, Performance, and the Making of Publics in Early African American Literature," in Lara Langer Cohen and Jordan Alexander Stein, eds., *Early African American Print Culture* (Philadelphia, 2012), 336; Tara Bynum, "A Silent Book, Some Kisses, and John Marrant's Narrative," *Criticism,* LVII (2015), 71–90; Karen A. Weyler, *Empowering Words: Outsiders and Authorship in Early America* (Athens, Ga., 2013), 255n; Gates, *Signifying Monkey,* 151.

century Cherokee country. Cross-referencing these three yields a more complex, multidimensional, nuanced, and necessarily speculative understanding of Marrant's *Narrative* as an account of a colonial encounter in which, rather than a symbolic representation, the Talking Book may be an element in a symbolic interaction.[5]

"Singing to the Lord"

The Talking Book scene is preceded by a series of similarly improbable representations. Near the outset of his wanderings Marrant met an Indian "hunter," whose company he kept for ten weeks, during which he "acquired a fuller knowledge of the Indian tongue." The hunter led him to "a large Indian town, belonging to the Cherokee nation," where he was promptly arrested and thrown into a "dungeon" to await execution for trespassing. But his prayers, which "the power and grace of God" inspired him to articulate in "their tongue," effected the conversion of his very executioner, who, after "five minutes" of stupefaction, declared: "'No man shall hurt thee till thou has been to the king.'" To the king they went, with an escort of "two hundred men with bows and arrows," through the "many windings" that led to "the king's outward chamber, and after waiting some time he came to the door, and his first question was, how came I there?" Marrant's account of his journey into Cherokee country in 1769 is engaging—but as a historical source, it may be all but useless.[6]

Marrant's *Narrative* already has the liability of being a traveler's tale, and it may also be compromised by mediation, as a written representation of an oral performance, although Aldridge's role as amanuensis lent an insider's credibility to a black provincial recounting an adolescent adventure. (Most scholars use the fourth edition of the narrative, which is seemingly authorized by Marrant's emendations and his "notes explanatory.") Mainly, it strains belief because of its outlandish, grandiose claims, fabulous descriptions, and ethnographically inappropriate diction. Aldridge himself acknowledged the narrative's incredibility through a disclaimer: "The novelty or magnitude of the facts contained in the following pages,

5. See Herbert Blumer, *Symbolic Interactionism: Perspective and Method* (Berkeley, Calif., 1986).

6. *UV,* 119. One historian who does use Marrant's *Narrative*—"one of America's most fascinating captivity narratives"—as a primary source is Christina Snyder, *Slavery in Indian Country: The Changing Face of Captivity in Early America* (Cambridge, Mass., 2012), 105.

may dispose some readers to question the truth of them." Sure enough, some contemporary readers did find Marrant's account to be unbelievable, just as modern, scholarly ones have pointed out that the *Narrative* seems driven more by "typological necessity"—comparisons with biblical figures such as Joseph, Lazarus, and Jesus—than by the events it portrays. However, Aldridge, who claimed he made "no more alterations" to Marrant's language "than were thought necessary," suggested that the live audience was privy to nonverbal indicators of authenticity unavailable to readers. "He appeared to me to feel most sensibly, when he related those parts of his Narrative, which describe his happiest moments with God, or the most remarkable interpositions of Divine Providence for him; and I have no reason to believe it was counterfeited." Aldridge frames Marrant's account with this testimony to its affective performance of sincerity.[7]

What Marrant's performance demonstrated, according to Aldridge, was that "God is with" Marrant in the telling, so that the audience and readers might infer that God was also with him in the event; otherwise, "Would it not follow, that the Almighty gave his sanction to a falsehood?" Yet the representation of the Cherokees is so clearly subordinated to Marrant's evangelical reputation building that it seems especially opaque. With a little work, however, it does show some patches of translucency, enough to speculatively discern historical Cherokees. Despite details such as Marrant's claim—decades after the Cherokees had adapted to colonial warfare—that his armed guard consisted of "two hundred men with bows and arrows," the narrative is less difficult to reconcile with other contemporary descriptions than it appears to be. Some of its romantic or scriptural touches are consistent with other, less contested sources. For example, there was nothing unusual about Marrant's designation of the Cherokee headman as a "king"—many eighteenth-century writers and statesmen referred to Cherokee leaders as kings. And although the entrance of "the king's eldest daughter" (who "came into the chamber, a

7. *UV*, 110, 111, 128; Weyler, *Empowering Words*, 78, 99, 107. On Marrant's subscription to conventions and use of typology, see also Benilde Montgomery, "Recapturing John Marrant," in Frank Shuffelton, ed., *A Mixed Race: Ethnicity in Early America* (New York, 1993), 106–108; Brooks, *American Lazarus*, 98–99; Miles, "'His Kingdom for a Kiss,'" in Stoler, ed., *Haunted by Empire*, 161; Bynum, "A Silent Book, Some Kisses, and John Marrant's Narrative," *Criticism*, LVII (2015), 75. Katy Chiles argues that attention to the narrative's conventional and figurative dimensions "obscures a deeper understanding of the interaction Marrant chronicles between himself and the Cherokee tribe, including his Cherokee captivity, his time spent among the various Southeastern tribes, and his learning of Cherokee ways." See Chiles, *Transformable Race: Surprising Metamorphoses in the Literature of Early America* (New York, 2014), 124.

person about nineteen years of age, and stood at my right hand") triggers cliché sensors, there is nothing improbable about the headman's having a daughter; Marrant himself never refers to her as a "princess." Literary conventions and precedents may condition the reading of Marrant's account as much as they did its composition. The challenge is less to distinguish literary representation from fact as to recognize the complicated interaction between the two.[8]

Marrant's unidentified Cherokee town may resemble the gothic setting of Horace Walpole's *Castle of Otranto* (1764), but other travelers' accounts offer some corroboration for the "many windings," "chamber," and "dungeon." Henry Timberlake, an emissary to the Cherokees during the Seven Years' War, similarly recounted that the entrance to the town house in the Overhills capital of Chota was preceded by "much winding and turning." Famed naturalist William Bartram, describing the "dwellings" in the Middle Town of Cowee, observed that they were "partitioned transversely, forming three apartments, which communicate with each other by inside doors." These parallels afford Marrant a little benefit of the doubt in his characterization of the "low dark place" where he was imprisoned as a "dungeon." As with "chamber," his diction might have been supplied by the Bible, and he might have applied it somewhat by analogy to a "low dark place" such as one of the hot houses that were adjacent to the Cherokee homes: "a little conical house," according to Bartram, "covered with dirt." With Marrant inside, praying through the night, a hot house might indeed become a dungeon: "I called upon thy name, O LORD, out of the low dungeon" (Lam 3:55). Despite its stylized representations, Marrant's narrative conveys a sense of having been there, although it is unclear where *there* is. His representation of a three-stage journey back to the frontier—"sixty miles," then "a hundred miles farther," then "seventy miles . . . to the back settlements of the white people"—seems compatible with travel along the so-called "Cherokee Path" from one of the "Middle Towns," such as Nikwasi or Cowee.[9]

8. *UV*, 111, 119; Miles, "'His Kingdom for a Kiss,'" in Stoler, ed., *Haunted by Empire*, 178 ("princess"). On Cherokee kings, see Timothy J. Shannon, "'This Wretched Scene of British Curiosity and Savage Debauchery': Performing Indian Kingship in Eighteenth Century Britain," in Joshua David Bellin and Laura L. Mielke, eds., *Native Acts: Indian Performance, 1603–1832* (Lincoln, Neb., 2012), 221–247. Bynum points out that her position at Marrant's right hand reproduces the "the biblical language of Revelation 5" ("A Silent Book, Some Kisses, and John Marrant's Narrative," *Criticism*, LVII [2015], 78).

9. Duane H. King, ed., *The Memoirs of Lt. Henry Timberlake: The Story of a Soldier, Adven-*

One of the implausible premises of the narrative is that, having traveled to this town voluntarily, in the company of a member of the community, Marrant was seized as a trespasser and sentenced to die. His interaction with the executioner, preliminary to his audience with the king, illustrates the complexity of the input and variables resulting in the textual composition of Marrant's narrative, including the conventions of captivity narratives (such as descriptions of horrible torture and death), scriptural precedents for experience as well as for representation, actual cultural encounters, rhetorical agendas, memory, and mediation. Marrant represents a layered metaphysical, cross-cultural, multimedia literacy event, in which most of the existents are confined to the inaccessible narrative dimension of Marrant's storyworld—but others, namely the English-language texts, also existed in the domains of Marrant's auditors at Bath Chapel and the Christian readers of his English-language *Narrative*.

These include the two books Marrant carried into captivity with him: the Bible and his Isaac Watts hymnal, likely one of the ubiquitous copies of *Hymns and Spiritual Songs* (1707). It is possible that biblical stories of "deliverance," such as the stories of Joseph or Daniel, suggested Marrant's account, which construes him as a virtuous soul undeserving of affliction, unlike Mary Rowlandson, John Williams, or Isaac Jogues. After all, when the executioner told him he was to be stuck with "pegs" of "turpentine wood," which would be burned down to his flesh, before he would be thrown entirely "into the flame," Marrant "burst into tears" and demanded to know "what I had done to deserve so cruel a death? To this he gave no answer." It is not a question that Rowlandson or Williams (despite the comparisons to Job) would have represented themselves asking: if they were afflicted, they deserved it. (As for Jogues, the question might have been, What had

---

turer, and Emissary to the Cherokees, 1756–1765 (Chapel Hill, N.C., 2007), 17; Francis Harper, ed., *The Travels of William Bartram: Naturalist Edition* (Athens, Ga., 1958), 232; *UV*, 121. Stephen Brandon also identifies Marrant's "dungeon" as a hot or winter house (Brandon, "Sacred Fire and Sovereign Rhetorics: Cherokee Literacy and Literature in the Cherokee and American Nations, 1760–1841" (Ph.D. diss., University of North Carolina at Greensboro, 2003), 67; John Gerar William de Brahm, *A Map of South Carolina and a Part of Georgia, Containing the Whole Sea-Coast: All the Islands, Inlets, Rivers, Creeks, Parishes, Townships, Boroughs, Roads, and Bridges . . .* (London, 1757); Henry Mouzon, *An Accurate Map of North and South Carolina with Their Indian Frontiers, Shewing in a Distinct Manner All the Mountains, Rivers, Swamps, Marshes, Bays, Creeks, Harbours, Sandbanks, and Soundings on the Coasts, with the Roads and Indian Paths . . .* (London, 1775); David P. George, Jr., "Ninety Six Decoded: Origins of a Community's Name," *South Carolina Historical Magazine*, XCII (1991), 69–84. See also John Stuart's 1764 "Map of the Cherokee Country," reproduced in *Memoirs of Lt. Henry Timberlake*, 50–51.

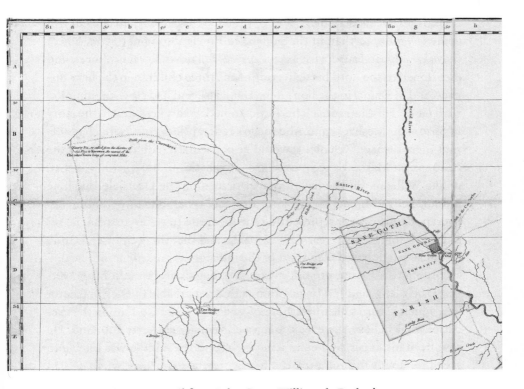

Figure 5 Detail from John Gerar William de Brahm's 1757
"Map of South Carolina and a Part of Georgia," showing the
"Cherokee Path" to western settlements in South Carolina.
Library of Congress, Geography and Map Division

he done *not* "to deserve so cruel a death?") It is also possible, however, that
Marrant's circumstances as a captive, his supposedly imminent execution
by fire, brought to his mind specific texts that are represented diegetically,
as in the other narratives. Already identifying with virtuous Old Testament captives, he might have experienced an allegorical convergence like
the ones that occurred between Psalm 137 and the specifics of Indian captivity for other Christian colonists. Indeed, a straightforward reading of
his narrative suggests that his circumstances compelled his identification
with the virtuous Jews in the Book of Daniel.[10]

10. On Watts, see Calhoun Winton, "The Southern Book Trade in the Eighteenth Century,"
in Hugh Amory et al., eds., *A History of the Book in America*, I, *The Colonial Book in the Atlantic
World* (Chapel Hill, N.C., 2000), 239; *UV*, 118, 129n.

Marrant recalled Daniel 3 and 6, which are especially apropos in this context—more so than in the preface to Rowlandson's narrative, where they also appear. Faced with execution, he "fell down upon my knees, and mentioned to the Lord his delivering of the three children in the fiery furnace, and of Daniel in the lion's den (Daniel 6), and had close communion with God." For Marrant, a "child" threatened with a fiery death, the story of Shadrach, Meshach, and Abednego's redemption from Nebuchadnezzar's "fiery furnace" (Daniel 3) would be particularly "suitable." One of the reasons that Marrant's account seems unrealistic—if not untrue—is that, unlike Williams (in the day of prayer preceding the Deerfield raid), he did not hedge his bets by invoking alternate types, one representing deliverance and another representing the fortitude to suffer. Instead, he requested a comparable treatment to Daniel and the "three children." God's response might have fallen short of the miraculous precedent, but he did, according to Marrant, prompt in him "a strong desire" to shift his prayers "into their language," endowing him with a remarkable fluency in Cherokee, which in turn unleashed the "power and grace of God" upon the executioner. "I believe the executioner was savingly converted to God. He rose from his knees, and embracing me round the middle was unable to speak for about five minutes; the first words he expressed, when he had utterance, were, 'No man shall hurt thee until thou hast been to the king.'" In Marrant's representation, the switch to Cherokee enabled a Whitefield-esque conversion.[11]

It's possible that this conversion of the so-called executioner is flat, like Gates's trope, meaning that it existed only in the plane of representation and served the rhetorical purpose of establishing Marrant's efficacy as a minister without necessarily originating in an event. It is also possible that it reflects his subjective, motivated understanding of the Cherokee man's response to his prayers. In this view, it suggests the dynamism of such a communicative interaction. His new convert momentarily became an equal—even a rival—participant in a triangulated communication with God. As they made their way to their audience with the king, the executioner, who had been struck dumb, was now "singing to

11. Aldridge refers to Marrant as a "child" and "stripling" (*UV*, 111, 118). According to Montgomery, "Throughout the narrative he remembers his experience as the antitype of scriptural events. Like Rowlandson's, his deliverance from the Indians is "the delivering of the three children in the fiery furnace, and of Daniel in the lion's den'" ("Recapturing John Marrant," in Shuffelton, ed., *Mixed Race*, 107).

the Lord" while Marrant himself was "at a loss to find words to praise him." One does not need to credit Marrant's interpretation of what was occurring to think that the executioner might have been as persuaded of Marrant's spirituality as his audience at Bath, and that he responded to Marrant's ecstatic prayer with a song; like other indigenous peoples, the Cherokees shared with the Christians a belief in the spiritual power of singing. While the executioner was thus engaged, Marrant had to defer his own connection with God, declaring, "I *will* thank thee for what is passed, and trust thee for what is to come. I *will* sing thy praise with my feeble tongue whilst life and breath shall last, and when I fail to sound thy praises here, I *hope* to sing them round thy throne above." Where could Marrant "find words"?[12]

He found them in a book he had carried with him into the "wilderness" and studied so often that he had committed its words (perhaps somewhat inaccurately) to memory: "With unspeakable joy," Marrant "sung two verses" of Isaac Watts's Hymn 54, "God's Presence is Light in Darkness." Like the diegetic scriptures in Rowlandson's narrative, the appearance of "Dr. Watts's" hymn in Marrant's is, not an allusion, but an occurrence. As with the references to the Book of Daniel in the preceding paragraph, an interaction with the Cherokee executioner might have prompted Marrant to call up a text. As in Daniel 3, the relation between the hymn and Marrant's account is allegorical. In the first instance, Nebuchadnezzar, the "children," and the "fiery furnace" correspond to the Cherokee king, Marrant, and the burning turpentine wood, respectively; in the second instance, "Darkness" more generally represents Marrant's predicament in Cherokee country. But when the allegory is so general and abstract, there is less reason to suspect that the levels of signification are inverted and that the figurative suggests the literal, instead of vice versa. That is, although there is a basis to infer that parts of Marrant's narrative were composed in order to suggest an allegorical parallel to the story of Joseph, for example, there is no appearance the narrative was influenced by Watts's hymn. Marrant's narrative raises doubts, but his claim to have sung that particular hymn is not one of its dubious details. On the contrary, the "two verses" corresponded across several levels—the book Marrant carried, his

12. *UV*, 118–120, emphasis added. Note the prevalence of songs in *James Mooney's History, Myths, and Sacred Formulas of the Cherokees: Containing the Full Texts of "Myths of the Cherokee"* (1900) *and "The Sacred Formulas of the Cherokees"* (1891) *as Published by the Bureau of American Ethnology* . . . (Asheville, N.C., 1992).

diegetic performance, his performance at Bath, the written account, the book that was familiar to his audience—as a demonstration of veracity.[13]

The text of the hymn that appears in Marrant's narrative actually diverges somewhat from the version published by Watts, but it is unclear whether the variation was introduced when Marrant sang the song in the Cherokee village; or perhaps during a repeat performance, when he sang it again in 1785 at Bath, as part of his oral history of his captivity; or perhaps in Aldridge's transcription. The version of the two verses of the hymn in the narrative substitutes third-person references to God with second-person addresses: instead of "In darkest Shades if he appear," Marrant's text reads, "In darkest shades, if thou appear." The effect is more intimate.[14]

The likelihood that Marrant sang out loud before his audience at Bath is suggested by Aldridge's statement in the preface, vouching for Marrant's veracity by attesting to his affective demonstration of spirituality. In that sense, the performance was not simply an account but a reenactment, and the *Narrative* was a textual record of it. At each step in mediation, so much is lost. The executioner's song, if there was one, is sealed off behind Marrant's limited powers of perception and representation and might have been exposed to an unintended interpretation—"singing to the Lord." Marrant's response, his inspired vocalization of Watts's published hymn, presumably drawn from memory, enabled Marrant to put words to feeling, in the event and again in the reenactment, a demonstration of his effusion of spirit. The textual reproduction of the hymn, in Marrant's *Narrative*, might have generated a corresponding feeling in his Christian readers, with an affective context supplied by their familiarity with the music and verses and their own experiences of the "religious sublime."[15]

The conversion of the executioner is the first demonstration of Marrant's ability, in Aldridge's phrase, to wield *"the arrow of prayer pointed with faith."* Further, it attests to the possibility for the sort of conversion

13. As Carretta points out, Marrant "slightly alters" the lyrics (*UV,* 129n). On the resemblance of Marrant's *Narrative,* especially its homecoming episode, to the story of Joseph, see Brooks, *American Lazarus,* 99; Chiles, *Transformable Race,* 124.

14. I[saac] Watts, *Hymns and Spiritual Songs: In Three Books. I. Collected from the Scriptures. II. Compos'd on Divine Subjects. III. Prepar'd for the Lord's Supper,* 16th ed. (Boston, 1742), 178; *UV,* 119.

15. David S. Shields, *Civil Tongues and Polite Letters in British America* (Williamsburg, Va., and Chapel Hill, N.C., 1997), 277; see also J. R. Watson, "The Hymns of Isaac Watts and the Tradition of Dissent," in Isabel Rivers and David L. Wykes, eds., *Dissenting Praise: Religious Dissent and the Hymn in England and Wales* (New York, 2011), 36.

event that regularly occurred at Whitefield's meetings to transcend the divide between Christianity and *"savage despotism."* Marrant was the lightning rod that drew down the Holy Spirit, which prompted him to pray in Cherokee, endowed him with a miraculous fluency, and struck down the executioner. If his auditors and readers credited this account, there could be little doubt about Marrant's ability to be an instrument of conversion in more favorable circumstances.[16]

"He Bid Me Read"

Marrant's audience with the king was a further, greater demonstration. The "king's eldest daughter" was drawn to the Bible he held in his hand: "She kissed it, and seemed much delighted with it. When she had put it into my hand again, the king asked me what it was?" This question led to a recital and a theological discussion:

> And I told him the name of my God was recorded there; and after several questions, he bid me read it, which I did, particularly the fifty-third chapter of Isaiah, in the most solemn manner I was able; and also the twenty-sixth chapter of Matthew's Gospel; and when I pronounced the name of Jesus, the particular effect it had upon me was observed by the king. When I had finished reading, he asked me why I read those names with so much reverence? I told him, because the Being to whom those names belonged made heaven and earth, and I and he; this he denied. I then pointed to the sun, and asked him who made the sun, and moon, and stars, and preserved them in their regular order; He said there was a man in their town that did it. I labored as much as I could to convince him to the contrary. His daughter took the book out of my hand a second time; she opened and kissed it again; her father bid her give it to me, which she did; but said, with much sorrow, the book would not speak to her.[17]

Marrant's account of the Cherokee woman's swing from delight to "sorrow" does seem to echo Albert Gronniosaw's autobiographical account of being "mightily delighted" by his master's book, and "very sorry and greatly disappointed when I found it would not speak." However, al-

16. *UV*, 111.
17. Ibid., 119.

though his autobiography was also published through the Huntingdon Connexion (his dedication is to the countess), there is no evidence that Marrant had read it by 1785, other than the Talking Book itself. Indeed, if we are looking for textual sources, there is no reason why the investigation should begin or end with Gronniosaw.[18]

Gronniosaw's and Marrant's narratives both belong to the larger discursive milieu of transatlantic British evangelical Protestantism. Marrant's explicit influences present a more probable source for the expectation that a Bible might speak to some and not to others: Whitefield, in his sermon on "The Duty of Searching the Scriptures" (1739), declared that, if "unbelievers" would read the Bible, "They would hear GOD speaking unto their souls by it, and, consequently, be built up in the knowledge and fear of him, who is the Author thereof." Gronniosaw, who also refers to Whitefield, would have read in a book he refers to in his narrative—Richard Baxter's *Call to the Unconverted* (1658)—that "Every leaf of the *blessed Book* of God hath, as it were, a voice, and calls out to thee, *Turn and live; turn, or thou wilt die.* How canst thou open it, and read a leaf, or hear a Chapter, and not perceive God bids thee *Turn?*" Understood as a revision of an evangelical trope of a speaking Bible, Marrant's silent book may figure his access to the life-saving word of God and the Cherokees' lack thereof.[19]

The evangelical language ideology expressed by Baxter's anthropomorphism, his attribution of speech to the Bible, might have informed not only Marrant's representation but also his perception of the Cherokees' responses to his Bible. Indeed, he represents his encounter with the Cherokee king and his daughter as an exemplary evangelical literacy event. Just as God had "accompanied the word with such power" that Whitefield's declamation of Amos 4:12 had laid low the unconverted Marrant, so, following Marrant's readings from Isaiah and Matthew, did the "glorious power" of the Lord accompany Marrant's prayers, such that "some of them cried out, particularly the kings' daughter, and the man who ordered me to be executed, and several others seemed under deep conviction of sin. This made the king very angry; he called me a witch, and commanded

18. Ibid., 38.
19. Of course, Marrant might be both borrowing from an established Protestant rhetoric and revising his predecessor's version. Bynum argues, "Marrant uses the tools of his faith (namely, the Word of God) to revise Gronniosaw's account of the talking book." See "A Silent Book, Some Kisses, and John Marrant's Narrative," *Criticism*, LVII (2015), 71; *Works of the Reverend George Whitefield*, I, 83; *UV*, 41; Richard Baxter, *A Call to the Unconverted to Turn and Live: And Accept of the Mercy while Mercy May Be Had* . . . (London, 1658), 134.

me to be thrust into the prison, and to be executed the next morning." With this account, Marrant, about to set out to "Preach the GOSPEL in Nova-Scotia" in 1785, attested before his English audience to his efficacy as a medium for the Holy Spirit. Of his first sermon at Birchtown, he would report that, after preaching from John 5:28–29, "God's spirit was very powerfully felt by the preacher and hearer, and for five minutes I was so full I was not able to speak. Here I saw the display of God's good spirit; several sinners were carried out pricked to the heart." Similar sequences unfold over and over again: specific Bible verses, preaching and prayer, powerful somatic displays from both "preacher and hearer."[20]

Marrant's *Narrative* similarly anticipates his *Journal*'s representation of "the power of God" not only "to wound" but also "to heal." Following Marrant's own conversion, the physiological effect of his "distress of soul" was such that he was unresponsive to all but soul medicine: his sister sent for three doctors, "but no medicine they prescribed could I take." Similarly, the king's daughter was laid low by the Holy Spirit, and she was unresponsive to Cherokee medicine: "They used the skill of all their doctors that afternoon and night; but physical prescriptions were useless." Her condition enabled Marrant to play the same role for her that the Baptist minister who visited him after his conversion had done for him: "I besought the Lord again, but received no answer: I cried again, and he was intreated. He said, 'Be it to thee as thou wilt;' the Lord appeared most lovely and glorious; the king himself was awakened, and the others set at liberty." This moment is the climax of the narrative. The supposed Talking Book, the focal point for critical attention, is part of the setup, but the language ideology of the narrative subordinates literacy to prayer and inspired speech.[21]

Yet to ascribe Marrant's representation of the Cherokees' responses to his book and his literacy practices to evangelical language ideology, or to any exogenous cultural tradition, favors the rhetorical context of the *Narrative*'s moment of production over the ethnohistorical context of its moment of representation. Such privileging indicates a general tendency in the textual analysis of nonfictional sources, especially representations of colonial encounters. This inclination arises from the long-standing recognition, by historians as well as literary historicists, that textual sources cannot be regarded as "transparent" records. But treating them as opaque

---

20. *UV*, 110, 119–120; Marrant, *Journal*, 12.
21. Marrant, *Journal*, 17; *UV*, 113, 118, 120.

representations is not necessarily more rigorous. It is certainly easier, increasingly so, in our era of digital scholarship, to trace "rhetorical paths of thought" among texts than it is to follow them across the epistemological barriers separating text and event. Thus the rhetorical and ideological sources for Marrant's representation seem more ascertainable than any empirical basis. However, the impossibility of determining what actually occurred in Marrant's colonial encounter—or even if there was such an encounter—does not mean that relationship between his representation and his experience should not be investigated. The first "hypothesis" to consider as an explanation for this written representation of an oral narrative account of a cultural encounter is the one put forward by the account itself: that it depicts the Cherokees' response to his Bible and, in particular, to his performative literacy practices.[22]

Interpretations of Marrant's *Narrative* should consider its apparent correspondence to other well-known descriptions of indigenous responses to European literacy in earlier colonial relations, which could suggest either another rhetorical influence upon his *Narrative* or a common experience of encounter. Well-known instances include Thomas Hariot's representation of the Roanoke Indians' reaction to the Bible in his *Briefe and True Report of the New Found Land of Virginia* (1590) ("Many be glad to touch it, to embrace it, to kisse it, to hold it to their brests and heades, and stroke over all their bodie with it; to shewe their hungrie desire of that knowledge which was spoken of") and similar accounts of awestruck indigenous peoples attributing the power of speech to European writing in John Smith's *General History of Virginia* (1624) and Gabriel Sagard's *History of Canada* (1636).[23]

22. Steven Mailloux, *Reception Histories: Rhetoric, Pragmatism, and American Cultural Politics* (Ithaca, N.Y., 1998), xiv. Allan Greer remarks that, although "the sources on Tekakwitha are incomparable, they are certainly not transparent." As a historian, he "found myself in the unaccustomed role of literary critic, attempting to analyze, critique, and decode enigmatic texts" (*Mohawk Saint: Catherine Tekakwitha and the Jesuits* [Oxford, 2005], viii). In writing of an arguably more mediated discursive form—the oral tradition—Jan Vansina suggests, "As long as traditions are not independently confirmed the evidence they present can best be described as 'on probation.' Such evidence is not worthless. It has a certain plausibility and forms a hypothesis that should be tested first, before any other hypothesis is considered. A body of tradition thus becomes an agenda for research" (Vansina, *Oral Tradition as History* [Madison, Wis., 1985], 160).

23. Thomas Hariot, *A Briefe and True Report of the New Found Land of Virginia* (Frankfurt, 1590), 27; Gabriel Sagard, *Histoire du Canada et voyages que les frères mineurs récollects y ont faicts pour la conversion des Infidelles* (Paris, 1636), 794; Karen Ordahl Kupperman, ed., *Captain John Smith: A Select Edition of His Writings* (Williamsburg, Va., and Chapel Hill, N.C., 1988), 62; James Axtell, "The Power of Print in the Eastern Woodlands," *WMQ*, 3d Ser., XLIV (1987), 300–309;

These reports in early colonial accounts have served as a disputed basis for generalizations about indigenous peoples' perceptions of European literacy, but one does not need to resort to these to illuminate Marrant's depiction of the Cherokees' responses to his Bible. Literacy is a prominent theme in Cherokee history, with their homegrown, widely adopted syllabary, bilingual newspaper, and printed constitution. The prehistory of these nineteenth-century developments, including the Cherokees' exposure to alphabetic literacy through Christian evangelization and treaty negotiations with Britain, is part of the ethnohistorical context for Marrant's account. If Marrant's captivity occurred in one of the Middle Towns, then the king he encountered would not have been someone as well known as Oconostota, the "Great Warrior" from the Overland town of Chota, but more likely a headman such as the "Chief of Cowe," whom Bartram reports meeting in 1773. Marrant's Bible in 1769 could hardly have been his first exposure to alphabetic literacy; by then, three embassies of Cherokee "kings" had been to London, in 1730, 1762, and 1765. Marrant claimed to have re-encountered his "old royal benefactor and convert" years after his captivity, riding in the company of General Henry Clinton after the English siege of Charleston. The possibility that he was there further fleshes him out as a historical figure participating in historical events, an actor in the Red Atlantic, rather than a one-dimensional element in a rhetorical figure emerging from the Black Atlantic. Either way, Marrant's representation of this king's response to the Bible may reflect a Cherokee language ideology—one substantiated by the accounts of the origin of the Cherokee syllabary.[24]

Patricia Seed, "'Failing to Marvel': Atahualpa's Encounter with the Word," *Latin American Research Review*, XXVI, no. 1 (1991), 7–32; Peter Wogan, "Perceptions of European Literacy in Early Contact Situations," *Ethnohistory*, XLI (1994), 407–429. Gustafson points out the resemblance between Marrant's representation and Hariot's (*Eloquence Is Power*, 108). Citing Axtell's "Power of Print," Miles observes, "An earlier occurrence of Gates's trope appears not in an African American context but in a Native American one." But Axtell certainly does not consider his instances to be figurative. See "'His Kingdom for a Kiss,'" in Stoler, ed., *Haunted by Empire*, 180. Leon Jackson suggests that the autobiographical Talking Book episodes Gates analyzes "reflect precisely the sort of noetic dissonance that emerges when representatives of primary oral cultures encounter written and printed artifacts" (Jackson, "The Talking Book and the Talking Book Historian: African American Cultures of Print—the State of the Discipline," *Book History*, XIII [2010], 267).

24. *Travels of William Bartram*, 231; Jace Weaver, *The Red Atlantic: American Indigenes and the Making of the Modern World, 1000–1927* (Chapel Hill, N.C., 2014). Brandon suggests that the headman might have marked Marrant for adoption, and that his "request that Marrant read from his Bible may well have been a test of his literacy" ("Sacred Fire and Sovereign Rheto-

These indicate that Cherokees did, indeed, attribute supernatural efficacy to European literacy into the nineteenth century. According to Samuel L. Knapp's account of an 1828 interview, Sequoyah's inspiration for his syllabary was a debate over the ontological status of alphabetic literacy. The debate itself was prompted by the discovery of a letter "on the person of a prisoner" taken at the 1791 battle of Wabash, popularly known as St. Clair's Defeat: "In some of their deliberations on this subject, the question arose among them, whether this mysterious power of the *talking leaf*, was the gift of the Great Spirit to the white man, or a discovery of the white man himself? Most of his companions were of the former opinion, while he as strenuously maintained the latter." In another version of this story, some Cherokee men "remarked how wonderful it was to think that simply by making marks on paper, and sending the paper to another, two persons could understand as well as if talking together face to face; and how these things were done, it was impossible to conceive." Sequoyah retorted, "'I can see no impossibility in conceiving how it is done. The white man is no magician.'" The various histories of the "invention of the syllabary"—purportedly issuing from the inventor himself, from associates, or from family members and put into writing after the introduction of the syllabary or after transmission as an oral tradition, in English or in Cherokee—largely agree in tracing the inception of the syllabary to a

---

rics," 63); on Cherokee embassies to London, see Shannon, "'This Wretched Scene,'" in Bellin and Mielke, eds., *Native Acts*, 227–228; *UV*, 126. In a footnote, Marrant addresses what he evidently felt was the most unlikely aspect of his description: "Though it is unusual for Indians to have a horse, yet the king accompanied the general on the present successful occasion riding on horse-back" (ibid., 131n). Bartram reports that he encountered Attacullaculla, "emperor or grand chief of the Cherokees" at the head of "a company of Indians, all well mounted on horse back" (*Travels of William Bartram*, 230). There is, however, no corroborating reference to the presence of a Cherokee leader in other firsthand accounts of the siege—nothing to help identify Marrant's "king"—and even Marrant's presence at this event is subject to doubt. See William T. Bulger, ed., "Sir Henry Clinton's 'Journal of the Siege of Charleston, 1780,'" *South Carolina Historical Magazine*, LXVI (1965), 164; see also Carl P. Borick, *A Gallant Defense: The Siege of Charleston, 1780* (Columbia, S.C., 2003); Bernhard A. Uhlendorf, ed., *The Siege of Charleston: Capts. Johann Ewald, Johann Hinrichs, and Maj. Gen. Johann Christoph von Huyn*, Eyewitness Accounts of the American Revolution (New York, 1968); William B. Willcox, ed., *The American Rebellion: Sir Henry Clinton's Narrative of His Campaigns, 1775–1782, with an Appendix of Original Documents* (New Haven, Conn., 1954). Whereas Carretta suggests that Marrant might have "fabricated his career 'in his Majesty's service,'" pointing out that his name does not appear on the muster lists for the ships he mentions in the *Narrative*, Joanna Brooks points out that a possible alternative spelling, "John Morant," does appear "on a list of prisoners taken from American privateers during the War of Independence" (*UV*, 130–131n; Brooks, *American Lazarus*, 210–211n).

debate over writing's supernatural properties, in which Sequoyah consistently takes the part of demystifier.[25]

Thus there is evidence of magical literacy on both sides of Marrant's encounter with the Cherokees. Where Marrant channeled the voice of the book whose "every leaf" could speak, the Cherokees might themselves have perceived, in Marrant's spirited demonstration, the "mysterious power of the talking leaf." Instead of a clever adaptation of a fellow Anglo-African writer's trope, then, we may see the record of a collision between different cultures of communication. The king's accusation that Marrant was a witch may indicate a significant aspect of this collision: the interaction between religious enthusiasm and traditional indigenous beliefs about shamanism and witchcraft. The king's attribution of his daughter's somatic responses to witchcraft, during a period in which witchcraft accusations were prevalent in Cherokee towns, is the most ethnographically plausible element in this episode. It offers a key to some of the other implausible features of the narrative, including the death sentence (if not necessarily the stay of execution) and the effect of Marrant's prayers on the executioner, the headman's daughter, and others.[26]

That Marrant was suspected of being a witch is indicated by the method of execution the Cherokees threatened him with. The turpentine stakes and fire suggest the Cherokee practice of destroying witches by "'lowering the soul,'" using "counter-active magic" such as "magically empowered arrows, sharpened stakes, or bullets that can pierce their flesh." The turpentine and fire find approximate corroboration in George E. Foster's *Reminiscences of Travels in Cherokee Lands* (1899). "I never understood why the Southern Indian always punished the souls of their wicked dead with fires of burning pitch," commented Foster, a New Englander who wrote prolifically (if not necessarily authoritatively) about the Cherokees, "until I visited their old stamping grounds, the turpentine forests of the South.

25. Samuel L. Knapp, *Lectures on American Literature with Remarks on Some Passages of American History* ([New York], 1829), 26; Major George Lowery, "Notable Persons in Cherokee History; Sequoyah or George Gist," ed. John Howard Payne, *Journal of Cherokee Studies,* II, no. 4 (Fall 1977), 388.

26. Stanley W. Hoig refers to Dragging Canoe's "people's suspicion that the [Chickamauga] towns were infested with witches" (Hoig, *The Cherokees and Their Chiefs: In the Wake of Empire* [Fayetteville, Ark., 1998], 64). For a detailed reading of Marrant's narrative in relation to Cherokee witchcraft, see Brandon, "Sacred Fire and Sovereign Rhetorics," 66–70. Gustafson points out, "Evangelicalism provided one of the most important sites of exchange between culturally diverse forms of magic and American Christianity" (*Eloquence Is Power,* 105).

Nothing earthly is much hotter than burning pitch." Thus Marrant's representation of the description of his impending death could have been informed by what the so-called "executioner" actually communicated to him and by his subsequent exposure to Cherokee traditional culture.[27]

The Cherokees' perception that Marrant was practicing magical literacy might have played a role in his identification as a witch. Sequoyah himself might have been suspected of witchcraft, arguably because of the belief that the syllabary was derived from a writing system that had been employed by an ancient, malevolent clan of priests, the Ani-Kutani. Possibly, the Ani-Kutani tradition led some Cherokees, during the "treaty-making era of conflicts with Europeans and Americans," to associate writing with witchcraft, and indeed Sequoyah's syllabary was immediately put to use as a medium for "medicomagical knowledge." In other words, there is a substantial correspondence between Marrant's representation of the Cherokees' responses to his Bible and his recitation—the daughter's attribution of the power of speech, in the form of her complaint that "the book would not speak to her," and the king's imputation of witchcraft—and more direct sources about Cherokee language ideologies concerning literacy.[28]

Marrant's narrative may reflect a dynamic that also played out on more familiar fronts of the Great Awakening—the interaction between witchcraft beliefs and religious enthusiasm. Evangelical "gatherings were once perceived by many as demonic." In a 1754 screed, the bishop of Exeter, George Lavington, declared that John Wesley was fortunate to escape

27. Alan Kilpatrick, *The Night Has a Naked Soul: Witchcraft and Sorcery among the Western Cherokee* (Syracuse, N.Y., 1998), 5, 94; Geo[rge] E. Foster, *Reminiscences of Travel in Cherokee Lands: An Address Delivered before the Ladies' Missionary Society of the Ithaca, N.Y., Congregational Church, 1898* (Ithaca, N.Y., 1899), 7.

28. Margaret Bender, *Signs of Cherokee Culture: Sequoyah's Syllabary in Eastern Cherokee Life* (Chapel Hill, N.C., 2002), 29; Rose Gubele, "Utalotsa Woni—'Talking Leaves': A Re-Examination of the Cherokee Syllabary and Sequoyah," *Studies in American Indian Literatures*, XXIV, no. 4 (Winter 2012), 61; Christopher B. Teuton, *Deep Waters: The Textual Continuum in American Indian Literature* (Lincoln, Neb., 2010), 3–6; Raymond D. Fogelson, "An Analysis of Cherokee Sorcery and Witchcraft," in Charles M. Hudson, ed., *Four Centuries of Southern Indians* (Athens, Ga., 1975), 114 ("medicomagical"). According to Fogelson, "The writing down of this material imbued it with tangibility and an aura of sanctity that insured a fairly literal transmission of the knowledge contained within these texts" (ibid.). Peter Wogan's study of "magical literacy" in a contemporary indigenous community in Ecuador concludes that the use of writing as an instrument of Church and State power might have fostered the belief in its efficacy in witchcraft. See Wogan, "Magical Literacy: Encountering a Witch's Book in Ecuador," *Anthropological Quarterly*, LXXI (1998), 186–202.

prosecution for witchcraft, in light of his boasted "'Power *to throw* [his] Followers *into Contorsions, Convulsions, Variety of* unaccountable Disorders *of Body and Mind, into the most* hellish Tortures; *and then to* release *them again.*'" Marrant himself, in his *Narrative*, boasted of comparable powers, insofar as his prayers brought about the headman's daughter's condition and released her from it.[29]

The headman's depicted discussion with Marrant indicates that he understood Marrant's reading in terms that corresponded to Marrant's own understanding—as an interaction with the spirit world. It would have been quite a performance. Marrant read "particularly the fifty-third chapter of Isaiah, in the most solemn manner I was able; and also the twenty-sixth chapter of Matthew's gospel." The Old Testament chapter, in Christian hermeneutics, predicted the sacrifice of Christ; the New Testament one includes the Last Supper and Jesus's delivery to the Jewish Court. From Isaiah, Marrant would have read: "He was taken from prison and from judgment: and who shall declare his generation? for he was cut off out of the land of the living: for the transgression of my people he was stricken" (53:8). From Matthew 26, he would have read the high priest's question—"Tell us whether thou be Christ, the Son of God"—and Jesus's response: "Thou has said: nevertheless I say unto you, Hereafter shall ye see the Son of man sitting on the right hand of power, and coming in the clouds of heaven" (26:63–64). Implicitly, Marrant's selections express his own messianic ambitions.[30]

The Cherokee hearers might not have understood the language, but they would have witnessed the emotional expression: in a footnote, Marrant explains that the king asked "what those parts were which seemed to affect me so much, not knowing what I read, as he did not understand the English language." Marrant's communication of feeling on that occasion may be indicated by a passage in his later journal, in which he describes preaching to a community of Indians in Nova Scotia out of Matthew 28:

29. Roark Atkinson, "Satan in the Pulpit: Popular Christianity during the Scottish Great Awakening, 1680–1750," *Journal of Social History,* XLVII (2013), 346. M. Thomas Hatley suggests that "Marrant's *Narrative* . . . provides a rare insight into the way in which the Great Awakening defensively absorbed disturbing intercultural memories" (*The Dividing Paths: Cherokees and South Carolinians through the Era of Revolution* [New York, 1993], 237); and see George Lavington, *The Enthusiasm of Methodists and Papists Compared: In Three Parts . . .* , II (London, 1754), xvii–xviii, cited in Atkinson, "Satan in the Pulpit," 347.

30. *UV*, 119. See Bynum, "A Silent Book, Some Kisses, and John Marrant's Narrative," *Criticism*, LVII (2015), 74.

19–20: "My soul was filled with the glorious power and love of God; I could perceive solemnity in the faces of all the people within the audience of my voice; so that the convincing power of God was manifested." Subsequently, describing how he invoked "the baptising Spirit," he reports, "I was not able to speak, being overpowered with the love of God; when, rising from my knees, I looked upon the people, and saw tears in their eyes, and the congregation at large, filled with solemnity." The "solemn manner" that Marrant refers to in his *Narrative* and the "solemnity" he attributes to his congregants in his journal connote, not merely a deep seriousness, but rather an engagement with the sacred. Whereas the represented affects and effects of Marrant's Bible reading and prayer are consistent with the evangelism of his day, the Cherokees might have recognized sorcery.[31]

If the Cherokees were convinced that Marrant was a witch, though, it seems unlikely that the headman's daughter would have picked up his Bible, kissed it, and lamented that it did not speak with her. It is equally unlikely that they would not only have spared his life but exalted him. Witches were "inherently evil" and "irredeemable"; they needed to be destroyed. Witches caused illness by manipulating spiritual power through "ritual incantations." Marrant's various invocations and "pentecostal" exhibitions might have appeared to be witchcraft, but if his account is to be accepted as authentic—if not necessarily accurate—then the Cherokees must have determined that he was, not actually a witch, but a different sort of spiritual agent.[32]

Conclusion

One cannot know what happened. The Talking Book episode may be subject to miscommunications and misrepresentations at multiple levels, affected by multiple factors. In the moment of representation, these factors include the intentions of the Cherokee actors, Marrant's understanding of Cherokee language and culture, his extreme stress, and his intense devo-

31. *UV*, 119, 130n; Marrant, *Journal*, 18; "solemn," *OED Online*.
32. Gustafson, *Eloquence Is Power*, xiv; Fogelson, "An Analysis of Cherokee Sorcery and Witchcraft," in Hudson, ed., *Four Centuries of Southern Indians*, 119. According to Fogelson, "to be discovered as a witch [was] the equivalent of signing one's death warrant" ("The Conjurer in Eastern Cherokee Society," *Journal of Cherokee Studies*, V, no. 2 [Fall 1980], 63). Duane Champagne similarly notes, "An accusation and community condemnation of witchcraft carried a death penalty" ("Institutional and Cultural Order in Early Cherokee Society: A Sociological Interpretation," ibid., XV, no. 1 [Spring 1990], 4).

tion; in the telling, they include memory, personal agendas, and a panoply of rhetorical and ideological influences; in the writing, they include Aldridge's own agenda, as well as his understanding and interpretation of Marrant's oral performance. The resulting depiction of a literacy event may be a highly subjective but literal representation of the Cherokees' response to a fourteen-year-old, Bible-bearing, Anglo-African, Christian enthusiast.

This "ethnohistoricist" reading brings the indeterminacy of literary language together with the dynamic uncertainty of colonial contact. Once again, seemingly apparent intertexts or allegorical points of reference—Bible stories, saintly lives, perhaps, in Marrant's case, an Anglo-African trope—should be considered alongside factors in representation that are more difficult to ascertain, especially those pertaining to the ethnohistorical moment of representation. If such stories may shape authors' representations of indigenous peoples, the actions and cultures of the indigenous peoples may suggest the points of reference, and these intertexts may occur during the course of events, represented diegetically, as in Marrant's allusions to the stories of Daniel and of the three children. Instead of a mere representation, this passage can be a representation of a literacy event in which Marrant reminded God of biblical precedents akin to the Cherokees' execution practices.

Instead of locating the Talking Book within a single literary tradition, we may put it in a chain of literacy events spanning the moments of representation and production. In a broad sense, all the episodes in the narrative are literacy events, since they eventuate in textual representation; but in a narrow sense, most of the narrative cruxes—including Marrant's conversion at Whitefield's revival meeting, his reprieve from execution, his climactic encounter with the king and his daughter, and, arguably, his reunion with his family—involve texts, whether as material objects or as references, invocations or interpretations that occur within the diegesis and again during the telling. This chapter has asked readers to consider an original, diegetic literacy event, centered around a Bible, as it might have been experienced by its colonial and indigenous participants: as a stunning manifestation of spiritual power.

CHAPTER SIX

"A Singular Gift from a Savage"

In August 1764, Colonel John Bradstreet dispatched Captain Thomas Morris on an embassy to "take possession also of the Ilinois country in his Britannic Majesty's name" in accordance with the Treaty of Paris ending the Seven Years' War. En route from Cedar Point on Lake Erie, Morris found that the Indians in the Ohio Country were hostile to the news "that their father, the king of France, had ceded those countries to their brother the king of England." He never made it to Illinois. He was detained and feared for his life. In flight, Morris forwarded to Bradstreet a manuscript journal of his aborted mission, requesting that a copy be made for his own use. The manuscript was eventually archived in the papers of Bradstreet's commanding officer. The copy became the basis for the "Journal of Captain Thomas Morris, of His Majesty's XVII Regiment of Infantry," first published as a component of Morris's belletristic *Miscellanies in Prose and Verse* (1791). In 1978, *Miscellanies* was republished as volume 20 of the Garland Library of Narratives of North American Indian Captivities; with its treatise on tragedy and its translations of Juvenal, it is one of the more anomalous items in that series.[1]

Morris's journal has been a valuable source for historians of Pontiac's War. They make note of two seemingly superfluous details. First, Morris reports that at the initial stage of his journey up the Maumee River, at a village where the Ottawa chief Pontiac was encamped with his army, the Potawatomi leader called the Little Chief "made me a present of a volume of Shakespear's plays; a singular gift from a savage." Next, he reports that, during his approach to a "Miami Fort" upstream, he was so engrossed in reading *Antony and Cleopatra* that he was oblivious to the gathering of Indians on the riverbank, waiting to kill him. He implies that Shakespeare

---

1. "Journal of Captain Thomas Morris, of His Majesty's XVII Regiment of Infantry," in Morris, *Miscellanies in Prose and Verse* (London, 1791), 1, 8; Gregory Evans Dowd, *War under Heaven: Pontiac, the Indian Nations, and the British Empire* (Baltimore, 2004), 159; Richard White, *The Middle Ground: Indians, Empires, and Republics in the Great Lakes Region, 1650–1815* (Cambridge, 1991), 298–300.

kept him at a safe remove, saving his life. (On these points, as will be discussed, the 1791 journal differs from the 1764 manuscript.)[2]

Rather than serving as merely a colorful detail in a narrative history, the appearance of this volume of Shakespeare in Morris's journal warrants further investigation, both as historical record and literary representation. It broaches topics that variously pertain to history, the history of the book, and literary scholarship. For example, Morris's representation that his book was a gift from an Indian can be construed as the record of an apparently unusual instance of frontier exchange, or of a remarkable juncture in the itinerary of a particular book. We may wonder about the significance both Morris and the Little Chief might have attached to the transaction, as well as the significance Morris subsequently attached to his reading as part of a performance of identity. We may also consider Morris's expedition during Pontiac's War as a particular context for a reception allegory of *Antony and Cleopatra*. How did the content of the book presented by the Little Chief relate to Morris's experience and to his narrative?

In addition to the account by Morris (1732–1808), three other narratives of captivity in the eighteenth-century Ohio Country and Old Northwest territory allow for broader speculations about the involvement of native Americans in the circulation of books and the significances both they and the colonists attached to the colonists' activities of reading and writing in Indian Country: James Smith (1737–1814) was a captive adoptee among Kahnawake Iroquois during the Seven Years' War, whereas Thomas Ridout (1754–1829) and Charles Johnston (1770–1833) were captured separately by Shawnees on the Ohio River during the Northwest Indian War (1785–1795). Each of their narratives inverts the iconic image of the colonial encounter, in which the European approaches the Indian with a book in hand.[3]

In light of the scope of the captivity narrative archive—as noted in the introduction, the Garland Library comprises 111 volumes and 311 titles—

2. Francis Parkman, *The Conspiracy of Pontiac and the Indian War after the Conquest of Canada: From the Spring of 1763 to the Death of Pontiac*, II (Lincoln, Neb., 1994), 190; Harvey Lewis Carter, *The Life and Times of Little Turtle: First Sagamore of the Wabash* (Urbana, Ill., 1987); White, *Middle Ground*, 298–299; Dowd, *War under Heaven*, 159–161; Morris, *Miscellanies*, 12.

3. "It has been said of the missionaries that when they arrived they had only the Book and we had the land," writes Vine Deloria; "now we have the Book and they have the land" (Deloria, *Custer Died for Your Sins: An Indian Manifesto* [Norman, Okla., 1969], 101). See also John Heckewelder, *History, Manners, and Customs of the Indian Nations Who Once Inhabited Pennsylvania and the Neighboring States* (Philadelphia, 1881), 188.

it would be an exaggeration to say that episodes in which the captors present their captives with books are a rhetorical commonplace. Yet in the canonical Puritan narratives, the books that provide the typological frameworks for the narratives also appear as represented objects within them. As discussed previously, Mary Rowlandson declared in *The Soveraignty and Goodness of God* (1682), "I cannot but take notice of the wonderfull mercy of God to me . . . in sending me a Bible. One of the *Indians* that came from the *Medfield* fight, had brought some plunder, came to me, and asked me, if I wou'd have a Bible, he had got one in his basket." Similarly, in *The Redeemed Captive, Returning to Zion* (1707), John Williams, emphasizing the contrast with the Jesuits, noted that his Indian "master gave me a piece of a Bible, never disturbed me in reading the Scriptures, or in praying to God," and that many of his "neighbors also found that mercy in their journey to have Bibles, psalm books, catechisms, and good books put into their hands with liberty to use them." These instances suggest the Indians' increasing familiarity with Christian devotional practices and the centrality of holy books within them.[4]

The Indian who, according to Rowlandson, handed her a Bible and assured her that the Indians would let her read might well have been a Protestant convert himself. But Weetamoo, whom Rowlandson represents as her imperious mistress, might have evinced a more traditionalist viewpoint when she returned from "the burial of a *Papoos*" and "snatched" Rowlandson's Bible "hastily out of my hand, and threw it out of doors." She might have suspected Rowlandson of practicing a malevolent spirituality. As for Williams, the Indians who gave holy books to him and his captive congregation apparently had no such fears. Neither, a half century later, did the Delawares who gave the French and Indian War captive Barbara Leininger a French Bible to prepare her for execution. When told she did not read French, "they gave her a German Bible." The Delawares would have been exposed to Bibles through Moravian missionaries, just as Rowlandson's and Williams's captors had been through Puritan and Jesuit ones, respectively.[5]

Whereas early colonial accounts and captivity narratives feature Bibles or other religious texts, the Ohio Country captives (with the exception of James Smith, whose narrative itself is predominantly secular) also read

---

4. *SGG*, 76; *CH*, 105.

5. *SGG*, 76, 86; "The Narrative of Marie Le Roy and Barbara Leininger, for Three Years Captives among the Indians," *Pennsylvania Magazine of History and Biography*, XXIX (1905), 409.

literary works. Morris, Johnston, and Ridout were participants in the cosmopolitan "literary culture" (whereas Smith, the Scots-Irish settler and adopted Indian captive, defined himself partly against it) that arose with the decline of the literary patronage system, the proliferation of coffeehouses and periodicals, and multiple additional factors that "made the circumstances of literary communication particularly visible to the educated classes." Theirs was a more "spacious" conception of discourse community than that of Rowlandson or Jogues, for example, but they similarly performed their affiliation from within captivity. Like their predecessors' sacred texts, their books functioned as material embodiments for their identities and lenses for their experiences. Moreover, Morris's and Ridout's narratives present secular recapitulations of the sort of allegorical parallelism that operates in the religious narratives, insofar as their stories seem to track, respectively, with Shakespeare's *Antony and Cleopatra* and Fenelon's *Adventures of Telemachus.*[6]

"I Felt My Heart Warm towards the Indians"

Book presentation scenes express the fundamental importance of literacy to the self-conception of some colonists and attest to the recognition of that importance by the Indians. Such significance is apparent in James Smith's description of an emotional swing attending the loss and recovery of his books.

Smith was captured while engaged in the construction of Braddock's Road, a passage cut westward through the Pennsylvania backwoods. This route led General Edward Braddock's expedition to take Fort Duquesne directly into a calamitous encounter with a French and Indian force at the Monongahela River. On July 9, 1755, the day of what became known as Braddock's Defeat, Smith was already a prisoner held in Fort Duquesne. He was afterward brought into the Ohio Country to a village of Kahnawake Iroquois—migrants from the Catholic Mohawk community of Kahnawake, near Montreal—and ceremonially adopted into the tribe. He remained among the Kahnawakes until the end of the war; increasingly, his narrative intimates, he became reconciled to his adoptive iden-

6. David S. Shields, "Eighteenth-Century Literary Culture," in Hugh Amory et al., eds., *A History of the Book in America*, I, *The Colonial Book in the Atlantic World* (Cambridge, 2000), 434–435.

tity. He published *An Account of the Remarkable Occurrences in the Life and Travels of Colonel James Smith* (1799) almost forty years after his return to the Pennsylvania settlement frontier.

Like Rowlandson and other predecessors, near the outset the Indians provided Smith, albeit indirectly, with discursive equipment for his journey. From Fort Duquesne, while he was convalescing from the beating he had suffered running the gauntlet, Smith watched the victorious return of the French and Indians from Braddock's Defeat. They brought "a great many bloody scalps, grenadiers' caps, British canteens, bayonets etc with them." They also brought at least one book. After witnessing the British prisoners being "burned to death," Smith returned to his chambers to find a copy of Robert Russell's *Seven Sermons*, "which they had brought from the field of battle, which a Frenchman made a present of to me." This popular sermon book, reprinted frequently throughout the eighteenth century, exemplified "the staple reading matter" of "middling" readers such as Smith or its previous owner, who was likely a common soldier.[7]

Weeks later, Smith acquired a second book. A Kahnawake party returned to Smith's village from a raid in Virginia with "an English Bible, which they gave to a Dutch woman who was a prisoner; but as she could not read English, she made a present of it to me, which was very acceptable." In these instances, Smith didn't receive the books from the Indians directly, but they found their way to him through Europeans who had. The books the Indians picked up as plunder had been cherished possessions of the soldiers and settlers who had carried them to the backcountry. Because of their strong identification with their owners, they might have served the Indians as trophies, items whose principle value is as tokens of victory—like the grenadiers' caps. Yet this same association with the colonists' culture, coupled with their relative lack of use or exchange value, undergirded the decision to give them away to Europeans. There was also an element of kindness in these bestowals, as Smith acknowledged once his books went missing and were restored and as the other captives discussed in this chapter also seemed to recognize.[8]

That Smith counted his books as necessities is illustrated by his mode

7. *An Account of the Remarkable Occurrences in the Life and Travels of Colonel James Smith (Late a Citizen of Bourbon County, Kentucky): During His Captivity with the Indians, in the Years 1755, '56, '57, '58, and '59* (Lexington, Ky., 1799), 12–13; Elizabeth Carroll Reilly and David D. Hall, "Customers and the Market for Books," in Amory et al., eds., *History of the Book in America*, I, 395.
8. Smith, *Account*, 12.

of transporting them, as he set out on a hunting trip with an adoptive older brother: "All the pack I carried was a pouch, containing my books, a little dried venison, and my blanket." Early on in his account, however, this pouch with his books went missing at a seasonal camp at the Falls of the Canesadooharie River. Smith's companions suggested "the puppies had carried them off," but he suspected that "they were displeased at my poring over my books, and concluded that they had destroyed them, or put them out of my way." Smith's reference to the intensity with which he read, and his apparently unfounded perception that this activity infuriated the Indians, indicates that his practice of literacy was, in his view, a conscious rejection of his adoptive society. This significance became a basis for paranoia. As he observed them building a wooden structure, he feared for his life. He "concluded it was a gallows. I thought that I had displeased them by reading my books, and that they were about putting me to death." (The structure turned out to be a scaffold for drying furs.)[9]

At this juncture in the narrative, Smith was still lingering reluctantly at the threshold of participation in his adoptive society. Perhaps, in his ignorance of their perspective, it became easy to project his own onto them. He was attributing to the Indians an intolerance of other cultural practices and spirituality that was more characteristic of his natal society. Appropriately, he fantasized about a form of execution that was an Anglo-American cultural practice, temporarily arresting the transformation of the Indians within his own perception.

Months later, this barrier broke down. Smith's party returned to the camp, and a small group of Indians called him, using his "Indian name, which was Scoouwa," and showed him where they had found his books. This passage contains the only reference to his "Indian name" in the narrative: he acknowledges his adoptive identity only at the point where he recounts his captors' affirmation of his natal cultural identity through the restoration of his books. This moment is a turning point in his relationship with the Indians: "I told them that I thanked them for the kindness they had always shewn to me, and also for finding my books. They asked if the books were much damaged? I told them not much." They showed him how the pouch had rested against a tree in such a way as to "turn off the water," and he observed that the "print was not much injured, though the binding was." Smith comments: "This was the first time that I felt my

9. Ibid., 13, 28–29.

heart warm towards the Indians. Though they had been exceeding kind to me, I still before detested them, on account of the barbarity I beheld after Braddock's defeat." Somehow, the only act of "kindness" that got through to Smith was the restoration of his books, the antidote to "barbarity": "I began now to excuse the Indians on account of their want of information." By referring to the Indians' "want of information," Smith attributes their faults to their lack of exposure to scriptural revelation.[10]

Thus the books, particularly the English Bible, signify to Smith an advantage that he has and that they lack. Yet, despite his professed intentions as a narrator, he repeatedly fails to demonstrate the "deficiency of the light of nature." On the contrary, he exhibits his own deficiencies. If the *telos* of most captivity narratives is the captive's redemption or escape, the climactic sequence in Smith's narrative is a false start toward home, a flight from deprivation rather than from captivity. Smith, the only able hunter, resolved to head toward the settlement frontier, abandoning his adoptive elderly brother, Tecaughretanego, and nephew, Nunganey, to starvation in their winter camp, when he struck upon "fresh buffaloe tracks." His point of reference for his relief in a time of need is, not a "place" in scripture, as in Rowlandson's narrative, but a formal exhortation that Tecaughretanego had delivered, imparting the Christianlike sentiment that "Owaneeyo some times suffers us to be in want, in order to teach us our dependance [sic] upon him" and assuring him "that you will be supplied with food, and that just in the right time." After bingeing on half-raw bison, Smith "considered how remarkably the old man's speech had been verified in our providentially obtaining a supply" and chastised himself "for my base inhumanity, in attempting to leave them in the most deplorable situation." The ascription of "base inhumanity" to the narrator, rather than the Indians, is a startling inversion of the conventions of the captivity genre.[11]

Moreover, Smith's lesson in the sovereignty and goodness of Owaneeyo illustrates how far his narrative departs from the scriptural framework of early captivity narratives. He might have pored over Russell's *Seven Sermons* and the Bible, but he didn't construe himself as captive Israel, like Rowlandson; or Job, like Williams; or Joseph or Daniel, like John Marrant. Smith makes several references to the act of reading, but, as noted in the introduction, he makes only a single diegetic reference to a Bible

10. Ibid., 39–40.
11. Ibid., 91–94, 98.

passage relating to his captivity: fellow captive Arthur Campbell's invocation of Lamentations 3:27, "where it is said, 'It is good for a man that he bear the yoke in his youth.'" (Campbell's captivity might have fulfilled this scripture more than Smith's did.) Instead, the standard Smith attempted to live up to was that of his Kahnawake predecessor, the "great man" in "whose room" he had been adopted. In this respect, he was more like Marguerite Kanenstenhawi than like any of the other aforementioned captives, yet since he was captured at an older age he was less susceptible to transculturalization. He would not become a Kahnawake Mohawk man characterized by "great actions." When all the men "from fifteen to sixty years of age" marched off to do battle on the "frontiers of Virginia," no one remained behind "but squaws and children, except myself, one very old man, and another about fifty years of age, who was lame." Unlike Kanenstenhawi, he was unlikely to take the sort of bridge-burning step that would fulfill his name. He also retained his literacy practices.[12]

The only other reference in Smith's *Account* to a particular act of reading is in a represented exchange with Tecaughretanego that similarly showcases the Indian sage's moral superiority. Again, Smith started out on the wrong foot by smiling when Tecaughretanego was burning tobacco as a material sacrifice to the "Great Spirit." Tecaughretanego chastised him: "'You know that when you were reading your books in town, I would not let the boys or any one disturb you; but now when I was praying, I saw you laughing.'" Here Smith indicates that Tecaughretanego recognized his reading as a devotional practice. Smith apologized and explained "the method of reconciliation with an offended God, as revealed in my Bible, which I had then in possession." Tecaughretanego respectfully declined to change his ways. Moreover, he got the rain and success in the hunt that he asked for and was "fully persuaded that all this came in answer to his prayers—and who can say with any degree of certainty that it was not so?" Smith's efforts to vindicate his own religion seem half-hearted.[13]

Whereas the contest between scriptural revelation and the "light of Nature" concerned spiritual matters, Smith's account also showcases an opposition between book learning and empirical knowledge, in which the latter typically prevails. For instance, Tecaughretanego refuted a book

12. Ibid., 16, 46–47, 49, 66. On transculturalization, see A. Irving Hallowell, "American Indians, White and Black: The Phenomenon of Transculturalization," Papers in Honor of Melville J. Herskovits, *Current Anthropology*, IV (1963), 519–531.

13. Smith, *Account*, 97–100.

Smith had read that contended beavers eat fish. "He laughed, and made game of me and my book. He said the man that wrote that book knew nothing about the beaver." Smith performed an autopsy on a beaver "but found no appearance of fish . . . therefore I acknowledged that the book I had read was wrong." Smith actually prefaces his narrative with such a statement, explaining that, since he had "but a moderate English education," he had been advised "to employ some person of liberal education to transcribe and embellish" his journal. He declined, insisting, "Nature always outshines art." In other words, Smith asserts that his narrative is unmediated and unembellished. This disclaimer is a conventional avowal of truthfulness, yet, in the narrative that follows, "nature" does consistently outshine education. It contrasts with the narratives of Morris, Ridout, and Johnston, who styled themselves sophisticated and educated men and accordingly displayed no ambivalence about identifying themselves with book learning nor distancing themselves from their captors.[14]

"Shakespeare at the Foot of a Water-Fall"

Captain Thomas Morris was himself a "person of liberal education" and was thus equipped to embellish his own journal of his failed expedition to the Illinois Country, which, as noted above, is extant in two versions: one produced in the field and one revised and expanded years later. The point of divergence in their provenance was Morris's request to Thomas Mante (Colonel Bradstreet's aide) that he make a copy of the manuscript Morris had forwarded Bradstreet to apprise the colonel of the region's dire state of affairs. Bradstreet forwarded the original to his commanding officer, Major General Thomas Gage, who preserved it among his papers; it ultimately appeared in print in 1945 as a transcription. Morris himself received Mante's copy; "For many years," he claimed, it lay "in a chest among other papers, unseen either by myself or my friends." Eventually, Morris revised it and published it in *Miscellanies in Prose and Verse* (1791).[15]

Although Morris's revised journal is not necessarily less reliable than

14. Ibid., 3, 59. "As a rhetorical commonplace," Michael Householder points out, "the admission of stylistic clumsiness both masks and marks a writer's sophistication" (Householder, "American Mordecai: Scriptural Association and the Work of Remembering in Lion Gardiner's Relation of the Pequot Wars," *Early American Studies*, IX [2011], 417).

15. Howard H. Peckham, "The Journal of Captain Thomas Morris, 1764," *Old Fort News*, VI (1941), 3–4. Besides Peckham, Dowd is perhaps the only scholar to cross-reference the versions of Morris's journal (*War under Heaven*, 159–161; Morris, *Miscellanies*, iii).

the original manuscript, he might have embellished or colored in some details that would be particularly striking for his intended audience of urbane British readers.[16] One of the principal discrepancies between the transcription and the revised edition is regarding a transaction involving the Little Chief, Morris, and Morris's Canadian interpreter, Godefroi. In the manuscript, Morris wrote:

> The little chief made me a present of some melons, and offered to sell me a volume of Shakespear, wch I bought for a very little powder. He told Godefroi that he would send his son along with him.

He later revised the episode as follows:

> An Indian, called the little chief, told Godefroi that he would send his son with me, and made me a present of a volume of Shakespear's plays; a singular gift from a savage. He however begged a little gunpowder in return, a commodity to him much more precious than diamonds.[17]

In this instance, we see the editor at work, and the original does seem more credible. Morris appears to relish the incongruity of "Shakespear" in an Ottawa village and as a gift from an Indian, and he expects his readers to do the same. As a literary artist might do, he polishes his material. The Little Chief's sale of the volume of Shakespeare was already, literally, a noteworthy event. In the manuscript, the book is somewhere in a relation of values involving the melons, the Little Chief's son, and the gunpowder. Perhaps the "present" of the melons might not have merited recording if it had not been part of this sequence, as it did not survive revision. But the Little Chief's apparent willingness to risk the life of his son was magnanimous and presumably inestimable (notably, in the original, the son was sent with Godefroi, not Morris). Morris's revision transforms the presentation of the book into a gesture that is somehow eligible for grammatical juxtaposition (he "told Godefroi that he would send his son with me, and made me a present of a volume of Shakespear's plays") with the provision of an escort into hostile territory.[18]

16. Peckham points out: "The reperusal of his diary might very well have recalled certain details which he had not written down at the time" ("Journal of Captain Morris," *Old Fort News*, VI, no. 1 [1941], 4).

17. Ibid., 6; Morris, *Miscellanies*, 12.

18. The spelling "Shakespear" was prevalent during the mid-eighteenth century. See John

In Morris's subsequent representation, Shakespeare became his escort; the book was a magical talisman that shielded him from harm during his approach to the Miami fort, as discussed below. However, in principle, the gunpowder he exchanged for it would have been a more practical accoutrement. Each might have been a scarce "commodity" in Indian Country, but the gunpowder's value to the Little Chief was utilitarian, whereas the book's value to Morris was profoundly nonutilitarian. In this regard, it stands apart from the other media he describes, including wampum (about which he offers no ethnographic explanation for his uninformed readers) and letters. He mentions that Pontiac sent a "great belt, forty years old, on which were described two hundred and ten villages," and reports that the Miamis refused "some strings of wampum, on which the French had spoken to spare my life," deferring instead to a "deputation" of hostile Shawnees and Delawares bearing "fourteen belts and six strings." He disparages a letter sent to Pontiac from New Orleans, "written in French, full of the most improbable falsehoods, though beginning with a truth." The volume of Shakespeare was different from the wampum belt in that it did not represent terms that Morris either agreed to by accepting it or refused by rejecting it. The book was different from the letter in that its utterances were not subject to verification and falsification—they had a different sort of truth value, belonging to a sphere apart from politics and diplomacy (even as Shakespeare's plays were profuse with representations of political and diplomatic speech).[19]

Beyond its content, the book was also a tangible material good with exchange value. In that sense, it was like wampum. Depending on its quality, condition, and availability, it would have fetched a certain price in London and perhaps a higher one in Philadelphia; but in the Ottawa village where he encountered the Little Chief, there was little discernable market. Importantly, also like wampum, as a material medium, the book had an aesthetic value that was independent of its content, and the Little Chief himself might have prized it as such. At the same time, in asking Morris for "a commodity" that was "to him much more precious than dia-

Louis Haney, *The Name of William Shakespeare: A Study in Orthography* (Philadelphia, 1906), 38; Morris, *Miscellanies*, 12.

19. Of Morris, Gordon M. Sayre writes, "England's greatest dramatist . . . saved his skin" (*The Indian Chief as Tragic Hero: Native Resistance and the Literatures of America, from Moctezuma to Tecumseh* [Chapel Hill, N.C., 2005], 160); Morris, *Miscellanies*, 7, 13, 18. Richard Middleton describes St. Vincent as "a half-breed trader and onetime drummer in the French army" (Middleton, *Pontiac's War: Its Causes, Course, and Consequences* [New York, 2007], 158).

monds," the so-called "little chief" apparently recognized the value that Morris would put upon the book. He might not have been aware of the precise cultural capital of "Shakespear," but he knew that the volume of his plays had been a prized possession of its former owner—who had, after all, chosen to carry it with him, as a true luxury item, inessential to either his physical or spiritual welfare.[20]

The Little Chief might have recognized the arrival of a prospective customer, and he might have felt that he had the better end of the transaction by far. For Morris, however, the value of the book, accentuated in his revised account, was largely symbolic. The Little Chief had handed him a volume that was nearly as central to his discourse community as the Bible in the basket was to Rowlandson's. Shakespeare was the most powerful synecdoche for English letters, the cultural vanguard of "the advancing frontier." This symbolism is apparent in Morris's writing, but it might also have resonated in his experience. On the one hand, by reading the book he had obtained from the Little Chief and by composing a journal, Morris set himself apart from the backwoods: he performed the identity of a man of letters amid people whom he regarded as savages. He construed his expedition down the Maumee, as always, already a tale of adventure: he aestheticized his experience. On the other hand, by doing so, Morris also distinguished himself—perhaps only in his own perspective—within the London literate circle to which he aspired to belong. "If the world ever afforded me a pleasure equal to that of reading Shakespeare at the foot of a water-fall in an American desert," he wrote in the letter that follows his journal in *Miscellanies*, "it was Du Menil's performance of tragedy." His reference was to the French actress Marie-Françoise Dumesnil (1713–1803), who was famous, in part, for her interpretation of the role of Cléopâtre in Pierre Corneille's *Rodogune*.[21]

20. Morris, *Miscellanies*, 12. For relevant discussions of wampum, see Germaine Warkentin, "In Search of 'The Word of the Other': Aboriginal Sign Systems and the History of the Book in Canada," *Book History*, II (1999), 1–27; Gordon M. Sayre, *Les Sauvages Américains: Representations of Native Americans in French and English Colonial Literature* (Chapel Hill, N.C., 1997), 114–217; Lynn Ceci, "The Value of Wampum among the New York Iroquois: A Case Study in Artifact Analysis," *Journal of Anthropological Research*, XXXVIII (1982), 97–107. See Elizabeth Maddock Dillon's discussion of the cross-cultural aesthetic valuations of Morris's volume of Shakespeare in Dillon, "Atlantic Aesthesis: Books and *Sensus Communis* in the New World," *EAL*, LI (2016), 367–395.

21. Alden T. Vaughan and Virginia Mason Vaughan, *Shakespeare in America* (New York, 2012), 71, 119–120, 208; see also Helene Wickham Koon, *How Shakespeare Won the West: Players and Performances in America's Gold Rush, 1849–1865* (Jefferson, N.C., 1989); Morris, *Miscellanies*, 63.

Morris's reading of his volume of Shakespeare, in the *pays d'en haut*, might have been informed by his youthful exposure to the French theater. At age twenty-one, residing in Paris, he "constantly attended the French theatre for fifteen months," fulfilling a vow to his late father to "make myself master of the French language." Like many others, he was deeply impressed by Dumesnil. She epitomized the sublime: her performances "transported all who had feeling hearts." As an avid fan, Morris was probably familiar with an "anecdote" regarding Dumesnil's Cléopâtre: during one performance, infusing the part with "the burning energy with which her soul was consumed," she caused the audience to recoil, "leaving a great empty space between the front rows and the orchestra, as if to put themselves out of reach of her terrifying expression." This Cleopatra was a noble savagess figure, a personification of nature. The strong association between the character of Cleopatra and Morris's favorite actress might have directed his selection of a play to read in the volume he had acquired from the Little Chief; in turn, Shakespeare's Cleopatra would have been embodied in his imagination by the sublime Dumesnil. In this sense, reading Shakespeare (already the epitome of natural genius), specifically *Antony and Cleopatra*, by "the foot of a water-fall" (a conventional symbol of the natural sublime) would have been the *ne plus ultra* of aesthetic experience.[22]

In his published journal's only reference to actually reading Shakespeare, Morris makes no mention of a waterfall—instead, the sublime accompaniment is supplied by hostile Indians. Morris was floating idly in a stretch of "easy water" on the Maumee River when his party was "met at the bottom of the meadow by almost the whole [Miami] village, who had brought spears and tomahawks, in order to dispatch me; even little children had bows and arrows to shoot at the Englishman who was come among them"; Morris "had the good fortune to stay in the canoe, reading

22. Morris, *Miscellanies*, 45, 63. Sayre suggests, "It is tempting to imagine that [Morris's] fluent spoken French and even his French cultural tastes might have won over Pontiac and saved his life" (*Indian Chief as Tragic Hero*, 161); see also Parkman, *Conspiracy of Pontiac*, II, 186. Dumesnil "excelled in playing passionate roles, blazing her eyes, expanding her gestures, and crying" (Paul Kuritz, *The Making of Theatre History* [Englewood Cliffs, N.J., 1988], 217). "La brûlante énergie dont son ame était dévorée ... laissant ainsi un grand espace vide entre les premiers rangs et l'orchestre, comme pour se mettre hors de l'atteinte de ce regard qui le terrifiait": Jean-Baptiste Pierre Lafitte, *Mémoires de Fleury de la Comédie-française (1757 à 1820)*, 6 vols. (Paris, 1836–1838), I, 173.

the tragedy of Anthony *[sic]* and Cleopatra, in the volume of Shakespear which the little chief had given me, when the rest went on shore." It was Shakespeare, he implies, that kept him at a safe remove from the Miamis.[23]

If the association with Dumesnil was one prompt for his selection of *Antony and Cleopatra*, its correspondence to his circumstances on his mission might have been another. The geopolitical context for *Antony and Cleopatra*'s doomed love story is the attempted secession of the exotic fringe of a nominally conquered empire—a neat parallel to so-called rebellion led by the Ottawa chief Pontiac. With Egypt already long established as a type for the American wilderness, Cleopatra, upon whose "tawny front" the once noble Roman Antony has become enthralled, becomes a compelling personification for the temptation of a descent into barbarism. Antony accordingly would be a figure for Europeans—the French, perhaps—who succumbed to barbarous decadence. As Caesar recalls in act 1, scene 4, Antony once survived famine in the Alps "with patience more / Than savages could suffer"; he ate the "roughest berry on the rudest hedge" and "strange flesh" without losing the bearing of a "soldier." But now, with Cleopatra, he had become unmanned.[24]

Most important for Morris, the index of Antony's descent was his treatment of messengers. *Antony and Cleopatra* is a locus classicus for the notion of shooting the messenger and, accordingly, had specific relevance for Morris as the bearer of a letter to the commander of Fort Chartres and as an emissary carrying unwelcome word of French capitulation (through the Treaty of Paris) into Indian Country. When, in act 1, scene 2, a messenger arrives in Alexandria with "stiff news," Antony assures him of fair treatment: "Who tells me true, though in his tale lie death, / I hear him as he flattered." This policy contrasts with Cleopatra's abuse, in act 2, scene 5, of the messenger who brought her the news of Antony's engagement to Octavia; the messenger protests, "I that do bring the news, made not the match." Cleopatra strikes this messenger but forbears from having him whipped, setting up a contrast with Antony's behavior in act 3, when he

---

23. Morris, *Miscellanies*, 16–17.

24. William Shakespeare, *Antony and Cleopatra*, ed. Burton Raffel, The Annotated Shakespeare (New Haven, Conn., 2007), 30–31. According to Emory Elliott, writers in colonial New England "identified their leaders with Biblical figures, the Atlantic with the Red Sea, and the American wilderness as the howling deserts of Egypt" (Elliott, "The Emergence of the Literatures of the United States," in Paul Lauter, ed., *A Companion to American Literature and Culture* [Malden, Mass., 2010], 20).

catches a messenger from Octavius Caesar kissing Cleopatra's hand and does have him whipped.[25]

Morris's part in the war in the pays d'en haut is most analogous to that of this messenger, Thidias, who attempts to induce Cleopatra to renounce her relationship to Antony and put herself under Octavius Caesar's protection: "It would warm his spirit / To hear from me you had left Antony, / and put yourself under his shroud, / The Universal landlord" (act 3, scene 13). In this allegorical reading, Antony, Cleopatra, and Caesar correspond to the French, the Indians (particularly Pontiac), and the British, respectively. Morris hoped to induce the Indians to stop pinning their hopes on the defeated French and to accept a subservient position of "friendship" with the British. He explained to an Ottawa chief that Colonel Bradstreet had summoned the Indians to Detroit because he "sought their friendship" and handed the chief a letter from Bradstreet to that effect.[26]

The parallels between the play and Morris's situation might have heightened his sense that the events in which he was participating constituted a story, albeit without any notion of antitypal fulfillment. Shakespeare might not have been his "Guid by day" as the Bible was for Rowlandson, yet his reading might have shaped his perspective and, accordingly, his portrayal of the Indians, whose orations seem to resonate with the discourse of the play. Morris claimed that Pontiac made "a speech to the chiefs, who wanted to put me to death, which does him honour; and shews that he was acquainted with the law of nations: 'We must not,' said he, 'kill ambassadors: do we not send them to the Flatheads, our greatest enemies, and they to us? Yet these are always treated to hospitality.'" This rendition of Pontiac's speech is consonant with the image of him as a tragic hero, a great man who was not representative of the Indians generally. Perhaps even more exceptional was Pacanne, the young "king of the Miamis nation," who, according to Morris, came forward and untied him from a stake, telling his tribesmen: "'If you want meat (for they sometimes eat their prisoners) go to Detroit, or upon the lake (meaning go face your enemies the English) and you'll find enough. What business have you with this man's flesh, who is come to speak to us?'" The account in the manu-

25. Shakespeare, *Antony and Cleopatra*, 13–14, 63, 66. On the prominent theme of messengers in *Antony and Cleopatra*, see Richard Madelaine, "'What Are You?' The Staging of Messenger-Function in Antony and Cleopatra," *Parergon*, XXV, no. 1 (2008), 149–170.

26. Shakespeare, *Antony and Cleopatra*, 122; Peckham, "Journal of Captain Morris," *Old Fort News*, VI (1941), 6.

script is nearly identical to the one in the published journal, but, at best, it is a subjective representation of what must have been a bewildering colonial encounter, based on an interpreter's subsequent translation and explanation of what had occurred. Morris's subjectivity emerged from his cultural education, including, quite possibly, his reading of *Antony and Cleopatra*.[27]

Morris follows the account of Pacanne's intervention with an allusion to a literary protagonist whose characteristic trait was a perspective warped by literature. Abused but not tortured, Morris repaired to the fort on the other side of the river. There, "Two very handsome young Indian women"—Pacanne's sisters—arrived to inquire after his welfare. "Happy Don Quixote," Morris wrote in the revised journal, "attended by princesses!" This is a conventional extradiegetic allusion, a gesture to a shared point of reference, and therefore to a community. It is also rich with implications, not necessarily intentional or even recognized. On the one hand, it can be read as a disparagement of Pacanne's sisters, suggesting that they were, not princesses at all, but more like the innkeeper's wife and daughter and the hideous Asturian damsel, "the compassionate Maritornes," who visited the wounded knight-errant in the inn he mistook for a castle. On the other hand, it is a self-deprecating reference to Morris himself. He was, after all, on a quixotic mission. More important, Don Quixote is the classical instance of a protagonist who is unable to separate reality from literary formulae. In this episode, even Morris's diction is Cervantean. The women "seemed to compassionate me extremely," he wrote. They asked Godefroi—Morris's Sancho Panza—"a thousand questions" concerning his welfare.[28]

If Morris, like Don Quixote, viewed his circumstances through the lens of literature—in his case, casting Pacanne, Pontiac, and other Indians as players in a Shakespearean tragedy unfolding in a colonial theater of war—he might also have "unwittingly" played a part in a native American "drama." Like other last-moment reprieves, including the famous one involving John Smith and Pocahontas, this one might have been a staged performance. Pacanne's mother might have orchestrated it, perhaps with the involvement of his half-sister, Tacumwah, one of the two women who

27. *SGG*, 90; Morris, *Miscellanies*, 10, 22; Peckham, "Journal of Captain Morris," *Old Fort News*, VI (1941), 4; and see Sayre, *Indian Chief as Tragic Hero*.

28. Morris, *Miscellanies*, 23; Miguel de Cervantes Saavedra, *The History of the Valorous and Witty Knight-Errant Don Quixote of the Mancha* (Basingstoke, U.K., 1908), 125.

later visited Morris. Morris's arrival might have provided a pretext for "a public act of authority" to mark the young Pacanne's assumption of the "head chieftainship," which transferred from the incumbent to his maternal nephew.[29]

Morris would have been ignorant of such machinations, but from his point of view, Shakespeare's *Antony and Cleopatra* presents such an apt allegory for Pontiac's War and his own expedition that his interpolation of that particular play into his narrative seems contrived. Morris might have chosen to embellish his account with a point of reference that his cosmopolitan readers in 1790 would have known well, although they would have had limited knowledge, at best, of its relevance to what they would have perceived as an obscure, backcountry aftershock of the Seven Years' War. If Morris did invent the detail that he was reading *Antony and Cleopatra* upon his approach to the Miami fort, it would have been a different sort of allusion than the one to *Don Quixote,* planted in the diegesis rather than exegesis: that is, the reader envisions the protagonist in a canoe holding the book rather than imagining the author in his study glancing at it while composing his narrative. If we take his narration at face value, however, then even as he physically journeyed within the storyworld of his own narrative, he might have imaginatively explored that of *Antony and Cleopatra,* similarly to earlier captives who found themselves transported to the "Rivers of Babylon." His circumstances might have informed his selection of that play to read, in the same way that Rowlandson's directed her attention (guided by God) to appropriate passages in the Old Testament, albeit without scripting his actions in the same way. If, for example, he held in his hands the third volume of the 1734 edition of *The Dramatick Works of William Shakespear,* he might have found *Antony and Cleopatra,* the first of the listed plays, also to be the most pertinent (Figure 6). As he floated down the Maumee River, he would have been simultaneously in

29. "Years later," according to Karen Marrero, "Tacumwah would take advantage of a similar situation in arranging for the rescue of a grateful American captive by her son Jean Baptiste Richardville, thus ensuring her son's smooth succession to the chieftainship of his uncle Pacanne" (Marrero, "'She Is Capable of Doing a Good Deal Of Mischief': A Miami Woman's Threat to Empire in the Eighteenth-Century Ohio Valley," *Journal of Colonialism and Colonial History,* VI, no. 3 [Winter 2005], paras. 21, 23); see also Carter, *Life and Times of Little Turtle,* 68; and see Laura L. Mielke's reading of the Pocahontas episode in John Smith's *Generall Historie* (Mielke, "Introduction," in Joshua David Bellin and Mielke, eds., *Native Acts: Indian Performance, 1603–1832* [Lincoln, Neb., 2012], 1–4, 35).

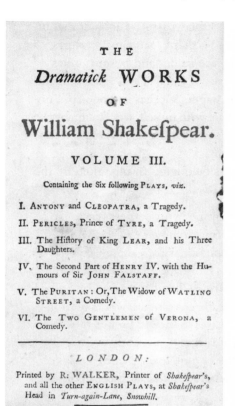

Figure 6 Title page of *The Dramatick Works of William Shakespear,* III (London, 1734), and frontispiece depicting the death of Cleopatra. By permission of the British Library, General Reference Collection 11762.aa.5

the ancient Mediterranean, his consciousness forming a nexus between disparate continents and between history and literature.[30]

A Captive Library

Thomas Ridout, the future surveyor general of Upper Canada, arrived in North America in 1787 as a thirty-something merchant gentleman. In 1788, he set out for Kentucky, via the Ohio River, bearing "£300 or £400 worth

---

30. *The Dramatick Works of William Shakespeare,* 7 vols., III (London, 1734).

of merchandise." His posthumously published narrative includes an inventory of these goods transcribed from his diary, featuring "27 shirts; 28 stocks; 26 pocket-handkerchiefs; 1 pair lace ruffles and bosom ruffles"; a "hair powder bag"; portable writing desks of English and French manufacture; a "portmanteau, containing my papers, clothes and books." Concludes Ridout: "The above things, together with myself, were taken by the Shawanese near the falls of the Ohio." His language seems to acknowledge his own objectification as plunder.[31]

Ridout gave a separate "list of books belonging to me taken by the Indians":

> A Bible, once my mother's, and read by me in my earliest years; Thompson's works, elegantly bound, four volumes; Chesterfield's Letters, four volumes; Posthlewaite's dictionary of Commerce, two volumes; Lex Mercatoria; Ainsworth's Latin and English dictionaries; Italian, Latin and French dictionaries; Chambaud's English and French dictionaries; Life of Petrarque, three volumes; works of Montesquieu, three volumes; Plutarque's Lives in the old French of Amyot; translation in French of Homer, eight volumes, elegantly bound; Corneille's Tragedies, in French, elegantly bound, five volumes; Essays of Montaigne, French, ten volumes; Rochefoucaulds. Of these books the Bible alone was returned.[32]

Here was an exemplary, conventional, and aspirational English gentleman's bookshelf—captive. Ridout lists the books categorically. A family Bible; two relatively recent British publications: the works of the eighteenth-century Scottish poet James Thomson, author of the poem "Rule, Britannia," and the fourth earl of Chesterfield's immensely popular *Letters to His Son on the Art of Becoming a Man of the World and a Gentleman* (1774); two mercantilist texts, George de Malynes's foundational *Consuetudo vel Lex Mercatoria* and the popular handbook Malachy Postlethwayt's *Universal Dictionary of Trade;* an assortment of reference books; and classical and French literary and philosophical works befitting a "Man of the World and a Gentleman." For example, Chesterfield advises his son: "Till you come to know mankind by your own experience, I know no thing, nor no man, that can in the mean time bring you so well acquainted with them

---

31. Thomas Ridout, *Ten Years of Upper Canada in Peace and War, 1805–1815: Being the Ridout Letters . . .* , ed. Lady Matilda Ridout Edgar (Toronto, 1890), 340, 346.
32. Ridout, *Ten Years of Upper Canada,* 346.

as le Duc de la Rochefoucauld: his little book of Maxims, which I would advise you to look into, for some moments at least, every day of your life." In this way, Ridout's captured books composed a set. Such book inventories would become a commonplace of frontier writing, a sort of bibliographic metonymy, where the bookshelf symbolizes the self, as participants in literary culture journeyed westward.[33]

As Ridout's notice of the "elegantly bound" editions suggests, his books were not only "objects of knowledge transfer" but also material goods with exchange value. That Ridout's captors recognized the worth of his collection is evident in their decision to restore to him the one edition whose value was strictly sentimental—the "family Bible I had read in when a child," which was in his possession when he composed his retrospective narrative "and has the covering which my dear mother sewed on it about the year 1766." Their restoration of his Bible to him is also consistent with the provision of Bibles in other captivity narratives: the only distinction between the Bible an Indian brought Mary Rowlandson from the "Medfield fight" and the one the Shawnees gave to Ridout is that it had previously belonged to him.[34]

Ridout's books were among the accoutrements that helped the Indians to recognize him, as well, as a valuable commodity. He was probably too mature to be eligible for adoption and integration into the tribe, and too wealthy to be subjected to torture and execution; he would be able to pay his own ransom, and at the outset of his captivity, a white man

33. Philip Dormer Stanhope Chesterfield, *Letters Written by the Late Right Honourable Philip Dormer Stanhope, Earl of Chesterfield, to His Son, Philip Stanhope, Esq. . . . ,* IV (Paris, 1789), 53. For examples of book inventories, see Vaughan and Vaughan, *Shakespeare in America,* 53, 75. For later instances, see Thomas C. Russell, ed., *The Shirley Letters from California Mines in 1851–52: Being a Series of Twenty-Three Letters from Dame Shirley (Mrs. Louise Amelia Knapp Smith Clappe) to Her Sister in Massachusetts* (San Francisco, Calif., 1922), 100; Frederick Anderson, ed., *Mark Twain's Notebooks and Journals,* I, *1855–1873* (Berkeley, Calif., 1975), 70, 70n. According to Ann C. Dean, Chesterfield's *Letters to His Son* "went through eight editions in its first year from publishers in London and Dublin, and by 1800 had been published in Edinburgh, Boston, Paris, Philadelphia, and Vienna, as well as continuing to appear in editions in London" (Dean, "Authorship, Print, and Public in Chesterfield's Letters to His Son," *Studies in English Literature, 1500–1900,* XLV [2005], 691); on Malynes and Postlethwayt, see Julian Hoppit, "The Contexts and Contours of British Economic Literature, 1660–1760," *Historical Journal,* XLIX (2006), 103–104. The works by Montaigne, Thomson, Malynes, Ainsworth, and Postlethwayt are all listed in Walter B. Edgar's study of book inventories: "Some Popular Books in Colonial South Carolina," *South Carolina Historical Magazine,* LXXII (1971), 174–178.

34. Germaine Warkentin, "Dead Metaphor or Working Model? 'The Book' in Native America," in Matt Cohen and Jeffrey Glover, eds., *Colonial Mediascapes: Sensory Worlds of the Early Americas* (Lincoln, Neb., 2014), 2; Ridout, *Ten Years of Upper Canada,* 356–357.

"who had been taken prisoner when a lad and had been adopted, and was now a chief among the Shawanese" assured him that he'd be brought to Detroit and given the opportunity to redeem himself. According to his account, individual Shawnees subsequently attempted to take his life, but he was always protected, and he helped himself by insisting that he was English, not American, and therefore not an avowed enemy in the Northwest Indian War. His proof of nationality was in his papers, which the Shawnees examined with the assistance of "an interpreter, a white man, who several years before had been taken prisoner." They might have similarly used interpreters to understand the books they were collecting.[35]

The Shawnees added the books they took from Ridout to others they had previously acquired to assemble a small, transient lending library. Wrote Ridout, referring to Kakinathucca, the Shawnee chief who held him for ransom: "To divert my solitary hours my Indian friend used to bring me books to read, some which had belonged to me." Among these books, Ridout especially appreciated one that had not been in his inventory: "the first edition of Telemachus in French, printed in Holland, with notes marking the living characters for whom the imaginary personages in that excellent work were intended." Ridout was referring to François de Salignac de la Mothe Fenelon's political allegory *Les aventures de Télémaque* (1699, 1717). The copy the Shawnees handed to him might have been from the edition printed in 1725 in Rotterdam, an ornate book that included twenty-four full-page prints and a folded engraved map, a gorgeous object whose aesthetic appeal was hardly confined to its literary content.[36]

Yet, as the Shawnees might have realized, the book would have had significance for Ridout that was not directly accessible to them. Fenelon used the story of the travels of Telemachus, son of Odysseus, to pose an allegorical critique of the absolute monarchy of Louis XIV (who accordingly banished Fenelon from Versailles), but its applicability outlived the context of its composition: its allegorical function was readily generalizable, referring to governments in different times and places. It was a seminal text of the French Enlightenment and was a very popular work in France, in Britain (whose system of constitutional monarchy it seemed to espouse), and in the British colonies. It had been commended by Montesquieu and

35. Ridout, *Ten Years of Upper Canada*, 348, 359.

36. Ibid., 356; François de Salignac de La Mothe-Fénelon and H. P. de Limiers, *Les avantures de Télémaque, fils d'Ulysse* (Rotterdam, 1725).

was a favorite of Thomas Jefferson. Ridout, reading in captivity, likely allegorized himself, just as so many previous captive authors had done with reference to biblical captivity stories.[37]

Ridout would have found the parallels in book 2 of *Télémaque* to be especially compelling. Here, Telemachus recounts to Dido the narrative of his captivity in Egypt. Just as Ridout's American boat on the Ohio had been boarded by hostile Shawnees, so Telemachus's Phoenician boat had been boarded by hostile Egyptians. Just as Ridout was at pains to declare that he was British, not American, and therefore not an enemy of the Indians, so Telemachus and Mentor attempted to prove that they were Greek, not Phoenician, and therefore not enemies of the Egyptians. Just as Ridout had to contend with "a black man, about twenty-five years of age, called Boatswain (or Boosini)"—an "exceedingly insolent" servant of Kakinathucca, whose "lies and artifices" posed the "greatest danger" to him—so Telemachus, condemned to pastoral servitude in the desert, with "nobody in this country but shepherds as savage as the desert itself," was confronted by "the brutal fury of the first slave who, in hopes of obtaining his liberty, incessantly accused the rest." The parallels are so forceful as to create interference, raising the possibility that Ridout's account of his captivity was partly modeled after his reading of *Télémaque*.[38]

For Ridout, perhaps the most resonant such parallel would have been to reading itself. Although Ridout was thankful that his captor brought him books "to divert my solitary hours," Telemachus recounted to Calypso how he had sought books to "better to support the chagrin of captivity and solitude." Telemachus explained to Calypso that, without books, "I was overwhelmed with melancholy for want of some instruction to nourish my mind, and to sustain it." The character then launches into a didactic encomium of the pleasures of reading, including these sentiments: "Happy are those who find amusement in search of instruction and take pleasure in cultivating their understanding with science! Wheresoever they are thrown by adverse fortune, they still carry along with them a fund of entertainment; and that chagrin that preys on other men even in

37. Douglas L. Wilson, "Thomas Jefferson's Library and the French Connection," *Eighteenth-Century Studies*, XXVI (1993), 673–674. It was listed in 17 of the 438 libraries surveyed by Edgar (*Paradise Lost* appears in 20). See Edgar, "Some Popular Books in Colonial South Carolina," *South Carolina Historical Magazine*, LXXII (1971), 175.

38. Ridout, *Ten Years of Upper Canada*, 354; François de Fénelon, *Telemachus, Son of Ulysses*, ed. Patrick Riley (Cambridge, 1994), 20.

the midst of pleasures, is unknown to those who can employ themselves with reading. Happy are those who love reading, and are not, like me, deprived of books!" Whereas Ridout's supplier of books was his principal captor, Telemachus, fresh from his soliloquy about reading, wandered into a forest, where he met an ancient priest of Apollo: "All of a sudden, I beheld an old man with a book in his hand." In *Télémaque,* a book handed to him by a Shawnee Indian, Ridout would have read and seen depictions of an indigenous person presenting a European captive with a book (Figure 7).[39]

Ridout does not refer to the content of *Telemachus,* but if he started at the beginning, he would have consumed these passages in his first sitting: one captive reader reading about another. He would have learned how the priest Termosiris inspired Telemachus to improve his circumstances by emulating the example of Apollo. "Like him," the priest enjoined, "make the desert flourish, and teach all those shepherds the charms of harmony; soften their savage hearts; display the amiable side of virtue, and make them feel how happy it is to enjoy, amidst their solitude, those innocent pleasures which nothing can deprive them of." Accordingly, Telemachus used music to convene the rough pastoral community: "Nothing savage now appeared amidst those deserts. All was agreeable and smiling: the lands themselves seemed to improve in proportion as the inhabitants were civilized." Applying the allegory, Ridout could have fantasized about civilizing his own captors.[40]

In July 1790, after about four months, Kakinathucca brought Ridout to Detroit to be ransomed. Having ventured westward to sell goods, Ridout himself had been subjected to commodification and transacted back eastward. In his narrative, however, his experience of objectification is contrasted by his representation of subjectivity as a reader and, implicitly, by his voice as a writer. Surely, like Smith and Morris, he represents an experience as a reader that is dramatically different from those of virtually all the other participants in his discourse community and yet is representative of a common language ideology, a shared belief in participation in literary culture as evidence of the utmost realization of human potential. Moreover, perhaps as Morris did with *Antony and Cleopatra,* with *Télémaque* Ridout might have had an experience unlike that of virtually any other

39. Fénelon, *Telemachus,* ed. Riley, 21–22.
40. Ibid., 24.

Termosiris console Telemaque dans son esclavage.

Figure 7 Termosiris, the priest of Apollo, handing the captive
Telemachus a book. Engraving from *Les avantures de
Télémaque, fils d'Ulysse* (Amsterdam, 1725), "Termosiris consoles
Telemachus in his enslavement." Courtesy of the Rare Book
Collection, Kislak Center, University of Pennsylvania

reader of a popular text. Of course, even within an interpretive community, no two individual readings of a given text can be identical. Yet, as participants in the communities of interpreters surrounding Shakespeare and
Fenelon, Morris and Ridout, in the particular contingent circumstances
recounted in their narratives, were assuredly outliers.[41]

41. Stanley Eugene Fish, *Is There a Text in This Class? The Authority of Interpretive Communities* (Cambridge, Mass., 1980).

"The Book in Which I Kept My Journal"

If, while Ridout was a captive, his books were in some sense material emblems of his civilized self, a different sort of book represented his captive self after his redemption. He recounts how his "mistress," Kakinathucca's wife, was fond of tea; with the wrapping paper ("tea paper"), he "made a book, stitched it with the bark of a tree, and with yellow ink of hickory ashes, mixed with a little water, and a pen made with a turkey quill, I wrote down the Indian names of visible objects" (Figure 8). He made two such books. In 1890, when his granddaughter Lady Matilda Ridout Edgar edited his captivity narrative for publication, she had one of these books in her possession. "This book still remains in good preservation," she observes in a footnote, "to testify to Mr. Ridout's ingenuity." She also, apparently, had access to Ridout's "Diary,–a little book restored to him by the Indians," which belonged to another Ridout descendant, his namesake Thomas Ridout, of Ottawa. The journal was a record of his captivity, and also—having passed through the hands of his captors—an artifact of it.[42]

Like Ridout, Charles Johnston—then nineteen or twenty—was captured by Shawnees on the Ohio River in 1790; he was traveling to Kentucky as the clerk of the lawyer John May, "a gentleman of great worth and respectability." This status indicates that Johnston had had more formal education than James Smith, for example, but that he did not have access to the sort of cultural capital represented by Morris's education in the French theater or Ridout's book collection. Like these other captives, Johnston kept a journal. For a young clerk starting out in life, this literacy practice might have been conventional, but Johnston's circumstances—beginning with the radical alteration in his prospects occasioned by the Shawnee ambush and the death of his employer "by a ball shot through his brain"—veered drastically from the mundane.[43]

The significance of Johnston's journaling as a performance of language ideology is apparent in his narrative's juxtaposition of the Shawnees' pas-

42. Ridout, *Ten Years of Upper Canada*, 360, 370.

43. Charles Johnston, *A Narrative of Capture, Detention, and Ransom*, Garland Library of Narratives of North American Indian Captivities, XLIII (1827; rpt. New York, 1975), 16. On American clerks and their diaries in the nineteenth century (I'm assuming some continuity from the late eighteenth), see Thomas Augst, *The Clerk's Tale: Young Men and Moral Life in Nineteenth-Century America* (Chicago, 2003); see also Michael Zakim, "The Business Clerk as Social Revolutionary; or, A Labor History of the Nonproducing Classes," *Journal of the Early Republic*, XXVI (2006), 563–603.

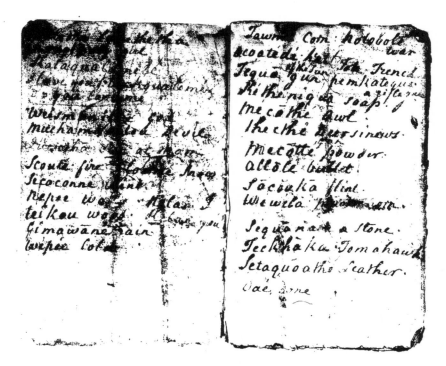

Figure 8 Page from Thomas Ridout's handwritten Shawnee-English Dictionary. Microfilm, courtesy of the Archives of Ontario

times beside his own. In the fourth chapter, having calmed down from his "apprehensions" of an immediate death, Johnston adopts the posture of cultural observer, remarking on the Shawnees' "habit of daily lounging" and describing "Nosey," a card game in which the winner was entitled to administer "fillips" (finger-flicks) to the nose of the loser. "It is astonishing to what an excess they were delighted with this childish diversion. After two had played for some time, others would take their places, and the game was often continued for hour after hour." Johnston's prose is redolent with his sense of the moral superiority of his cultural practices: "While the Indians were employed in this amusement," he writes, "I endeavoured to begin, and intended to keep, a journal of my travels." As Ridout did with his tea-paper notebook, Johnston improvised his materials. He wrote in the margins of a "copy of the Debates of the Convention of Virginia, assembled to decide on the adoption or rejection of the Federal Constitution"—a volume he had salvaged from a plundered boat on the Ohio "to serve as a source of amusement." He fashioned a pen from a turkey quill, and furnishing himself "with ink by mixing water and coal dust together," he began, as he recounts in the language of his profession, to keep "daily minutes of our progress and its incidents." His writing "attracted the attention, but did not excite the disquiet, of the Indians." His captors passed the book around. "They seemed gratified and surprised at what indicated, in their opinion, something extraordinary about me, which, however, they could not comprehend." Like Smith, Johnston imagined his literary practices through the eyes of his captors.[44]

Thus, while the Shawnees played Nosey, Johnston, writing in the margins of the "Debates of the Virginia Convention," kept company with agents of Enlightenment. His book was likely a copy of *Debates and Other Proceedings of the Convention of Virginia* (1788), "to which is prefixed the Federal constitution" (Figure 9). In Johnston's use, this book showcased the rationality of Johnston's United States, weighing their governance against the Indians' lack thereof. Johnston's palimpsestic journal keeping put him on common, civilized ground with American statesmen. An implicit contrast is to Peggy Fleming, a fellow captive who was allotted to the Cherokees, and who to Johnston's amazement seemed at first to be delighted with the prospect of her captivity: "She enjoyed a high flow of spirits;—and, indeed, I had never seen anyone who appeared to be more contented and happy." Johnston met her again after his redemption (and before hers): "Her stay with us was only for a few hours, during which time, I could not extract a word from her, except occasionally the monosyllables *yes* and *no*." She had undergone a complete revolution: she was emaciated, despondent, and literally speechless.[45]

Johnston had made his book, a compendium of exemplary enlightened discourse, supplemented by his own coal-ink inscriptions, into a personal

44. *A Narrative of the Incidents Attending the Capture, Detention, and Ransom of Charles Johnston . . .* (New York, 1975), 20, 29–32.

45. Ibid., 33, 65. Johnston's use of literacy corresponds to David Sewell's formulation, according to which captivity authors write to demonstrate the retention of their "strong language," and to offset the lack of control over their experience by controlling its representation. As Sewell points out, Johnston's journal keeping made this process liminal rather than retroactive. See "'So Unstable and Like Mad Men They Were': Language and Interpretation in Early American Captivity Narratives," in Frank Shuffelton, ed., *A Mixed Race: Ethnicity in Early America* (New York, 1993), 42–43. See also *Debates and Other Proceedings of the Convention of Virginia, Convened at Richmond, on Monday the 2d Day of June, 1788, for the Purpose of Deliberating on the Constitution Recommended by the Grand Federal Convention: To Which Is Prefixed, the Federal Constitution*, 3 vols. (Petersburg, Va., 1788–1789).

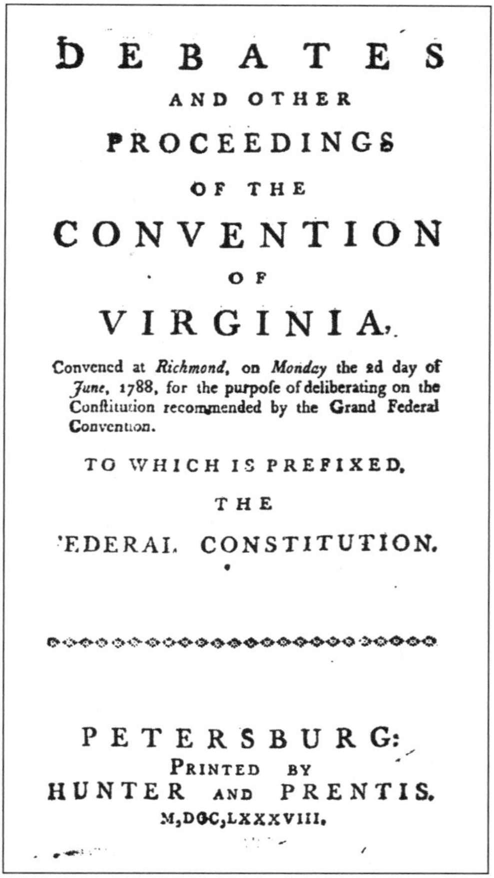

> # D E B A T E S
> ### AND OTHER
> ## PROCEEDINGS
> #### OF THE
> # C O N V E N T I O N
> #### O F
> # V I R G I N I A,
>
> Convened at *Richmond,* on *Monday* the 2d day of
> *June,* 1788, for the purpose of deliberating on the
> Constitution recommended by the Grand Federal
> Convention.
>
> ### TO WHICH IS PREFIXED,
>
> ### THE
>
> ### 'EDERAL CONSTITUTION.
>
> ◆◇◆◇◇◇◆◇◆◇◇◆◆◆◆◆◇◆◇◇◇◆◇◆◇◆
>
> ## P E T E R S B U R G:
> #### PRINTED BY
> ## HUNTER AND PRENTIS.
> #### M,DCC,LXXXVIII.

Figure 9 Title page of *Debates and Other Proceedings of the Convention of Virginia, Convened at Richmond, on Monday the 2d Day of June, 1788 . . .* (Petersburg, Va., 1788), Early American Imprints, Ser. 1, no. 21551. Reproduced with permission of Readex, a division of NewsBank, Inc.

totem. This function is illustrated by a sequence of loss and restoration, fear and reassurance, as in Smith's narrative. Near the end of his captivity, Johnston lost his book after his Shawnee captors temporarily transferred possession of him to a "Mingo Indian" and then, in an angry confrontation, appeared to reclaim him. The Shawnees brought him to a village, where he appealed to the Canadian trader Francis Duchouquet to redeem him. His captors refused Duchouquet's offers, though; the "failure of this negotiation" drove Johnston to despondency. "All the terrors of a cruel death, inflicted by merciless savages, ingenious in the invention and practice of torture, recurred to my imagination, and filled me with despair." This moment seems at least partly a contrivance. The narrative of the "incidents" of his captivity never quite substantiates the characterization of the Indians as "merciless savages"; it is as if, on the cusp of his redemption, he is invoking the familiar conventions of the captivity narrative genre.[46]

The passage appears at the close of his seventh chapter, setting up a sudden change of fortune at the beginning of the eighth. There, he reports the return of "the Mingo Indian"; recalling his dispute with his Shawnee captors, Johnston feared that "his views were not propitious to my safety; and I was disposed to avoid him. My fears, however, were entirely dispelled, when, on his approach towards me, he drew from his bosom the book in which I had kept my journal, and presented it to me with a smiling face." Johnston could scarcely have attributed to him a more reassuring gesture.[47]

Yet this book presentation did not seem to carry quite the significance for Johnston that the Kahnawakes' recovery of his books did for Smith. Somehow, finally on his "homeward route," Johnston again left his journal behind. "If I had brought it with me," he later wrote, "according to my intentions and wishes, my narrative would probably have been more minute, and my record would have supplied many things, for which I now draw, in vain, on my memory." Apparently, however, as a redeemed captive, he did not find the use he might make of his journal as an author to be a compelling enough rationale to keep hold of it—it was as if it had served its purpose in guiding him through his captivity.[48]

As a symbolic interaction, the Mingo Indian's restoration of Johnston's journal receives more emphasis in an alternative account of his captivity, published by François Alexandre Fréderic, duc de La Rochefoucauld-Liancourt, in his *Voyage dans les États Unis d'Amérique* (1799). Johnston explained that he was motivated to compose and publish his account only because of this "extremely incorrect and imperfect" version. He had met La Rochefoucauld, a descendant of the author of Ridout's book of maxims, in exile from revolutionary France, on a transatlantic voyage in 1793, and told him his story of captivity. There is indeed a lot of variance between the two versions, and Johnston's is more authoritative. However, the duke's briefer account gives an idea about which details Johnston featured in his oral history and which came across the language barrier ("he spoke the English language very imperfectly, and I was utterly ignorant

46. Johnston, *Narrative of the Incidents*, 58.
47. Ibid., 96.
48. Ibid.

of the French"). Although he apparently misconstrued some of the circumstances, the duke made much of the restoration of Johnston's book—"a code of laws of Virginia that his masters had allowed him during his journey." It was the sort of gesture of civility that would have been rare in a civilized country, "even among Europeans"; it marked the close of Johnston's ordeal, heralding "a complete security." There was, perhaps, no act that could annul the barbarity and violence associated with Indian captivity (or, La Rouchefoucauld hints, with the Reign of Terror) as the presentation of a book.[49]

But this particular book, unlike, for example, Ridout's copy of *Télémaque*, did not allow for the incorporation of supposedly savage peoples into its imagined discourse community. The federal Constitution apportioned representation and taxation by adding up "free persons," indentured servants, and, infamously, "three fifths all other persons"—chattel slaves—but excluded "Indians not taxed"; the debates over its adoption invoked the threat of "the inroads and depredations" of the "savage Indians." Johnston's handwritten marginalia, presumably, concurred with this characterization. His narrative, published in 1827, contributed to the case for Indian Removal, and its conventional, derivative appendix on "Indian Character and Manners"—allowing that in isolated instances Indians might be "susceptible of civilization"—opined, "To reform them by tribes, or by nations, is an enterprise not so easily achieved." Of the four authors, Johnston was the most fervent exponent of the language ideology whereby his literacy practices marked an insuperable, essential difference between himself and the Indians.[50]

Conclusion

The representations of book presentations analyzed in this chapter are a seeming counterpoint to the "trope of the Talking Book" discussed in the preceding one. In one set of depictions, the non-European others evince naïve, awestruck responses to colonial literacy practices; in the other, they

49. Ibid., iv. "Un code des loix de la Virginie, qui lui avait été laissé par ses maîtres pendant la voyage"; "recherché meme parmi les Européens"; "une entire sécurité": François-Alexandre-Frédéric La Rochefoucauld-Liancourt, *Voyage dans les États-Unis d'Amérique, fait en 1795, 1796, et 1797*, I (Paris, 1799), 347–348.

50. *Debates and Other Proceedings of the Convention of Virginia*, I, 3, 137, 158; Johnston, *Narrative of the Incidents*, 254–255.

express familiarity and even kindness, and the colonists themselves exhibit unfounded fears. Arguably, for all the authors, whether of early colonial relations, slave narratives, or captivity narratives, the significance of
these depictions is much the same: they reaffirm the identification with
and mastery of the written word that is also expressed through the act of
authorship. Yet one reason that the term "trope," or any other term in the
lexicon of literary studies, is inadequate is because these representations
refer to actualities of colonial contact. They are literary representations of
apparent symbolic interactions, and the significances of the representation and event are not necessarily coincident, nor did the event have the
same meaning for all the participants.[51]

   If the book presentation did not originate as a trope, it became one. In
a culminating sequence of Kevin Costner's 1990 film *Dances with Wolves*,
which is based on a novel by Michael Blake, the Lakota youth Smiles A Lot
rescues the journal of John Dunbar (aka Dances With Wolves) from the
river. Smiles A Lot first "holds the book close to his face amazed at the
sight of words" and then rides up to restore it to Dances With Wolves.
The gesture signals that, despite taking the bridge-burning step of joining the Sioux in killing U.S. soldiers—bad men, whose willingness to defile
books is as much an index of their nature as their Indian hating—Dunbar
will not become an Indian. Instead, he will remain part of the community
implied by the repeated scenes of journal writing and voice-over narration—a community, comprising the film's audience, premised on shared
moral values including a common language ideology.[52]

   The appearance of this book restoration in the hackneyed plot of a
"white savior" film illustrates its persistent function as a symbolic device.
In colonial narratives, book restorations and presentations similarly operated as rhetorical figures. They were an update on the earlier representations of indigenous encounters with European literacy. If John Smith's
depiction of the Powhatans' "wonder" at his written communication signified, to his readers, the superiority of their communication technology

   51. Henry Louis Gates, Jr., *The Signifying Monkey: A Theory of African-American Literary Criticism* (New York, 1988), 127–169.
   52. Michael Blake, "Dances with Wolves," screenplay (May 23, 1989), 125. According to Jim
Collins, Dunbar's journal "serves as a guarantee of the authenticity of his position as ethnog-
rapher and as a symbol of his difference from other white men—a point made especially obvious when his journal is literally used as toilet paper by a pair of the most repulsive cavalrymen"
(Collins, "Genericity in the Nineties: Eclectic Irony and the New Sincerity," in Collins, Hilary
Radner, and Ava Collins, eds., *Film Theory Goes to the Movies* [New York, 1993], 257).

and the fundamental alterity of America's natives, the representations of Indians' handing a white man a book signify the native peoples' affirmation of that difference—and perhaps imply their acknowledgment of inferiority.[53]

In the context of colonial encounters, however, the Indians themselves were the authors of these symbolic interactions, the book presentations. Their motives might have been varied and contingent, but these several representations allow for general inferences about indigenous perceptions of literacy practices during the colonial period (as opposed to early contact situations). Because of his own degree of immersion and acculturation, James Smith's discernment of "kindness" on the part of the Kahnawakes is more credible than Johnston's claim that the Shawnees were "gratified and surprised" by his act of writing in a book. Such kindness—also implicit in Ridout's characterization of his book provider, Kakinathucca, as his "Indian friend"—is premised on the recognition of the status of reading as a cultural practice, a devotion. From the Little Chief's trade of a volume of Shakespeare to Morris, and the Shawnees' confiscation of Ridout's deluxe editions (and loan to him of others), we may infer that the Indians learned to associate certain kinds of books with certain kinds of readers and understood the value of books as status symbols.

For the captives, the content of the proffered or restored books had additional levels of meaning. Exactly the right book came into each of these captives' hands. Morris's Shakespeare was as apt for him as Rowlandson's King James Bible was for her. Smith's books might have been found in the home of any of his Presbyterian neighbors. The books featured in Ridout's and Johnston's narratives are epitomes of their respective discourse communities. This concept—the discourse community—is the common denominator between religious and secular literacy practices. The captive's reading is of a piece with the captive's concurrent or subsequent writing, a means to perform belonging even as he or she was experiencing alienation.

Morris and Ridout, especially, provide grounds to speculate about a further correlation between devotional and secular reading. Unlike Rowlandson, Williams, or Marrant, they do not explicitly cross-reference their own stories with the narratives they were reading, but the parallels that emerge

53. Kyla Schuller, "Avatar and the Movements of Neocolonial Sentimental Cinema," *Discourse,* XXXV (2014), 182; Karen Ordahl Kupperman, ed., *Captain John Smith: A Select Edition of His Writings* (Williamsburg, Va., and Chapel Hill, N.C., 1988), 62.

between Morris's and Ridout's narratives and *Antony and Cleopatra* and *Télémaque*, respectively, resemble Puritan typology as an allegorical correlation between text and history. Indeed, of all the elements in the story-worlds of their captivity narratives, the texts of the books that they read are the only ones that are accessible to readers today. Reading them, in light of these accounts, may afford some sense of what they meant to captive readers.

CONCLUSION

A Lakota war party captured Fanny Kelly in a raid on her wagon train on July 12, 1864, in what is now Wyoming. Her captivity lasted nearly five months. In her *Narrative of My Captivity among the Sioux Indians* (1871), she recounts that one morning, during a period of severe deprivation as her Oglala captors fled from General Alfred Sully's devastating invasion of the Dakota Territory, she left camp to fetch water and returned to find a mirror image of herself: "a fair-faced, beautiful young girl sitting there, dejected and worn, like myself, but bearing the marks of loveliness and refinement, despite her neglected covering." Astonished, "doubting my reason," Kelly "stood spell-bound," gazing in the white captive's "sad brown eyes and drooping, pallid face." Kelly's principal captor, a Lakota chief, who had been "watching the interview with amusement," offered her "a book, which chanced to be one of the Willson's readers, stolen from our wagons, and bade me show it to the stranger." She "approached the girl, who instantly held out her hand, and said: 'What book is that?'" According to Kelly, "The sound of my own language, spoken by one of my own people, was too much for me, and I sank to the ground by the side of the stranger, and, endeavoring to clasp her in my arms, became insensible." (The "stranger" was subsequently identified as Mary Boyeau, a captive from Iowa.) Here, the diction and action make Kelly resemble her counterparts in fiction, except that the physiological conditions for fainting — fatigue, lack of nourishment — were historically determined, and the lady who revived her by sprinkling water on her face was "a kindly squaw." In Kelly's account, as with the narratives discussed in the preceding chapters, rhetorical formulae meet ethnohistory.[1]

1. Fanny [Wiggins] Kelly, *Narrative of My Captivity among the Sioux Indians . . . ,* Making of America Books (Hartford, Conn., 1871), 112–113; Kelly, *To the Senators and Members of the House of Representatives of Congress . . . ,* American Broadsides and Ephemera, 1st Ser., no. 13050 ([Washington, D.C.], 1871). On Sully and the 1864 Northwest Sioux Expedition, see Doreen Chaky, *Terrible Justice: Sioux Chiefs and U.S. Soldiers on the Upper Missouri, 1854–1868* (Norman, Okla., 2012), 199–240. On fainting in fiction, see Frances Etheridge Oakes, "The Swoon, the Kayo, and the Blackout," *Georgia Review,* IX (1955), 433–442; Naomi Booth, "Feeling Too Much: The Swoon

This work of western Victorian Americana illustrates the broader claims of *Allegories of Encounter*. Kelly's *Narrative* completes a small inventory of captivity texts that feature representations of literacy practices and events. This set, assembled across ethnohistorical, discursive, and temporal contexts, includes the canonical narratives by Mary Rowlandson, John Williams, and John Marrant, the first- and secondhand accounts of the captivity of the Jesuit Isaac Jogues, and the lesser-known narratives of James Smith, Thomas Morris, Thomas Ridout, and Charles Johnston. It's a small sample of the large archive of captivity narratives, which itself represents the experiences of only a small proportion of Euro-American captives. Four chapters present close textual analyses of these works, whereas two follow leads from these analyses into related topics: the captives' repeated evocations of Psalm 137 and the cultural transformations of Eunice Williams and Kateri Tekakwitha.[2]

As a close reading of a curated selection of texts, *Allegories of Encounter* may invite some of the general critiques that historians have leveled against literary scholars' interventions into historical topics — namely, that the selection of evidence is often thesis driven, and the explanatory value of close textual analysis is often taken for granted. Yet I hope this book demonstrates the rewards of this mode of inquiry: inductive, speculative, associative, *slow*. Its premise is that the extreme circumstances and pressures of Indian captivity reveal as much about settler-colonial literacy and discursive practices as vice versa. Moreover, the correlations in the representations of literacy and discursive practices among these diverse texts are manifestations of overarching language ideologies shared across the discourse communities of the captive authors, from seventeenth-century Jesuits and Puritans to nineteenth-century "pioneers."[3] My deliberate

---

and the (In)Sensible Woman," *Women's Writing*, XXI (2014), 575–591. Christopher Castiglia describes Kelly's narrative as "undoubtedly one of the most detailed and complex accounts authored by a nineteenth-century captive" (Castiglia, *Bound and Determined: Captivity, Culture-Crossing, and White Womanhood from Mary Rowlandson to Patty Hearst* [Chicago, 1996], 69). Marcius Willson (1813–1905) was a prolific American producer of readers and history textbooks.

2. As discussed in the introduction, there are "more than a thousand separate captivity titles." See Annette Kolodny, "Review Essay," *EAL*, XIV (1979), 232.

3. See Eric Slauter's synthesis of historians' reviews of books by literary scholars published in the *William and Mary Quarterly*: "History, Literature, and the Atlantic World," *WMQ*, 3d Ser., LXV (2008), 146–150. In *The Slow Professor*, Maggie Berg and Barbara K. Seeber refer to Stefan Collini's distinction between the production of knowledge and the development of understanding; according to Collini, scholarly publication in the humanities "is often the expression of the deepened understanding which some individual has acquired, through much reading, discussion, and reflection, on a topic which has been in some sense 'known' for many genera-

readings develop the significances of literacy events across multiple moments and dimensions—in the past-tense actuality of colonial contact and in the present-tense process of retrospection and composition; in terms of the contingent intersections between one's own story and other stories and representations, and the value-laden symbolism of writing and books.

Indeed, captivity narratives represent conditions of estrangement and deculturation—construed as dehumanization—that bring to the fore the value of literacy as a means of participation in what Kelly refers to as "civilization": a construction of culture in which the use of letters and literature was a defining feature. To a lesser degree, these conditions were already associated with the experience of colonists and emigrants, which was why Kelly was so gratified, shortly before the Lakota attack, to have another family, the Larimers, break off from a larger wagon train to join hers. The "addition of one of my own sex," Sarah Larimer, enabled Kelly to realize a cultural community en route: "Our amusements were varied. Singing, reading, writing to friends at home, or pleasant conversation, occupied our leisure hours," she wrote, adding, with irony: "So passed the first few happy days of our emigration to the land of sunshine and flowers." Kelly and Larimer formed a sort of discourse community in capsule, ideationally connected to a larger network of "friends" through the act of writing (and, when the opportunity presented, sending) letters—and to a larger, imagined community of fellow readers. Captivity disrupted these already attenuated connections.[4]

More precisely, captivity put Kelly, like her predecessors, in a situation where native Americans mediated her access to books and correspondence. Like Rowlandson and Williams, she represented Indians presenting salvaged or plundered texts, and like Smith, Morris, and Johnston, she associated such presentations with a swing from perceived mortal danger to an assurance of safety. After the attack on her train, a "young Indian, Wechela," brought her two pairs of shoes from the wrecked train and gave them to Kelly and her adopted daughter, Mary, "intimating by his gestures that our lives were to be spared"; he also brought her "some books and

---

tions" (Collini, *What Are Universities For?* [New York, 2012], 123, cited in Berg and Seeber, *Slow Professor: Challenging the Culture of Speed in the Academy* [Toronto, Ont., 2016], 55–56). "Pioneers": Kelly, *Narrative of My Captivity*, v. My use of the phrase "settler-colonial" is predicated on the basic continuity of patterns of settlement and dispossession between the colonial and national periods. See Patrick Wolfe, "Land, Labor, and Difference: Elementary Structures of Race," *American Historical Review*, CVI (2001), 866–905.

4. Kelly, *Narrative of My Captivity*, v, 13.

letters, all of which I thankfully received." Mary soon, at Kelly's urging, fled from captivity, but Kelly herself, as a sole captive, was carried deeper into Dakota Territory, so that, as with Rowlandson, her redemption correspondence relied on Indians as couriers. Her response to the arrival of a "friendly Indian" bearing a letter—"My heart leaped with unaccustomed hope"—echoes Rowlandson's: "My heart was so heavy before that I could scarce speak or go in the path; and yet now so light, that I could run." But, as with the Jogues and Williams accounts, most letters failed to reach their destination; she later learned of all the undelivered letters from her husband.[5]

The use of writing and literacy as a contradistinctive sign of identity is epitomized in Kelly's remarks on a letter that an Indian brought her to read. He had taken it "from a soldier killed by him," possibly along with his scalp; almost precisely recapitulating Smith's account of his view from Fort Duquesne after Braddock's Defeat, Kelly describes the Indians returning from battle with Sully's army, "bearing their trophies, reeking scalps, soldiers' uniforms, covered with blood, which told its sad story to my aching heart." Kelly's representation is the sum of a concatenation of literacy events: the soldier writing a letter home, in the midst of a ruinous invasion of Dakota territory; Kelly reading the dead soldier's letter to the Indian who had killed him; the former captive at her writing desk, composing her narrative. Implicitly, the description to the reader was a paraphrase of what she recited to the Indian: "that the topographical engineer was killed, and that General Sully's men had caught the red devils and cut their heads off, and stuck them up on poles." The grotesque communication to the Indians formed a hideous counterpoint to the intended communication to the home front: Kelly comments, concluding the ninth chapter of her narrative, "The soldier had written a friendly and kind letter to his people, but, ere it was mailed, he was numbered with the dead." Here, the loss of life is expressed in terms of a broken communicative circuit.[6]

It's a short, metonymic step from the use of literacy to sustain interpersonal (or spiritual) communication to the symbolic investment of writing or print with the significance of personhood. This language ideology is instantiated by the Jesuit superior's encomiums of the letter he received

5. Ibid., 41, 104, 105, 129, 130; *SGG*, 94.
6. Kelly, *Narrative of My Captivity*, 101, 104–105.

from Isaac Jogues—"this letter contains more substance than words"—
and might have underlain Smith's fears prompted by the disappearance
of his books. Kelly observes that her husband, who had fled the Lakota
attack, returned to salvage "a few relics from our demolished train," including the diary she had kept "from the time we were married until the
hour that the Indians came upon us. This he prized, as he said, more than
he did his life." Kelly herself literally invested (in the etymological sense
of that word, putting into clothing) the papers that Wechela gave her
about her person. She told Sarah Larimer, who had also been captured,
her plan: she would hide the papers in her clothing and would "drop them
at intervals along the way we are taken, as a guide, and trust in God that
our friends may find and follow them to our rescue, or if an opportunity to
escape offer, we will seize it, and by their help retrace our steps." Larimer
soon escaped; Kelly sent Mary on her way, as well (she was captured and
killed), and tried, unsuccessfully, to escape herself, so she was never able
to follow her paper trail.[7]

Kelly's representation of receiving books from Wechela indicates, as
in the earlier narratives, the Indians' recognition of the settler-colonists'
urgent attachment to books: they were items to salvage from the wreckage
of a "demolished train," perhaps on the same order of priority as shoes. The
chief's gesture in giving her a book to present to a fellow captive indicates
that he saw reading as constituting whiteness, perhaps especially white
femininity—a cultural performance, like drinking tea. In another episode,
Kelly encountered a "white" woman who had been adopted at a young age
and brought up "with habits of savage life"; the woman's husband, Black
Bear, "suggested the idea that white women always drank together, so she
made us a cup of herb tea, which we drank in company." The chief's introduction of a book into an encounter between two captive white women
might have been predicated on a similar logic.[8]

Kelly herself, despite some intimations of empathetic identification
with the Lakotas, especially the women, was nevertheless resolutely in-
sistent on "the superiority of the white race." She demonstrated her allegiance with her disposition of the book her captor handed to her by gifting it to her counterpart, Mary Boyeau, who was a captive of the Yankton
Sioux. Their meeting was comparable to Smith's encounter with the

7. *JR*, XXIV, 298–299; Kelly, *Narrative of My Captivity*, 33, 41.
8. Kelly, *Narrative of My Captivity*, 139.

Wyandot captive Arthur Campbell, as discussed in the introduction: a "chance interview" with the captive of another band. It was an opportunity to compare notes; Kelly learned that Boyeau had been captured in the 1857 Lakota attack on the settlement on Spirit Lake, Iowa—the Spirit Lake Massacre—and she had become "the unwilling wife of a brutal savage." Thus the interview was a literacy event, in the sense that it contributed to the production of a text. Perhaps Kelly recorded Boyeau's story in the "memoranda" she "kept during the period of my captivity" and used to compose her manuscript. It supplied her *Narrative* with its most lurid details, toward its apparent rhetorical purpose of justifying war and dispossession. The episode was also a representation of a literacy event, beginning with the presentation of the book, a copy of a volume in the popular series of readers published by Marcius Willson, and ending with her gifting "my little book and half of my pencil" to Boyeau.[9]

With this gift, Kelly seemed to wish to lend the permanence of writing to their brief encounter, to keep a captive sister company on the page. "I wrote her name in the book, together with mine, encouraging her with every kind word and hope of the future." But previously, Kelly had used the book—filled with stories and illustrations to promote basic literacy— "to teach the Indians," whom it made "very angry to have me part with it." She recounted that she had spent "hours" "showing them pictures and explaining their meaning, which interested them greatly." According to Kelly, her literacy "inspired them with a degree of respect and veneration" for her, whereas she, in turn, was impressed by their promise: "I found them apt pupils, willing to learn, and they learned easily and rapidly. Their memory is very retentive—unusually good." By giving the book to Boyeau, she chose one discourse community over another, nascent one.[10]

Kelly observes that her reading tutorials alerted her captors to her "usefulness in writing letters and reading for them." This capacity illuminates the connection between the more subjective, self-contained significance of literacy in settler colonialism that has been an emphasis of this book (as part of the performance of affiliation or cultural identity) and writ-

9. Ibid., vi, 113, 116, 118, 139. I can't find any historical references to Mary Boyeau and her family. See Abbie Gardner-Sharp, *History of the Spirit Lake Massacre and Captivity of Miss Abbie Gardner* (Des Moines, Ia., 1885). The book she refers to was one in the popular series of readers by Marcius Willson. Her characterization of it as "little" makes me think it might have been the first, which was only ninety-three pages. See Willson, *The First Reader of the School and Family Series* (New York, 1861). On Kelly's empathy, see Castiglia, *Bound and Determined*, 69–79.

10. Kelly, *Narrative of My Captivity*, 118–119.

Jumping Bear Promising by the Moon, to Carry My Letter to tho
White Chief at Fort Sully.

Figure 10 Engraving from Fanny Kelly, *Narrative of
My Captivity among the Sioux Indians* (Cincinnati, Oh., 1871).
Library of Congress, Prints and Photographs Division

ing's more widely noted function as an instrument of deception. In Kelly's
representation, though, writing was a means to "circumvent" the Indians'
"malicious designs." Tasked with writing a letter to Captain James Liberty Fisk, pretending to offer a truce, Kelly employed a "clerical strategy":
although "the wily chief counted every word dictated," she combined
words, inventing compounds, "to warn the officer" of the Lakotas' hostile
intentions and to "tell him briefly of my helpless and unhappy captivity."
Later, after she had been transferred to the custody of the Sihásapas, or
Blackfeet Sioux, she foiled their strategy to take her to Fort Sully as a ruse
to gain access to the fort. Kelly persuaded Jumping Bear, a Lakota suitor,
to deliver a letter of warning "into the hands of the great chief there."

She wrote on a page torn from a notebook, using a lead bullet as a pencil, and "assured" Jumping Bear that the letter contained nothing that would harm him or his people; "and invoking the bright moon as a witness to my pledge of honor and truth, he started on his journey, bearing the letter, which I believed was to seal my fate for weal or wo." Her "Daring and venturesome deed" is reminiscent of the captive John Smith's trick, two and a half centuries earlier, of having the Powhatans carry a note to Jamestown warning the colonists of their own intended attack. By this means, Kelly reportedly instigated her own rescue, prompting the soldiers to immediately close the gates after a small group of Sihásapas had escorted her into the fort, leaving "a large body of Indians" shut out.[11]

Kelly's romantic, stylized representation, as expressive of the literary conventions of her day as Smith's *Generall Historie* was of his, is indicative of the multiple purposes of her *Narrative*. On the one hand, it was a commercial venture, written to appeal to a wide audience; on the other hand, it supported her case for congressional reparations, as a victim of Indian wars who had abetted the United States. She pointed out in footnotes that her letters from the field were deposited in federal archives, and she included appendices containing "extracts from the correspondence" and supporting documentation—including a deposition signed by officers from the Sixth Iowa Cavalry that credited her with preventing a "massacre." She was successful in both endeavors, producing a "widely circulated narrative" and obtaining federal compensation. The popularity of the narrative brought her an audience with President Grant, and in 1871, Congress awarded her $5,000 as compensation for the property stolen or destroyed in the attack on her train, to be drawn from funds nominally allotted to the Lakotas.[12]

The occasion for Kelly's narrative was similar to that of Thomas Morris, who also composed a literary narrative in conjunction with a "memorial" advancing "a claim on government"—in his case, petitioning the king for compensation for his service in America. More generally, her narra-

11. Kelly, 147, 149, 199, 200, 280; Karen Ordahl Kupperman, ed., *Captain John Smith: A Select Edition of His Writings* (Williamsburg, Va., and Chapel Hill, N.C., 1988), 62n. On Fisk's 1864 expedition, see Chaky, *Terrible Justice*, 228–233; W. Turrentine Jackson, "The Fisk Expeditions to the Montana Gold Fields," *Pacific Northwest Quarterly*, XXXIII (1942), 272–276.

12. Kelly, *Narrative of My Captivity*, 152, 201. Kelly, *To the Senators;* Janice Schuetz, *Episodes in the Rhetoric of Government-Indian Relations* (Westport, Conn., 2002), 101; Chaky, *Terrible Justice*, 240.

tive performed the same function as those of all the other captive authors in attempting a discursive integration that had been impossible during the captivity. A *Narrative of the Incidents* of one's captivity is also a performance of discourse conventions. Citations and allusions are one such mode of enacting community, and in that regard, the religious references in the narratives of Jogues, Rowlandson, or Marrant serve the same function as the literary references in those of Morris, Ridout, or Johnston.[13]

Kelly's *Narrative* illuminates this functional parallel, with devotional passages that also signal her participation in a cosmopolitan, Christian literary culture. Recounting how, at the onset of her ordeal, "all the horrors of Indian captivity that we had ever heard crowded on our minds with a new and fearful meaning," she notes that she nevertheless was able to "collect the soul in prayer." In the telling, however, instead of a verse of scripture, she cites an aphorism derived from Elizabeth Barrett Browning's "Lay of the Brown Rosary":

> When woe is come, the soul is dumb,
> That crieth not to God.

Similarly, in describing her hunger and exhaustion as well as the "toil and fear" she experienced by day, she asserted that she "was not wholly denied spiritual food" and that she was "visited with many bright visions" at night. She expressed the lesson she drew from her "communion with the heavenly world" during her "midnight, wakeful hours" by citing "The Angel of Patience" (1847) by the contemporary American poet John Greenleaf Whittier (1807–1892):

> He walks with thee, that angel kind,
> And gently whispers, be resigned;
> Bear up, bear on, the end shall tell,
> The dear Lord ordereth all things well.

The sentiment is consonant, for example, with the exhortation John Williams derived from scripture on behalf of the Deerfield captives: to assume "a patient bearing" of their "afflictions." However, instead of citing scrip-

---

13. Charles Johnston, *A Narrative of Capture, Detention, and Ransom*, Garland Library of Narratives of North American Indian Captivities, XLIII (1827; rpt. New York, 1975). Morris was unsuccessful; "having in vain sought a mediator between Majesty and me, I dropt all thoughts of the memorial" (Thomas Morris, *Miscellanies in Prose and Verse* [London, 1791], iv).

ture, Kelly evokes it through Whittier's "free paraphrase" of a German hymn, a reference that is simultaneously devotional and literary.[14]

Kelly further remarked that the Sihásapas had treated her as well as "their circumstances and condition would allow, and the women were very kind, but 'their people were not my people,' and I was detained a captive, far from home, and friends, and civilization." She continued: "With Alexander Selkirk I could say, 'Better dwell in the midst of alarms, than reign in this horrible place.'" The first citation is doubly significant. Denotatively, it means that she could never recognize the Indians as her "people"; but it was also a shibboleth, an indication that her "people" would recognize the allusion to Ruth 1:16 ("thy people *shall* be my people"). The reference was oddly inappropriate, insofar as, unlike Ruth, Kelly was not a convert but one who was refusing any notion of conversion. Similarly, the second citation, alluding to an iconic castaway, is from William Cowper's poem "The Solitude of Alexander Selkirk"; it expresses her sense of estrangement and enacts her belonging. The syntax is reminiscent of Rowlandson's, only she speaks with "Alexander Selkirk" instead of "Job" or "David."[15]

Unlike several of Rowlandson's scriptural references, however, there is no ambiguous "now" introducing Kelly's references to Browning, Whittier, and Cowper. These belong to her discourse rather than her story; they are part of the telling and not of the narrated action. In other instances, Kelly's narrative exemplifies the sort of reception allegories discussed in the chapters above. In one passage, recounting her exhaustion, exposure, and extreme thirst as they rode "through dry and sandy hills, upon which the sun glared down with exhausting heat," she includes a diegetic allusion to Luke 16:19–25: "When, in famishing despair I closed my eyes, a cup of cool, delicious drink would seem to be presented to my lips, only to be cruelly withdrawn; and this torture seemed to me like the agony of the rich man, who besought Lazarus for one drop of water to cool his parched

14. Kelly, *Narrative of My Captivity*, 40, 111; "The Lay of the Brown Rosary," in Elizabeth Barrett [Browning], *Poems*, 2 vols. (London, 1844), I, 200; "The Angel of Patience: A Free Paraphrase of the German," in *The Poetical Works of John Greenleaf Whittier*, 4 vols. (Boston, 1892), II, 217; *CH*, 100. Kelly might not have known the precise attribution, since the poem also appears anonymously in compendiums such as Virginia De Forest, ed., *The Young Lady's Cabinet of Gems: A Choice Collection of Pieces in Poetry and Prose* (New York, 1860), 147; Iola Kay Eastburn, *Whittier's Relation to German Life and Thought*, Americana Germanica, N.S., no. 20 (Philadelphia, 1915), 97–101.

15. Kelly, *Narrative of My Captivity*, 213; "Verses Supposed to Be Written by Alexander Selkirk, during His Solitary Abode in the Island of Juan Fernandez," in William Cowper, *Poems* (London, 1782), 305; Salisbury, *SGG*, 74, 82.

tongue." Whereas the rich man had lived in luxury while the beggar Lazarus suffered at his gate, in the afterlife, the rich man saw "Abraham afar off, and Lazarus in his bosom"; he pleaded with Abraham to "send Lazarus, that he may dip the tip of his finger in water, and cool my tongue; for I am tormented in this flame." But Abraham said, "Son, remember that thou in thy lifetime receivedst thy good things, and likewise Lazarus evil things: but now he is comforted, and thou art tormented" (Luke 16:23–25). The allegory casts the Indians as Lazarus and Kelly as the rich man: "Turning my eyes despairingly to my captors, I uttered the word 'Minne,' signifying water in their language, and kept repeating it imploringly at intervals." It picks up, from the immediate rhetorical context, on some reflections on "the chief's blasphemous language," which "would all be English; a sad commentary on the benefits white men confer on their savage brethren when brought into close contact." The allegory suggests that, momentarily, she experienced her suffering, not as an innocent victim, but as a representative of the "white men," experiencing just retribution for the conferring on the Indians only "evil things" and not "good things."[16]

As this example illustrates, following intertextual leads from the diegesis of nonfictional narrative accounts can afford speculative insights into the protagonist authors' subjective experience. A further step is the notion that experiences and even actions are informed by allegoresis; I have argued that several of the captives, as well as the converts Kateri Tekakwitha and Marguerite Kanenstenhawi, self-consciously followed parallel plotlines, even to the point of convergence. In Kelly's representation, however, she was more concerned with the divergences between her prior reading and her own ongoing story. Although her experience corroborated some of the "horrors of Indian captivity" she had heard about — "the slow fires, the pitiless knife, the poisoned arrows, the torture of famine" — she pointed to the "strange contrast" between the noble savages she had read about in her youth and "the flesh and blood realities into whose hands I had fallen." Referencing the "stately Logan, the fearless Philip, the bold Black Hawk, the gentle Pocahontas," she argued, "The true red man, as I saw him, does not exist between the pages of many volumes. He roams his native wastes, and to once encounter and study him there, so much must be sacrificed that I could scarcely appreciate the knowledge I was gaining at such a price." Like her predecessors, Kelly offered

16. Kelly, *Narrative of My Captivity*, 59–61.

her readers a representation of experience she had gained at great cost—one they couldn't access "between the pages of many volumes," but they could, at a safe remove, through her *Narrative*. She could never really communicate her experience: the "sorrowful accompaniments" of her "Indian home" were "certainly engraved upon faithful memory, to last forever; but no touch of pen could give any semblance of the realities to another." Her narrative was a mere allegory for the story she had experienced.[17]

In writing, she would slip from one track to another, from the marks on the paper to the grooves on her memory. "It has seemed, while writing it, as if with the narration of each incident, I was living over again the fearful life I led while a captive; and often I have laid aside the pen to get rid of the feelings which possessed me." Now, in completing her "task," she hoped "to lay aside forever all regretful remembrances of my captivity." Taking up the pen—or, rather, employing a pointed bullet as a pencil—had been a way out her captivity, and now, by laying aside her pen, she hoped to seal off the virtual reality she had created. Henceforth, she wrote in the last line of her narrative, she hoped to "enjoy the happiness which every one may find in child-like trust in Him who ordereth all things well." As with Rowlandson's narrative, which concludes with a reference to Exodus 14:13, Kelly's four final words, sampling her earlier citation from "The Angel of Patience," were shared words. They closed the circle between the former captive, her readers, and their God.[18]

Like much scholarship in the humanities, especially literary studies, *Allegories of Encounter* dwells on shared words, texts in common. I hope that it puts narratives of captivity in a new light that illuminates the roles of literacy and literature in the captive authors' experiences; that it complicates our understanding of intertextuality by demonstrating that stories can inform actions and perceptions as well as representations; and that scholars working in other genres and other contexts will find a useful model for the analysis of other narrative primary sources, which may also feature literacy events and reception allegories and which may also constitute discursive performances of cultural affiliation. I hope, finally, that readers will recognize this book as a successful contribution to a discourse community from one of its participants.

17. Ibid., 40, 77–78, 110.
18. Ibid., 254.

NOTE ON THE SOURCES

Allegories of Encounter draws mainly on published sources. For the most part, I have analyzed and consulted this material online. This practice raises the emergent, complex, unresolved issues surrounding the use and acknowledgment of online resources in scholarly publications.

These issues are tangentially related to the discussions in this book, because there are language ideologies at play in research and citation practices. In much historical scholarship, there is a prestige hierarchy that arguably elevates scribal archival material over print and definitely values books over digital media. Archival research connotes discovery, intensive labor, expensive travel, exclusive access, fellowship awards; it positions the scholarly author not simply as interpreter but as mediator. (This valuation plays into the tensions within early American studies between historians and literary scholars, whose work, albeit to a lesser degree than in later literary-historical periods, consists largely of the reinterpretation of a shared set of texts.) Citations of rare books similarly evoke the foam supports and weighted strings that protect them, temperature control, and lunch breaks with fellow scholars. Increasingly, however, such citations may amount to a gratuitous suggestion of academic cultural capital, because more and more out-of-print and rare books are available as digital facsimiles. Many of these facsimiles are in subscription-based repositories like Early English Books Online (EEBO), but others are available open-access. One of the rarest books that I cite above is Phillipe Alegambe's *Mortes illustres et gesta eorum de Societate Jesu* (1657), which reproduces Isaac Jogues's 1643 letter from Rensselaer. According to WorldCat, the nearest edition is 3,500 miles away from my Brooklyn home, in Madrid. This citation might indicate expensive travel (in addition to misleadingly implying competency in Latin), except that *Mortes illustres* is also available through Google Books.[1]

The prevalent practice, in scholarly publishing, is to forego acknowledgment of digital repositories. This omission is continuous with predigital conventions; typically, scholars acknowledge archives but do not identify the libraries for cited books. Depending on one's methodology and aims, it may not matter

---

1. Jonathan Blaney and Judith Siefring, "A Culture of Non-Citation: Assessing the Digital Impact of British History Online and the Early English Books Online Text Creation Partnership," *Digital Humanities Quarterly*, XI, no. 1 (2017), para. 1, http://www.digitalhumanities.org/dhq/vol/11/1/000282/000282.html. For literary scholars' perspective on the disciplinary tensions in early American studies, see Ed White and Michael J. Drexler, "The Theory Gap," *American Literary History*, XXII (2010), 480–494, https://doi.org/10.1093/alh/ajq007.

which copy of a particular edition of a primary source one uses nor whether one accesses a physical book or a microfilm, a digital facsimile of an individual copy (such as those in EEBO), or a digital edition (such as those in Project Gutenberg). But the absence of acknowledgment, the broad pretense that we are using physical books instead of electronic ones, drastically underrepresents the impact of e-resources and may have negative consequences for both subscription-based services and open-access initiatives. It's important to recognize the contributions of initiatives such as the Internet Archive, Electronic Texts in American Studies (ETAS), or the EEBO Text Creation Partnership (TCP). Furthermore, I want to alert my readers to readily accessible editions of my primary sources. Finally, I want to own up to a furtive use of electronic resources. I know I'm not the only researcher, for example, to use an electronic edition and then find a print one to cite (sometimes by searching in Amazon.com or Google Books). Such citation practices convey a tacit disapprobation of digital sources, but I could not have written this book without them.[2]

From an editorial and production standpoint, however, DOIs and URLs in footnotes can be awkward, unsightly, and sometimes transitory. I am instead appending a list of repositories and works. For the full bibliography, including links, please visit allegoriesofencounter.hcommons.org.

Electronic Repositories

Archive of Americana (www.readex.com/content/archive-americana)
Documenting the American South (docsouth.unc.edu)
Early Canadiana Online [ECO] (http://eco.canadiana.ca)
Early English Books Online [EEBO] (eebo.chadwyck.com)
EEBO Text Creation Partnership [EEBO TCP] (https://quod.lib.umich.edu
  /e/eebogroup)
Eighteenth-Century Collections Online [ECCO] (https://www.gale.com
  /primary-sources/eighteenth-century-collections-online)
ECCO Text Creation Partnership [ECCO TCP] (https://quod.lib.umich.edu
  /e/ecco)
Electronic Texts in American Studies [ETAS] (http://digitalcommons.unl.edu
  /etas)
Evans Early American Imprint Collection Text Creation Partnership [Evans
  TCP] (https://quod.lib.umich.edu/e/evans)
Gallica (gallica.bnf.fr)
Google Books (https://books.google.com)
Internet Archive (https://archive.org)

2. Blaney and Seifring report that "many scholars, particularly in the humanities, fail to cite or otherwise acknowledge their use of digital resources" ("A Culture of Non-Citation," *DHQ*, XI, no. 1 [2017], para. 18). On the "myriad transformations" between print copy and digital facsimile, see Diana Kichuk, "Metamorphosis: Remediation in *Early English Books Online (EEBO)*," *Literary and Linguistic Computing*, XXII (2007), 297, https://doi.org/10.1093/llc/fqm018.

Library of Congress (https://www.loc.gov)
Making of America Books (https://quod.lib.umich.edu/m/moa)
North Carolina Maps (https://web.lib.unc.edu/nc-maps)
Power Library: Pennsylvania's Electronic Library (http://www.powerlibrary.org)

Electronic Texts

An Account of the Remarkable Occurrences in the Life and Travels of Colonel James Smith (Late a Citizen of Bourbon County, Kentucky): During His Captivity with the Indians, in the Years 1755, '56, '57, '58, and '59. Lexington, Ky., 1799. Internet Archive.

Baird, Charles W. *History of the Huguenot Emigration to America.* I. New York, 1885. Google Books.

Baker, Charlotte Alice. *True Stories of New England Captives Carried to Canada during the Old French and Indian Wars.* Cambridge, Mass., 1897. Google Books.

Baxter, Richard. *A Call to the Unconverted to Turn and Live: And Accept of the Mercy while Mercy May Be Had. . . .* London, 1658. EEBO.

Beard, Thomas, and Tho[mas] Taylor. *The Theatre of Gods Judgements: Wherein Is Represented the Admirable Justice of God against All Notorious Sinners. . . .* London, 1648. EEBO.

Bleecker, Ann Eliza. *The History of Maria Kittle.* Hartford, Conn., 1797. ECCO.

Brahm, John Gerar William de. *A Map of South Carolina and a Part of Georgia, Containing the Whole Sea-Coast: All the Islands, Inlets, Rivers, Creeks, Parishes, Townships, Boroughs, Roads, and Bridges. . . .* London, 1757. LOC.

Calvin, Jean. *Commentary on the Book of Psalms.* Ed. and trans. James Anderson. Calvin's Commentaries, V. Edinburgh, 1847. Google Books.

Chesterfield, Philip Dormer Stanhope. *Letters Written by the Late Right Honourable Philip Dormer Stanhope, Earl of Chesterfield, to His Son, Philip Stanhope, Esq. . . .* IV. Paris, 1789. ECCO.

Cholenec, Pierre. "Lettre du Père Cholenec, missionnaire de la Compagnie de Jèsus, au père Augustin le Blanc, de la même compagnie, procureur des missions du Canada, 1715." In *Lettres édifiantes et curieuses, écrites des missions étrangères.* IV, *Mémoires d'Amérique.* Lyon, 1819. Google Books.

———. *Vie de Catherine Tekakouita: (Traduction iroquoise).* Trans. Joseph Marcoux. [Montréal, Que.], 1876. ECO.

Cotton, John. *Singing of Psalmes, a Gospel-Ordinance; or, A Treatise, wherein Are Handled These Foure Particulars. . . .* London, 1647. EEBO TCP.

Cowper, William. *Poems.* London, 1782. ECCO TCP.

Debates and Other Proceedings of the Convention of Virginia, Convened at Richmond, on Monday the 2d Day of June, 1788, for the Purpose of Deliberating on the Constitution Recommended by the Grand Federal Convention: To Which Is Prefixed, the Federal Constitution. . . . 3 vols. Petersburg, Va., 1788–1789. ECCO.

A Dialogue, between Andrew Trueman, and Thomas Zealot: About the Killing the Indians at Cannestogoe and Lancaster. Philadelphia, 1764. Evans TCP.

Directions How to Hear Sermons, Preach'd by the Reverend Mr. George Whitefield, A.B. . . . Boston, 1740. Evans TCP.

Drake, Samuel Gardner. *The History and Antiquities of Boston.* [Boston, 1856]. Google Books.

The Dramatick Works of William Shakespear. 7 vols. London, 1734. ECCO.

England, John. *The Roman Missal: Translated into the English Language for the Use of the Laity. . . .* Philadelphia, 1843. Google Books.

Gardner-Sharp, Abbie. *History of the Spirit Lake Massacre and Captivity of Miss Abbie Gardner.* Des Moines, Ia., 1885. Internet Archive.

Glaire, l'Abbé J.-B, trans. *La Sainte Bible Polyglotte: Contenant le texte hébreu original, le texte grec des Septante, le texte latin de la Vulgate et la traduction francaise de M. l'Abbé Glaire.* Paris, 1900. Internet Archive.

Hannay, James, ed. *Nine Years a Captive; or, John Gyles' Experience among the Malicite Indians, from 1689 to 1698.* Saint John, N.B, 1875. Internet Archive.

Hariot, Thomas. *A Briefe and True Report of the New Found Land of Virginia.* Frankfurt, 1590. Documenting the American South.

Heckewelder, John. *History, Manners, and Customs of the Indian Nations Who Once Inhabited Pennsylvania and the Neighboring States.* Historical Society of Pennsylvania, *Memoirs*, XII. Philadelphia, 1881. Internet Archive.

The Holy Bible Containing the Old Testament and the New: Translated into the Indian Language and Ordered to Be Printed by the Commissioners of the United Colonies in New-England. Cambridge, Mass., 1663. EEBO.

Johnson, [Susannah Willard]. *A Narrative of the Captivity of Mrs. Johnson. . . .* 3d ed. Windsor, Vt., 1814. Internet Archive.

Johnston, Charles. *A Narrative of Capture, Detention, and Ransom.* Garland Library of Narratives of North American Indian Captivities, XLIII. 1827; rpt. New York, 1975. Internet Archive.

Julian, John. *A Dictionary of Hymnology.* II. New York, 1907. Internet Archive.

Kelly, Fanny [Wiggins]. *Narrative of My Captivity among the Sioux Indians.* Hartford, Conn., 1871. Making of America Books.

———. *To the Senators and Members of the House of Representatives of Congress. . . .* Washington, D.C, 1871. Archive of Americana.

Kirkpatrick, A[lexander] F[rancis]. *The Book of Psalms, with Introduction and Notes.* Cambridge, 1901. Internet Archive.

La Rochefoucauld-Liancourt, François-Alexandre-Frédéric. *Voyage dans les États-Unis d'Amérique, fait en 1795, 1796, et 1797.* I. Paris, 1799. Internet Archive.

Lafitau, Joseph-François. *Moeurs des sauvages amériquains, comparées aux moeurs des premiers temps.* [Paris, 1724]. Google Books.

Lafitte, Jean-Baptiste Pierre. *Mémoires de Fleury de la Comédie-française (1757 à 1820).* I. Paris, 1836. Internet Archive.

Lavington, George. *The Enthusiasm of Methodists and Papists Compared: In Three Parts. . . .* II. London, 1754. ECCO.

Marrant, John. *A Journal of the Rev. John Marrant from August the 18th, 1785, to the 16th of March, 1790. . . .* London, 1790. Power Library.

Mather, Cotton. *Magnalia Christi Americana; or, The Ecclesiastical History of New-England, from Its First Planting in the Year 1620, unto the Year of Our Lord, 1698.* I, book 2. Hartford, Conn., 1820. Google Books.

Mather, Increase. *An Earnest Exhortation to the Inhabitants of New-England.* Boston, 1676. ETAS.

Mather, Richard, Hugh Peters, and John Davenport. *An Apologie of the Churches in New-England for Church-Covenant; or, A Discourse Touching the Covenant between God and Men, and Especially concerning Church-Covenant. . . .* London, 1643. EEBO TCP.

Morris, Thomas. *Miscellanies in Prose and Verse.* London, 1791. Internet Archive.

Mouzon, Henry. *An Accurate Map of North and South Carolina with Their Indian Frontiers, Shewing in a Distinct Manner All the Mountains, Rivers, Swamps, Marshes, Bays, Creeks, Harbours, Sandbanks and Soundings on the Coasts, with the Roads and Indian Paths. . . .* London, 1775. North Carolina Maps.

"P. Isaacus Jogues." In Philippo Alegambe, ed. *Mortes illustres et gesta eorum de Societate Jesu.* Rome, 1657. Google Books.

Priezac, Salomon de. *La vie de Sainte Catherine de Sienne.* Paris, 1665. Google Books.

Raymond of Capua. *Life of Saint Catharine of Sienna.* Trans. Regis Hamilton. New York, 1862. Internet Archive.

Ridout, Thomas. *Ten Years of Upper Canada in Peace and War, 1805–1815: Being the Ridout Letters. . . .* Ed. Lady Matilda Ridout Edgar. Toronto, 1890. Google Books.

Rous, F[rancis]. *The Booke of Psalmes in English Meeter.* London, 1641. EEBO.

Russell, Thomas C., ed. *The Shirley Letters from California Mines in 1851–52: Being a Series of Twenty-Three Letters from Dame Shirley (Mrs. Louise Amelia Knapp Smith Clappe) to Her Sister in Massachusetts.* San Francisco, Calif., 1922. Internet Archive.

Sagard, Gabriel. *Histoire du Canada et voyages que les Frères Mineurs Récollects y ont faicts pour la conversion des Infidelles.* Paris, 1636. Gallica.

Shea, John Gilmary. *Perils of the Ocean and Wilderness; or, Narratives of Shipwreck and Indian Captivity, Gleaned from Early Missionary Annals.* Boston, 1857. Internet Archive.

Sternhold, Thomas. *The Whole Booke of Psalmes Collected into Englysh Metre by T. Starnhold, I. Hopkins, and Others. . . .* London, 1562. EEBO.

Tate, N[ahum], and N[icholas Brady]. *A New Version of the Psalms of David, Fitted to the Tunes Used in Churches.* London, 1696. EEBO.

Thomassin, Louis. *Traité dogmatique et historique des edits et des autres moiens spirituels et temporels . . . pour établir, et pour maintenir l'unite de l'Eglise catholique. . . .* Paris, 1703. Google Books.

Thwaites, Reuben Gold, ed. *The Jesuit Relations and Allied Documents: Travels and Explorations of the Jesuit Missionaries in New France, 1610–1791.* Cleveland, Oh., 1898. ECO.

Underhill, John. *Newes from America; or, A New and Experimentall Discoverie of New England; Containing, a True Relation of Their War-Like Proceedings These Two Yeares Last Past, with a Figure of the Indian Fort, or Palizado.* London, 1638. ETAS.

Waddell, J. A. *Annals of Augusta County, Virginia. . . .* Richmond, Va., 1886. Google Books.

Walworth, Ellen Hardin. *The Life and Times of Kateri Tekakwitha: The Lily of the Mohawks, 1656–1680.* [Buffalo, N.Y., 1893]. Google Books.

Watts, I[saac]. *Hymns and Spiritual Songs: In Three Books. I. Collected from the Scriptures. II. Compos'd on Divine Subjects. III. Prepar'd for the Lord's Supper.* 16th ed. Boston, 1742. ECCO.

[Wigglesworth, Michael]. *Day of Doom; or, A Description of the Great and Last Judgment: With a Short Discourse about Eternity.* Cambridge, Mass., 1666. EEBO.

Willson, Marcius. *The First Reader of the School and Family Series.* New York, 1861. Internet Archive.

INDEX

Page numbers in italics refer to illustrations.

Waddell, Joseph Addison, 63, 72–73

Walworth, Ellen Hardin, 111n, 119n, 120

Wampanoags, 6, 19, 36

Wampum, 4, 120, 170

Waongote (Mohawk name), 113, 129–131. *See also* Marguerite Kanenstenhawi

Wars, 2, 8, 56. *See also individual conflicts*

Watts, Isaac, 139, 144, 147–148

Wechela (Lakota), 195, 197

Weetamoo (Wampanoag), 6, 36–37, 39, 162

Wendats (Hurons / Wyandots), 6, 8, 12, 57, 61, 63, 67, 76, 80–82, 84, 91, 198

Wesley, John, 156

Whitefield, George, 138–139, 146, 149–150, 159

Whittier, John Greenleaf, 201–202, 204

Wigglesworth, Michael, 31, 98n

Williams, Eleazer, 116, 128

Williams, Eunice: and allegory, 16, 116, 129–131; and naming, 17, 113, 116, 119, 127–131; cultural transformation of, 77, 100–101, 110–111, 113–114, 116, 194; scholarship on, 114; and literacy, 114n, 136; and Kateri Tekakwitha, 116; mother of, 127–128; marriage of, 131, 132n; visits of, to New England, 135. *See also* Marguerite Kanenstenhawi

Williams, Eunice Mather, 102, 127–128

Williams, John: narrative of, 15, *16*, 55, 75–78, 81, 87, 96–97, 104, 110, 114, 162, 194; and literacy, 17, 78–79, 104–110, 136, 196; and psalms, 55–56, 59, 73–74; and infanticide, 66; and Deerfield raid, 75; and allegory, 77, 86–87, 144, 146, 166, 191; postcaptivity sermon of, 77, 96n, 110; and Jesuits, 80; and scripture, 90, 95–100, 102–103; and Eunice Williams, 101, 110–111, 113, 129; and converts, 101–102; wife of, 102, 128; poem by, 107–108; and book presentations, 162, 195; and letters, 196

Williams, Samuel, 104, 106

Williams, Solomon, 135

Williams, Stephen, 56, 100, 125n

Willson, Marcius, 193, 198

Winthrop, John, 51–52

Witchcraft, 150, 155–158

Women's studies, 113

Writing, 2, 3, 5–6, 78–79, 86, 92, 104–106, 108–109, 114n, 171, 190–191, 198–199; and speech, 4, 87, 140, 152; definition of, 7; as symbol, 109, 195–196; supernatural properties of, 155–156; in journals, 190. *See also* Literacy practices

Wyandots. *See* Wendats (Hurons / Wyandots)

Xeres, Francisco, 5

Zion, 13, 50–51, 54–55, 60–62, 74, 86